# The Job Developer's Handbook

## Practical Tactics for Customized Employment

by

**Cary Griffin**

**David Hammis**

and

**Tammara Geary**

*with invited contributors*

·P·A·U·L·H·
**BROOKES**
PUBLISHING Cº ®

Baltimore • London • Sydney

**Paul H. Brookes Publishing Co.**
Post Office Box 10624
Baltimore, Maryland 21285-0624

www.brookespublishing.com

Typeset by Spearhead Global, Inc., Bear, Delaware.
Manufactured in the United States of America by
Victor Graphics, Inc., Baltimore, Maryland.

The individuals described in this book are composites or real people whose situations have been masked and are based on the authors' experiences. Names and identifying details have been changed to protect confidentiality.

Second printing, February 2009.

**Library of Congress Cataloging-in-Publication Data**

Griffin, Cary.
The job developer's handbook: Practical tactics for customized employment / by Cary Griffin,
David Hammis, and Tammara Geary; with invited contributors.
    p.    cm.
    Title from table of contents Customized job development
    Title from table of contents Customized employment
    Includes index.
    ISBN-13: 978-1-55766-863-9
    ISBN-10: 1-55766-863-9
    1. People with disabilities—Employment—United States—Handbooks, manuals, etc.
2. People with disabilities—Services for—United States—Handbooks, manuals, etc. 3. People with disabilities—Rehabilitation—United States—Handbooks, manuals, etc. 4. People with disabilities—Social networks—United States—Handbooks, manuals, etc. 5. People with disabilities—Vocational guidance—United States—Handbooks, manuals, etc. I. Hammis, David. II. Geary, Tammara. III. Title. IV. Title: Customized job development. V. Title: Customized employment.

HD7256.U5G747 2007
362.4'04840973—dc22                                                    2007015317

British Library Cataloguing in Publication data are available from the British Library.

# The Job Developer's Handbook

Practical Tactics for Customized Employment

# Contents

# About the Authors

**Cary Griffin,** Senior Partner, Griffin-Hammis Associates, LLC, 5582 Klements Lane, Florence, MT 59833

Mr. Griffin is Senior Partner at Griffin-Hammis Associates, LLC, a full-service consultancy specializing in building communities of economic cooperation, creating high-performance organizations, and focusing on disability and employment. He is also Codirector of the U.S. Department of Labor's National Self-Employment Technical Assistance, Resources, and Training project with Virginia Commonwealth University and former Director of Special Projects at the Rural Institute at The University of Montana. He is also past director of an adult vocational program in southern Colorado, former Assistant Director of the Rocky Mountain Resource and Training Institute, and former Founder and Executive Director of CTAT in Colorado.

**David Hammis,** Senior Partner, Griffin-Hammis Associates, LLC, 317 Franklin Street, Middletown, OH 45042

Mr. Hammis is Senior Partner at Griffin-Hammis Associates, LLC, a full-service consultancy specializing in building communities of economic cooperation, creating high-performance organizations, and focusing on disability and employment. He maintains an ongoing relationship with the Rural Institute at The University of Montana, where he served as Project Director for multiple self-employment, employment, and Social Security outreach training and technical assistance projects, including the Rural Institute's Rural Entrepreneurship and Self-Employment Expansion Design Project. He works with organizations nationally and internationally on self-employment, benefits analysis, supported employment, and employment engineering. Mr. Hammis has worked in supported and self-employment since 1988 and is personally responsible for the implementation of thousands of Plans to Achieve Self-Support leading to employment, self-employment, and enhanced personal resources for people with disabilities. In July 1996, Mr. Hammis received the International Association for Persons in Supported Employment Professional of the Year Award for his "outstanding support and commitment to people with disabilities, especially in the areas of career development and the use of Social Security work incentives."

**Tammara Geary, M.S.,** Lead Associate, Griffin-Hammis Associates, LLC; Editor/Publisher, *InfoLines*/Geary Publishing, P.O. Box 286, Yorktown, VA 23690

Ms. Geary is a nationally recognized trainer and consultant focusing on creating and supporting community, employment, and economic advancement of people with disabilities. She specializes in customized and self-employment. She is Lead Associate with Griffin-Hammis Associates, LLC. She also publishes *InfoLines,* a newsletter highlighting practical and successful strategies for customizing employment. Besides providing various conference and training presentations, Ms. Geary is also currently working with an organization in Maryland to improve its outcomes via implementing discovery-based customized employment; heading up a National Institute on Disability and Rehabilitation Research (NIDRR)–funded self-employment project for people with brain injuries through the Brain Injury Association of America; and consulting with several statewide customized and self-employment projects in Florida. One of these projects is Start-Up Florida, one of three Office of Disability Employment Policy–funded state self-employment projects.

Ms. Geary was formerly with APSE: The Network on Employment, where she served as Executive Director for 10 of her 12 years with the organization. In that role, she traveled around the country, meeting with individuals and organizations and providing training and presentations at numerous conferences and events. In addition, Ms. Geary has been a leader in protecting the recent advancements in public policy that affect employment of people with disabilities.

Prior to her work with APSE: The Network on Employment, Ms. Geary worked in direct service and program management for a local community services board in Virginia, where she maintained a 100% job retention rate for her entire tenure. She was recognized by APSE for her work, receiving the first award for "excellence in direct service provision" in 1989, and later was honored as the "outstanding graduate student" in her graduate degree program.

Ms. Geary also serves as the primary support for her sister with disabilities, who uses supported employment, supported living, and other community supports, and has had many experiences within her own family with school accommodation, thus giving her a thorough personal understanding of the issues facing people with disabilities as they seek to gain access to employment and all areas of life.

# About the Contributors

**Nancy Brooks-Lane,** Director, Developmental Disability Services and Supports, Cobb and Douglas Counties Community Services Boards, 2051 Greenridge Street, Smyrna, GA 30080

Ms. Brooks-Lane is the director of Developmental Disability Services and Supports through the Cobb and Douglas Counties Community Services Boards in Georgia. She has spent the last 5 years developing expertise in the area of self-employment with the guidance of Cary Griffin. She has assisted persons with significant disabilities start their own businesses through work on U.S. Department of Labor Customized Employment and WorkFORCE Action Grants. She is affiliated with Technical Assistance to Providers through Virginia Commonwealth University and the Institute for Community Inclusion at the University of Massachusetts Boston, providing her with the opportunity to train other providers in the processes of self-employment for persons with disabilities. She serves on the editorial board of the *Journal of Vocational Rehabilitation* and is an associate of Griffin-Hammis Associates, LLC. She has co-authored chapters in a book on customized employment edited by Dr. Paul Wehman and colleagues (*Real Work for Real Pay: Inclusive Employment for People with Disabilities*, 2006, Paul H. Brookes Publishing Co.). She has presented extensively throughout the country on conversion, systems change, and customized employment, including self-employment, resource ownership, and business within a business.

**Michael Callahan,** President, Marc Gold & Associates, 4101 Gautier-Vancleave Road, Suite 102, Gautier, MS 39553; MiCallahan@AOL.com

Mr. Callahan is a native Mississippian and has consulted throughout the United States, Canada, and Europe in the areas of employment and transition for the past 25 years. He has worked with Marc Gold & Associates (MG&A) for 27 years and has served as the president of the organization since Marc Gold's death in 1982. MG&A is a network of consultants that provides technical assistance to systems, agencies, and families interested in ensuring the complete community participation of persons with severe disabilities. In 2000, Michael joined three other colleagues to form a nonprofit organization called Employment for All (EFA). EFA is dedicated to ensuring full access to employment for all persons with disabilities. He is a co-author of two popular "how-to" books on employment for persons with significant disabilities: *Getting Employed, Staying*

*Employed* (Paul H. Brookes Publishing Co., 1987) and *Keys to the Workplace* (Paul H. Brookes Publishing Co., 1997). He has written numerous articles, chapters, manuals, and curricula pertaining to employment.

**Ellen Condon,** Rural Institute, The University of Montana, 634 Eddy Avenue, 009 CHC, Missoula, MT 59812; condon@ruralinstitute.umt.edu

Ms. Condon is Project Director at The University of Montana's Rural Institute, where she has worked since 1996 on transition and employment for youth with significant disabilities. Ms. Condon is also a consultant with Marc Gold & Associates and is on the board of Employment for All. Her experience prior to joining the university includes working as an employment consultant, managing a large supported employment program, and providing technical assistance and training to employment staff.

**Doug Crandell,** Director, Project Exceed, Cobb and Douglas Counties Community Services Boards, 2051 Greenridge Street, Smyrna, GA 30080

Mr. Crandell is employed at the Cobb and Douglas Counties Community Services Boards. He currently directs Project Exceed, a Customized Employment Grant funded by the U.S. Department of Labor, Office of Disability Employment Policy. In addition, he directs a Work Incentives Grant funded by U.S. Department of Labor, Employment and Training Administration. He has presented extensively on systems change and best practice. He has co-authored chapters in a book on customized employment edited by Dr. Paul Wehman and colleagues (*Real Work for Real Pay: Inclusive Employment for People with Disabilities*, 2006, Paul H. Brookes Publishing Co.).

# Foreword

In *The Job Developer's Handbook: Practical Tactics for Customized Employment*, authors Cary Griffin, David Hammis, and Tammara Geary offer advice to those of us who care about the employment of someone with a disability. After you educate yourself about who this very real person with a disability is, then please consider the possibility of this person working. Now, think of 10 people you know who have a disability. Take the time to think of each person working for him- or herself, for a small company, or for the government. Pretty amazing, isn't it? How could we have gone so long without considering all of the possibilities? It's obvious that we were looking for employment only through the lenses of our own employment and could only imagine employment as a version of our own employer–employee relationships.

Cary Griffin, David Hammis, and Tammara Geary, along with invited contributors Michael Callahan, Ellen Condon, Doug Crandell, and Nancy Brooks-Lane are offering us a new set of tools—proven techniques—that open up a whole world of employment possibilities for citizens with disabilities. Some tools, like tapping the obvious but overlooked contacts, connections, and other assets of the person's own family and friends, have always been there. Other tools, like those used by Doug Crandell and Nancy Brooks-Lane in Georgia, will give you powerful techniques to create jobs that have real career potential.

For too long, citizens with disabilities have been grouped together by well-meaning (yet frankly naïve) professionals who thought the best they could do for citizens with physical, mental, and intellectual challenges was to group them together for employment. Bluntly put, professionals in the past grouped these citizens together and hoped for the best. Some of these professionals never really believed citizens with disabilities could work as well or better than their counterparts without disabilities in this world of employment. Most critically, it was assumed that citizens who could do but a part of what someone without a disability could do would benefit from being with a lot of other substandard performers and then two, or three, or four people could do the work of someone without a disability. Relegated to sheltered workshops and paid far less than a fair wage for their work—less than minimum wage—people with disabilities *themselves* blew up these low expectations! Sheltered workshops became profitable off of the backs of people with disabilities. They were so profitable that today people with disabilities are still being exploited behind a veil of benevolence in sheltered workshops.

Twenty-five years have passed since the very first studies on supported employment. These studies showed the power of an employee with a disability learning his or her job at the real jobsite. This latest book by Cary Griffin, David Hammis, and Tammara Geary says in no uncertain terms that citizens with disabilities not only can work in real jobs throughout our communities but also can succeed once the ideal conditions of employment are determined, explored, created, or captured. Here, in the pages that follow, is how you can help people succeed.

People who work on behalf of citizens with disabilities who need employment should consider spending some time with this book. This resource can open up a whole world of possibilities that probably have never been considered. Taxpayers are asking us to deliver high-impact services that actually help citizens with disabilities have better lives and become taxpayers. These are the kinds of employment services that states should be paying for, instead of continuing to use taxpayer funds to maintain sheltered facilities, disability center–sponsored cleaning crews, and other congregate work approaches that forever lock these citizens into low-status and low-paying jobs without health benefits. We have known for a few years now that one of the smartest investments is in carefully crafted and customized individual employment. Unfortunately, too many of us just haven't known how. Now we will. This is great work.

*Stephen R. Hall, Ph.D.*
*Director*
*Georgia Office of Developmental Disabilities*
*Atlanta, GA*

# Introduction

It is estimated that only about half of all Americans read a book last year. We hope this statistic does not include the many great people in the rehabilitation field, because the fact is that knowledge is power, and powerful knowledge is what will change the lives of people with disabilities. The staggering unemployment rate of people with disabilities begs our field to innovate, explore new methods, and think differently. This book is offered in the hope that some old pros as well as new enthusiasts in the world of rehabilitation will discover a few unique tactics, use them, modify them, and create new employment opportunities.

Customized employment (CE) represents the next phase in the developmental process of understanding how to meld job seekers and employers for mutual benefit. This book presents no strict recipes for success; no dogmatic menus that must be followed point by point. No cookbook for job development exists, nor should one; while respecting individual complexities, interests, and talents is required, rigid linear approaches will not do. Instead, we offer guidelines for best practice for this particular point in time. After a combined tenure of over 60 years in community employment, we finally feel competent to offer our suggestions and hope these techniques lead to better, more effective outcomes.

Chapter 1 frames the current state of employment for individuals with disabilities, introduces CE, and suggests a planning framework for job developers. Chapter 2 is contributed by Michael Callahan of Employment for All and Ellen Condon of The University of Montana, two people who understand that where one begins in this process largely determines where one ends up. This book revolves around their chapter on discovery; read it intently.

In Chapter 3, the Job Analysis Record is introduced. We believe that some written form for justifying a job match and for planning on-site training and support strategies is essential for customizing employment. The critical thought necessary when organizing and recording one's observations brings order to the steps taken in the worksite. For thoughts to live, be defended, and be shared, they should be written down.

Chapter 4 presents a roadmap for job developers and employment specialists. This map is designed to accommodate detours and offers suggestions and milestones rather than absolute directions. Be forewarned: Applying shortcuts to these methods can cause serious delays and retracings of one's route. The ideas presented here withstood the test of time, and we suggest they be improved through experimentation but not shortchanged in the interests of time or money.

The chapter on active employer councils, unlike most of the others, is reasonably prescriptive. Just as in the job development processes extolled in Chapter 4, the information in Chapter 5 does not lend itself well to shortcuts of time and effort. Still, we do expect that practitioners will, and must, improve on our formula.

Chapter 6 addresses the topic of resource ownership. After over 15 years of using resource ownership, we caution readers to apply it sparingly. The Rehabilitation Act of 1973 (PL 93-112) enables people with disabilities to request tools, equipment, and training that enhance their employability, and the Workforce Investment Act of 1998 (PL 105-220) and Social Security Act of 1935 (PL 74-271), along with Social Security Act Amendments of 1967 (PL 90-48) and 1994 (PL 103-432), reinforce this notion. This chapter establishes a method for person-centered employment enhancement through the ownership of exploitable resources. Doug Crandell and Nancy Brooks-Lane, along with their remarkable team in Georgia, used this information wisely to create jobs with career potential.

Chapter 7 presents numerous tactics for problem-solving and interest-based negotiation, the linchpin of CE. Life is a series of negotiations. Yet, few front-line staff receive appreciable training or guidance in this discipline. Asking nicely for jobs is not enough in today's world; the ability to put employers and job seekers together, creating profitable employment, requires considerable skill and thought made possible by the negotiation process.

Chapter 8 breathes new life into job-carving approaches by presenting this restructuring technique in terms of matching the job seeker's ideal conditions of employment with the employer's need to get work out the door. Combining the elements of interest-based negotiation, discovery, job analysis, and sound job development strategy, job carves represent a practical outcome for individuals with complex support needs.

Negotiation also plays an important role in helping consumers, families, and the Social Security Administration (SSA) understand the impacts of wages on public benefits and the creative implementation of Social Security work incentives to maximize benefits through the use of a Plan to Achieve Self-Support (PASS). People with disabilities, families, and rehabilitation staff labor under destructive folklore about benefits. Chapter 9 provides both the rationale and concentrated instructions for leveraging these resources in pursuing good jobs.

When considering support needs, few resources are as necessary and powerful as those of the immediate family. For far too long, families have either been self-exiled from the rehabilitative process driven by the belief that the system will provide for their adult child or dismissed as troublesome or unrealistic advocates for their sons and daughters. Chapter 10 provides pointers for engaging families while respecting the right of the individual with disabilities to emancipate as an adult.

Finally, Chapter 11 explores the critical thinking and actions necessary for organizations to support CE. Rethinking leadership responsibilities, fiscal appropriations to augment employment success, public image, staff development and power, and consumer direction are all elements essential to creating an agile community rehabilitation program that focuses on one person at a time and thinks broadly about the future.

Thanks for reading this book and applying its lessons. Please contact the authors with suggestions for improvement. We are all learning together.

## REFERENCES

Rehabilitation Act of 1973, PL 93-112, 29 U.S.C. §§ 701 *et seq.*
Social Security Act Amendments of 1994, PL 103-432, 42 U.S.C. §§ 1305 *et seq.*
Social Security Act Amendments of 1967, PL 90-48, 42 U.S.C. §§ 1396 *et seq.*
Social Security Act of 1935, PL 74-271, 42 U.S.C. §§ 301 *et seq.*
Workforce Investment Act of 1998, PL 105-220, 29 U.S.C. §§ 794 *et seq.*

# Acknowledgments

This book is over 25 years in the making. If there is any credit to be given for particular insights or successes, it goes to the many individuals with disabilities and their families who have allowed us the privilege of assisting them with job development. For the mistakes that we have made along the way (and there were many!) we apologize. This book is also the work of many, many people who explored ideas with us, who challenged us, and who did the hard work with us in the field. We cannot name them all, and have likely and inadvertently missed a couple folks.

Thanks go to numerous colleagues, customers, and funders who took the risk of trusting us with their resources and reputations, including the following:

Our colleagues at the Rural Institute at The University of Montana: Roger Shelley, Marsha Katz, Mike Flaherty, Nancy Maxson, Connie Lewis, Timm Vogelsberg, Ellen Condon, and Kim Brown

Meg Sibert-Hammis at Connections to Quality

Doug Crandell, Nancy Brooks-Lane, Tod Citron, Kate Brady, Grant Jerkins, Wanda Standridge, Melissa Jones, Michelle Robison, Ella Scott, Lizzi Prioleau-Davis, Nicole Bass, Deborah Marshall, Gail Harris, Doris Smith, Brian Palumbo, Vicki Phillips, Chris Hunt, Lujan Brooks, and Delora Bennett at Cobb/Douglas CSB in Georgia, which often serves as our idea incubator

John Helton, Executive Director of CobbWorks!

Susan Parker, Chris Button, Speed Davis, and Faith Kirk at the U.S. Department of Labor, Office of Disability and Employment Policy

Alex Kielty at the U.S. Department of Labor, Employment and Training Administration

Paul Wehman, John Kregel, Vicki Brooke, Katty Inge, Grant Revell, and everyone at the Research & Training Center on Workplace Supports at Virginia Commonwealth University

Steve Hall, the Director of Developmental Disability Services in Georgia

Rich Toscano and Patty Cassidy at the University of Georgia

Katherine Carol at Tango Consulting in Denver

Casey Jeszenka at the SBDC in Guam

Celane McWhorter at APSE

Mike Callahan at Employment for All, who is always a step ahead of the rest of us

Corey Smith at VIA in Pennsylvania

Joe Longcor with the Medicaid Infrastructure grant in Michigan

Dave Roberts and Diana Beckley at RCEP VII in Missouri

Andy Houghton at Disability Inclusion Solutions

Jill Houghton, Berthy De La Rosa Aponte, and Stephen Fear at the Social Security
   Administration (SSA)

SSA Plan to Achieve Self-Support (PASS) specialists Timothy McEvoy, Vera Brodsky,
   Wanda Berry, Paula Ryan, Randall Griffin, Stephen Doty, Roxanna Hunt, Diane
   Vider, and Moui Nguyen and all of the other SSA PASS Specialists who wake up
   each day with the task of directly financially supporting SSA beneficiaries and
   recipients to become successfully employed

All of the benefits planning specialists across the country

Pat Boyle and Dawna Teeguarden at Rise, Inc., in Utah

Carol Beatty and the staff at The Arc of Howard County, Maryland

Brian DeAtley, Larissa Timmerberg, Therese Stein, Denise Perka, Debbie Ignatz, Tony
   Young, and others at NISH

Karen Lee, Steve Blanks, and the team at SEEC in Silver Spring, Maryland

Rich Leucking and staff at TransCen

Steve Savage and Theresa Stinson in Indiana

Cheryl Green at Provail in Seattle, for originally proposing the idea of the Big Sign
   Syndrome

Dale Dutton, Sherry Beamer, and Vickie Vining in California

Dale DiLeo at TRN, Inc.

Dee Prescott and her team at Easter Seals, Southern California

Dave Guido, Tara Thompson, and Beth Keeton at the University of South Florida

Bill Kiernan, Sheila Fesko, John Butterworth, David Hoff, Cori DiBiase and the folks
   at ICI in Boston

National Brain Injury Association

Alabama's Full Life Ahead Foundation

Partners in Policymaking across the country

All our friends who attend the annual Best-Go-West Rendezvous and leave communication with the outside world behind

… and a thousand others who helped!

*To two individuals wise beyond their years who made us better
people for having known them:*

*Rick Douglas was a tireless advocate for the employment of people with disabilities. He was
Vocational Rehabilitation Director for the state of Vermont, Executive Director of
the President's Committee on Employment of People with Disabilities, and Director of
Disability Initiatives for the Department of Labor. He played a key role in teaching us
about working successfully with business and was our friend and mentor.*

*Marty Trujillo grew up in Colorado's beautiful San Luis Valley. She reflected that beauty
as a lifelong advocate for meaningful lives who, on a local level, changed many of us
forever with her commonsense approach to rehabilitation, her compassion, her intelligence,
her humor, and most of all, her unwavering respect for people. She made life better for
everyone she knew, and there's no higher accomplishment than that.*

# The
# Job Developer's
# Handbook
## Practical Tactics for
## Customized Employment

# 1

# Introduction to Customized Job Development

*Cary Griffin, David Hammis, and Tammara Geary*

## THE CURRENT STATE OF AFFAIRS

The high unemployment rate for people with disabilities is not the result of a flaw in the system, it is the system. In order to change the realities of poverty and isolation endured by people with significant disabilities, changes in our approach to employment services must take top priority. Many community rehabilitation programs (CRPs) have adopted supported employment (SE) and even microenterprise development in the attempt to address the high unemployment and underemployment rate. However, the fact remains that the majority of people entering CRPs never leave. They are subjected to a system that is predicated on low expectations, that is sometimes unresponsive to individual needs, that invests in buildings instead of personalized supports, and that accepts group placements and stereotypical and entry-level jobs as the rule, rather than the exception. Regardless of disability type, be it developmental, psychiatric, brain injury, sensory, or physical, no particular group of people with disabilities is flourishing. Despite the ever increasing funding for disability-related programs and the additional layers of enabling legislation, the overall unemployment rate remains at approximately 65% (Metzel, Boeltzig, Butterworth, Sulewski, & Gilmore, 2007). College graduates with disabilities do not do remarkably better than the average and remain unemployed at a rate of over 54% (DeLoach, 1992). Individuals with psychiatric disabilities find jobs at a rate of less than 15% (Bond et al., 2001). The University of Alabama National Spinal Cord Injury Statistical Center (2006) reported that individuals with spinal cord injury experience a 58.1% unemployment rate, and armed services veterans with spinal cord injuries face an astounding unemployment rate of over 60% (Trieschmann, 1987).

The Individuals with Disabilities Education Improvement Act of 2004 (PL 108-446), Rehabilitation Act of 1973 (PL 93-112), Workforce Investment Act (WIA) of 1998 (PL 105-220), Americans with Disabilities Act of 1990 (PL 101-336), and the 1999 *Olmstead v. L.C.* decision from the Supreme Court all hold the potential and promise of equal access to careers and substantive employment (Wehman, 2006). Still, most transition-age youth from special education programs graduate without paying jobs, and most adults with significant disabilities remain unemployed or severely underemployed throughout their lifetimes (U.S. Census Bureau, 2001). During the 1990s, a decade that witnessed the strongest economy in the history of the United States, enrollments for sheltered workshops increased and the number of special education students graduating into paid jobs remained abysmally low (Butterworth, Gilmore, Kiernan, & Schalock, 1999; McGaughey, Kiernan, McNally, Gilmore, & Keith, 1994; Wehman, 2006). The trend continues today, with a meager 26% of adults with developmental disabilities securing community employment annually, primarily through the efforts of CRP-supported employment personnel (Metzel et al., 2007).

This same time period witnessed the success of SE techniques, with over 150,000 individuals in community jobs (Mank, Cioffi, & Yovanoff, 2003; Wehman & Kregel, 1998). These workers were once considered to be too disabled for employment, but the techniques of offering ongoing workplace and personal supports, coupled with matching people to jobs they enjoy, eroded previous stereotypes held by the rehabilitation professions and the business community (Callahan & Garner, 1997; Griffin et al., 1999; Wehman & Kregel, 1998). Prior to the Rehabilitation Act Amendments of 1986 (PL 99-506), funding for CRPs serving individuals with significant disabilities focused mainly on services in work activity centers and sheltered workshops (Brooks-Lane, Hutcheson, & Revell, 2005). These sheltered work settings performed a variety of outsourced or subcontracted assembly and handwork tasks drawn from various local businesses. Instead of seeking jobs for people with disabilities, job developers believed then, and still do, that people with disabilities need such intensive training and support that the best approach to rehabilitation was to keep them in segregated settings surrounded by staff. The 1986 amendments to the Rehabilitation Act, in Title VI, Part C, established the SE formula grants to all state vocational rehabilitation (VR) agencies. These funds were used to provide SE job development, coaching, and worksite supports to the person with a significant disability in order to maintain a job (Brooks-Lane et al., 2005).

In the 2 decades since the passage of the Rehabilitation Act Amendments of 1986, the number of individuals with significant disabilities working in community employment has increased steadily and the funding for SE has grown substantially. However, growth has also occurred in the number of persons in day and work programs in segregated settings (Braddock et al., 2004). In fiscal year 1988, only 23,000 individuals with developmental disabilities were engaged in SE, while almost 250,000 individuals were in sheltered day programs. By 1992, SE had grown over 200% to 75,000. And, from 1992 to 2002, SE enrollment for adults with developmental disabilities grew to almost 120,000 individuals. However, in the same period, another 365,000 individuals with developmental disabilities were being served in segregated work programs, and the majority of individuals with severe psychiatric disabilities receiving services remained in nonwork day treatment programs, even though the cost of SE success ranges from only $2,000 to $8,000, an amount less than the typical annual cost of day programs. The percentage of individuals with developmental disabilities in SE leveled off at 24% in fiscal year 2002 (Braddock, Hemp, Parish, & Rizzolo, 2002; Braddock, Rizzolo, & Hemp, 2004). For every single person in integrated employment earning competitive wages, three individuals remained in sheltered settings. Earnings for those in sheltered employment were, on average, substantially below minimum wage (Brooks-Lane et al., 2005).

The funding of SE progressed in proportion to the growth in participation but was substantially less than that available for traditional day programs. The Balanced Budget Act of 1997 (PL 105-33) provided for funding of SE through the Home and Community-Based Medicaid Waiver (Brooks-Lane et al., 2005). In fiscal year 1998, federal Medicaid funding for SE was only $35 million. By comparison, $514 million was allocated for segregated day program services. From 1998 through 2002, funding for community-based SE grew to $108 million, whereas funding for day programs was reduced to $488 million. Still, for every $1 spent on SE, $4 are allocated to segregated day programming (Braddock et al., 2002; Braddock et al., 2004).

## THE LABOR MARKET

People with disabilities and job developers face the vagaries of the labor market daily. Past competitive employment approaches to achieving employment, while generally accepted as the standard approach to accessing work, are largely ineffective and ill-advised for people with disabilities who are living complex lives (Callahan & Garner, 1997; Griffin & Hammis, 2003). Many traditional employment readiness programs still emphasize grooming and hygiene classes, hours of résumé writing and interview role playing, and various preparatory steps. Although these approaches work for some job seekers, they largely fail people with disabilities. SE best practices sought to mitigate the most brutal aspects of the competitive job search

1.  By introducing person-centered job development strategies

2.  By assuming that everyone can work and that the concept of *work readiness* ignores the work world's broad acceptance of a range of worksite behaviors and skills

3.  By providing for on-site job coaching and training

4.  By emphasizing the unique qualities and talents of each individual job seeker and individualizing the employment process

5.  By seeking a match between the worker's desires and the employer's needs (Callahan & Nisbet, 1997; Griffin & Hammis, 1996; Wehman & Kregel, 1998)

Even so, job developers and employment specialists still rely heavily on traditional methods of identifying employment opportunities (Bissonnette, 1994). These strategies include searching out openings in the want ads of local newspapers, canvassing human resources managers of local industry, attending U.S. Chamber of Commerce functions and other networking events, and sitting on local job development councils where members share job leads. And still, the labor market rejects the majority of people with disabilities. Even during the 1990s, when this country created over 20 million new jobs, the employment rate for people with disabilities remained as motionless as it does today during a time of economic stagnation (Kraus, Stoddard, & Gilmartin, 1996; Metzel et al., in preparation; Minnesota Governor's Council on Developmental Disabilities, 2005). The fact is, the labor market has almost no impact on the employment rate of people with significant disabilities. The formal disability service system in the United States isolates people with disabilities from the economic life of communities; erects buildings and programs that hide people with disabilities from the community; and fosters stereotypes through fundraising appeals, segregated recreation and social events, and the hegemony of specialized services that harms people by making them objects of pity (Shapiro, 1993). The labor market is malleable and accessible, and good job development techniques will reduce the stigma induced by the ongoing clienthood of people with disabilities.

## BIG SIGN SYNDROME

As consultants to community employment programs across the United States, we often observe both the congestion of job developers descending upon the most visible employers in their communities, as well as the profusion of entry-level and stereotypical jobs for people with disabilities. This is an unfortunate result of growing caseloads, unrealistic time lines, and inadequate training and supervision provided to employment specialists, who adapt and mitigate the circumstances by approaching the same box stores, grocery chains, and discount vendors for ready-made, often high-turnover, entry-level jobs, on the ubiquitous commercial strips across the country. When job searches are person centered, the focus turns instead to helping the job seeker use his or her personal genius to advantage. The need to seek out existing job descriptions wanes, and job creation rises to the forefront of the job developer's duties. Job creation demands creativity and one-off thinking, hence the term *customized employment* (CE), which will be explored later in this chapter. When searching for adaptability, minimized bureaucracy in hiring, and prompt decision making, there is no substitute for the small business environment.

Small businesses in the United States create more jobs than big industry, and of the estimated 20 million businesses in this country, only 14,000 have more than 500 employees (Thornton & Lunt, 1997). The U.S. Chamber of Commerce estimates that almost 80% of their members are small business owners (Donohue, 2006). So, here is where the jobs are, in these companies scattered throughout the urban, suburban, and rural landscapes of America.

## THE BIG BANG

Job developers often revel in the accomplishment of finding jobs in large corporations. Establishing relationships with huge companies can mean multiple placement successes once an "in" is nurtured with the vice president for human resources or some similarly well-placed champion. It is true that these companies, including Wal-Mart, McDonalds, IBM, Hewlett-Packard, Citicorp, Home Depot, and others, mean good jobs for people. It also means significant time and effort spent cracking the hiring code and competing with 200 applicants for each job. Changes in shift managers or department heads, something all too common in big business, can signal a change in corporate culture on the local store or factory level that leads to folks with significant disabilities losing their jobs or suffering reduced hours and opportunities. Still, the seductiveness of landing a dozen jobs scattered throughout a company with just one good shot, the Big Bang, is too hard for most job developers to resist. And a few Fortune 500 company references on one's résumé guarantee continued personal career advancement.

Experience teaches us that working with big companies can yield significant payoffs for people with disabilities. In the early 1990s in Colorado, co-author David Hammis and the team at the Center for Technical Assistance and Training, along with the state VR agency and the late Rick Douglas from the U.S. Department of Labor, established the prototype for what would become the Business Leadership Network (BLN). At their monthly meetings, this group of employers was actively involved in meeting job seekers, using their personal and professional networks, and creating employment up and down their supplier and customer chains. With David taking the lead, these members of the BLN, many from very large corporations, helped find work for about 50 people with significant disabilities in 1 year's time. The small business members were just as active as the others, but the complications in creating employment were significantly reduced. By seeking the Big Bang of a corporate account, job developers may be creating more work than necessary.

## THE PROBLEM

Looking for jobs in big companies makes sense. Cultivating relationships with human resources people is one important aspect of identifying opportunities for employment that often result in fringe benefits and long-term employment tenure. But this is just one part of the equation.

Driving down the strip in any community reveals all the same box stores: the home improvement company, the department store, the discount store, and the fast food giants. Although these employers are happy to employ people with disabilities, they can also be the toughest to break into. Big companies have standardized approaches. Their job descriptions are developed far away at corporate headquarters by human resources people and labor attorneys, and when they advertise available positions, 200 applicants show up for the same job opening. The competitiveness of this job market, the sluggishness of the corporate office to approve a local job modification that accommodates an applicant with a disability, and the dead-end nature of ubiquitous part-time positions must be a consideration for job seekers and developers alike.

In a recent job development seminar, one of the authors was reminded by over 40 employment specialists working in a community of 6 million people that human resources staff complain regularly that someone from a human services agency is always knocking on their doors, looking for jobs. These developers suffer from Big Sign Syndrome. Over the course of a year, every agency visits every store numerous times, seeking ready-made jobs. Meanwhile, the small businesses, many hidden from view and requiring a networking effort to crack open, remain beyond the vision of these job cruisers—although these businesses often have no set application method, they hire based on word of mouth, and a written job description can be a rarity.

## THE SMALL BUSINESS FIX

Getting off a town's main thoroughfare is the most obvious fix for Big Sign Syndrome. Getting to that point sometimes requires a network. To develop a professional network, consider some of the following options.

1. Use a CRP Board of Directors member to have lunch or get an informational interview with small business owners they know who might have employment opportunities related to the interests of a job seeker.

2. Join Lions Club, Rotary, the chamber of commerce, or a similar organization and get to know the diversity of businesses and industries in the local community.

3. Complete a relationship map with others in the agency to identify staff, family, and friends who own or work for local businesses. (A relationship map is a listing of individual, social, and professional connections that can be accessed during job development activities.)

4. Complete a relationship map with families and consumers to identify the local companies where they purchase goods and services, and those family members who either own businesses themselves or who can serve as entrees into businesses they frequent or work for.

5. Identify the suppliers of the many goods and services the rehabilitation agency buys and enlist them as employers or as connectors to other potential employers in their networks.

Identifying smaller employers who may fit the employment needs of specific consumers is just one step in curing Big Sign Syndrome. A job creation approach is required to create jobs or intrigue employers of small businesses that are undercapitalized and surviving on limited profit margins. Breaking the cycle of entry-level employment for people with disabilities mandates creative rethinking of positions and opportunities to avoid the typical scenario of part-time, minimum-wage jobs (Boeltzig, Gilmore, & Butterworth, 2006). One successful approach that we have used for years now is *resource ownership* (see Chapter 6). This approach recognizes that a small business might sell more goods, better satisfy customers, or increase market share by adding a person with particular talents or technology. For instance, a baker we worked with recently heard customers complaining that they could not buy an espresso to go with their fresh pastry. The baker simply could not afford a $4,000 espresso maker. But then a young lady itching to go to work in a coffee shop through a CE project in Georgia and some VR dollars was able to purchase the machine and create a new position within the company (Griffin, Brooks-Lane, Hammis, & Crandell, 2006). This mutually beneficial approach helped a struggling entrepreneur and created a career track based on an individual's work preferences. And, happy customers mean more business, which means higher wages all around.

In this case, the espresso machine is the same lever that a college degree or a welding certificate represents for other job seekers with or without disabilities. For the job seeker, possessing exploitable resources, whether it be brain power or a color Xerox machine that boosts customer satisfaction at the local copy shop, is critical for the creation of jobs a few rungs up the career ladder from entry level. Resource ownership means acquiring the materials, equipment, or skills that an employer can use to make a profit. For instance, many people spend $50,000 or more on a college degree, and that degree is a symbol of exploitable resources. Employers reason that they can profit from a graduate's intellect, so people with degrees get hired and earn substantially higher wages than employees without degrees (Kamenetz, 2006). The graduate gives the employer that degree in trade for wages. The same occurs when a truck driver who owns a tractor trailer applies for a hauling job. Without the trucking equipment, the trucker is possibly forced to face unemployment, or a less satisfactory, lower paying trucking job in which the employer has to buy the equipment.

Large companies, such as IBM and Boeing, can afford their own equipment, and negotiation using resource ownership as a job creation tactic will likely end in a bureaucratic tangle of policy and regulation. Small businesses, however, are perfect for job creation strategies such as this, because the job developer and job seeker are dealing with the owner or manager. There are few, if any, layers of approval to be navigated, and management is less likely to change and reverse previous hiring decisions. A small business owner can see immediate results in the bottom line by adding valuable products or services, and employers still tell us that they enjoy creating jobs for people. Giving back to the community by employing one's neighbors is one of the joys of owning a business.

## CUSTOMIZED EMPLOYMENT

SE has produced outstanding but constrained results. As noted, the disability system still emphasizes segregation over inclusion, and funding methodologies reinforce this circumstance (Braddock et al., 2004). The lessons learned from SE are important: People can and want to work; a little support in job seeking and worksite training stabilizes employment; people in community jobs report higher quality of life and greater economic participation in their communities (Priebe, Warner, Hubschmid, & Eckle, 1998). CE grew from the broad foundation laid by SE and relies upon the same guiding values.

### Zero Exclusion

All people, regardless of severity or type of disability, have the right to live, work, and recreate in settings integrated with their chosen community.

## Partial Participation

All people have something or some part of something that they can do and enjoy doing. It is our job to see that this spark or personal genius is put to practical and profitable use in order to begin the development of real work and civic involvement.

## Zero Instructional Inference

For many people with disabilities, the best place to learn is in environments where the target skills will be utilized. Therefore, the use of developmental continuum and earning the right to a job or a social activity is eliminated, based upon the solid evidence that preparatory training has little validity. Segregated settings are not necessary and are indeed a detriment to teaching and learning (Brown et al., 1979).

## Mutuality

We must at all times attribute thinking and feeling to all people regardless of level or type of disability. The Golden Rule should be kept in mind consistently in all planning and in all interactions with people with disabilities, their friends, and family. Service alternatives that individuals with disabilities or anyone else find undesirable should not be proposed.

## Interdependence

All people rely upon a social network that assists them in daily life and in times of personal crisis. People with disabilities who have limited social networks and few friends can benefit from opportunities to participate and exhibit competence in a variety of settings with nondisabled citizens (Condeluci, 1991).

## Customized Employment and Communities

CE is being demonstrated in communities across the nation and numerous questions and concerns are being raised as this advanced employment strategy expands. The U.S. Department of Labor, Office of Disability and Employment Policy (ODEP), explained that

> CE means individualizing the employment relationship between employees and employers in ways that meet the needs of both. It is based on an individualized determination of the strengths, needs, and interests of the person with a disability, and is also designed to meet the specific needs of the employer. (ODEP Customized Employment Grants Notice, 2002)

It may include employment developed through job carving, self-employment or entrepreneurial initiatives, or other job development or restructuring strategies that result in job responsibilities being customized and individually negotiated to fit the needs of individuals with a disability. CE assumes the provision of reasonable accommodations and supports necessary for the individual to perform the functions of a job that is individually negotiated and developed (ODEP Customized Employment Grants Notice, 2002).

The principal hallmarks and activities of CE include

Identifying specific job duties or employer expectations that are negotiated with employers

Targeting individualized job goals in order to negotiate based on the needs, strengths, and interests of the employment seeker

Meeting the unique needs of the employment seeker and the discrete, emerging needs of the employer

Starting with the individual as the source of information for exploring potential employment options

Offering representation, as needed, for employment seekers to assist in negotiating with employers

Finding employment that occurs in integrated, inclusive environments in the community or in a business alongside people who do not have disabilities

Finding employment that results in pay at the prevailing wage or better (no subminimum wages)

Creating employment through self-employment and business ownership

Facilitating an amalgam of supports and funding sources that may include Workforce Investment (One-Stops), VR, Medicaid, CRPs, schools, the Social Security Administration (SSA), families, and other partners coordinated in ways to meet the needs of the individual (Callahan, 2004; Condon & Brown, 2005; Griffin & Hammis, 2005)

## MAKING CUSTOMIZED EMPLOYMENT WORK

Making CE work raises numerous questions. Is CE just a new name for SE? As Mike Callahan of Employment for All said, CE "stands on the shoulders of supported employment" (Callahan, 2003). CE is a refinement of SE but varies in important ways. SE still reacts to the labor market, although in best practice it should not (Condon, Gelb, & Gould, 2005). That is, the job search process is largely driven by what jobs are available, advertised, or easy to find in that community or region. By contrast, CE develops the employment seeker's profile without consideration of what might be available for work in the community. The first step is getting to know the employment seeker without the prejudice of "appropriate work" or "realistic goals." Once the person is known, then work can be explored on his or her terms. In other words, employment situations are sought that meet the needs of the individual, and a negotiation follows that melds the desires of the worker with those of the employer. Under the SE model, the existence of a labor market mindset drives the kinds of jobs sought for people with disabilities, hence the high proportion of food service, custodial, and high-turnover jobs. CE counteracts this impulse of filling available jobs and instead uses *discovery,* a process in which discovery of the individual is the driving force in the job creation process. Discovery seeks to create mutually beneficial employment relationships (Callahan, 2004; Condon & Brown, 2005; Griffin, Brooks-Lane, Hammis, & Crandell, 2006).

Whereas SE makes allowances for congregate or group settings, such as mobile crews and enclaves, where subminimum wages may be paid, CE is specifically individualized and accepts commensurate wages only, in integrated settings. CE also includes business ownership as an employment option (Griffin & Hammis, 2003).

### How Does One Get to Know the Employment Seeker?

The most widely used process is called discovery (Callahan, 2004; Condon & Brown, 2005). Discovery is not planning, but rather it is an assessment process that seeks to answer the questions "Who is this person?" and "What are the ideal conditions of employment?" (See Figure 1.1 for a plan that uses the discovery process; a blank version of this form is located in the appendix at the back of the book.) The process often starts at home by taking an inventory of the surrounding neighborhood. Because transportation and natural supports are ongoing employment and inclusion issues, it makes sense to look first for interests and opportunities nearby. The discovery process then expands to places where interests can be explored through informational interviews, paid work experiences, or engagement in social activities. One vital point to remember during discovery is that the CE team members (i.e., the employment specialist, the employment seeker, family members, and all others involved) are looking for not only a job description and employment but also an outcome that reflects the complexity of human life. In other words, multiple employment directions, vocational interests, and skills should be revealed, which can then be used to create employment in the community. (Discovery is also covered in Chapter 2.)

## Wouldn't a Standardized Vocational Evaluation Be More Scientific than Discovery?

Standardized vocational evaluation has never been proven to predict employment success. Discovery replaces the predictive validity assertion of vocational evaluation and psychometric testing with the ecologically valid process of witnessing an individual's needs, skills, desires, interests, and contributions in real community environments. Witnessing an individual's skills, talents, and behaviors in typical community and work environments (ecological validity) is much more functional and therefore more cost effective than traditional approaches to assessment, which often screen people out of employment services instead of capturing their potential as workers and human beings.

## Isn't Customized Employment Too Expensive?

CE is too new to have generated any definitive cost data. The question is a good one but might be further refined by asking, "Too expensive for whom?" As of 2005, approximately 74% of adults with developmental disabilities remain unemployed, served largely in sheltered work or non–work-related day programs operated across the country (Metzel et al., 2007). The unemployment rate for individuals with psychiatric disabilities is worse and estimated at close to 85%, even though individuals with psychiatric disabilities list being employed as their greatest need and desire (Becker & Drake, 2003; Bond et al., 2001). The tremendous expense of building over 5,000 day programs, segregated transportation systems, and associated services has not delivered gainful employment, adequate training for employment, or social inclusion, and it has cost taxpayers a great deal of money. CE can be accomplished for those needing such an intensive approach by blending day program funding, VR and WIA supports, and/or Social Security work incentives, such as a Plan to Achieve Self-Support (PASS). Examples to 2005 do not reveal extraordinary costs at all. In fact, it can be effectively demonstrated that using a year's typical day program funding can easily fund wage employment or business ownership for an individual with significant disabilities.

For instance, the national average rate for a person in a day program is approximately $12,000. The average cost of an SE placement for VR is just under $5,000. Using $12,000 just from the day program could cover the costs of discovery, job development or small business start-up, and coaching. Even using a couple thousand dollars a year for ongoing supports (i.e., extended employment), renders the cost of employment significantly lower. For example, let's say that an individual enters a day program at a cost of $12,000 per year. Outcomes data suggest this person will likely be there for 30 years or more (Braddock et al., 2004). Assuming no increases in funding (highly unlikely), the taxpayer bill for this program is $360,000, plus Supplemental Security Income payments in excess of $208,440 (again assuming no increases and not including the cost of Medicaid). Using the CE approach, the cost scenario might be as much as $12,000 for employment development services, plus $2,000 a year in additional vocational supports, or $72,000 over 30 years. (These expenses will no doubt vary based on the complexity of support needs, competence of the trainers, and job match precision.) At earnings of just $6 per hour for 30 hours per week (the typical weekly enrollment hours for a day program), this person would be expected to earn $9,360 per year, or $280,800 over the next 30 years, plus SSA savings of over $100,000, conservatively figured. Even assuming the person changes jobs three or four times, CE is still less expensive.

## Is Customized Employment About Helping People Find Their Dream Jobs?

People with disabilities, just like everyone else, live complex lives. The more exposure they have to ideas, diverse environments, people, and activities, the more interests they develop. Believing that any of them has only one dream job is quite limiting when careers are considered. We once worked with a young man and asked a question we should no longer be asking, "Tell us, Bill, what's your dream job?" He told us that he wanted to rewind videotapes for Blockbuster Video. That seems like a very limiting position, one that is likely isolated from other workers, that is repetitious and boring, and that holds little potential for natural support development or career and skill advancement. In truth, this dream job answer was the result of the job developer asking this question of someone with limited life experiences (other than weekly outings to the movie theater), and it reflected the limited skills of the agency's personnel, who could help someone master video rewinding but who could teach few tasks of more complexity. Following the discovery process, Bill revealed that he really aspired to be a movie director, and this opened up discussions about entertainment, acting, and theatrical production. Now there were many jobs open to Bill for exploration. Focusing in on a dream job is too limiting and can sometimes prove misleading. CE reveals themes in people's lives and is open to combinations of interests that lead to new and diverse career directions (Griffin et al., 2006).

## What Are the Roles of Workforce Investment Act Programs and Vocational Rehabilitation in Customized Employment?

CE is specifically designed for anyone living a complex life. In this instance, we are considering people with significant disabilities. Both WIA and VR programs are vital partners in creating wage employment and small business ownership. Both systems can singularly and collaboratively blend funding with other systems (e.g., CRPs, school transition programs). The WIA system, which encompasses both the WIA One-Stop and the VR systems, directs its counselors to seek out similar benefits or resources and to use WIA or VR funds to purchase job acquisition resources not covered or underfunded by the other systems. For example, one young man with a diagnosis of autism needed funds for a small business start-up, as well as ongoing support to make deliveries across town. The CRP funded an employment specialist to do the driving several hours a day for the first year, until the young business owner could afford to hire his own employee to do the driving. VR purchased auto repairs for a vehicle donated by his family, and WIA, under a CE demonstration project, purchased several thousand dollars in production equipment. In other cases, a PASS can also be used in combination with VR, CRP, and WIA funds to purchase equipment, put cash into a small business, pay for various supports, and also to assist with the identification and maintenance of a wage job (Griffin et al., 2006).

## Customized Employment Sounds Creative, but What About Today's Labor Market?

Over the past 5 years there has been a net loss of jobs in the United States. The unemployment rate for people with disabilities, however, remains unchanged from the 1990s when this country created over 20 million new jobs (Hatch & Clinton, 2000). The labor market has almost no impact on the employment rate of people with disabilities. What does have an impact is the will of leadership at all levels to make employment a priority. The money exists, the technology and techniques exist, and the employment opportunities exist.

CE is significantly different from competitive employment. Whereas the competitive employment process has been brutal to people with disabilities, CE recognizes that employers are always hiring. There is always room in a company for people who match the culture and values of the company, and who perform work that ultimately produces a profit. Without profit there are no jobs, so matching people with duties that create revenue overshadows the power of job descriptions that historically screened out people with significant disabilities. CE demands that we focus on economic development and job creation as the antidote to reacting to the alleged demands of the fickle labor market.

## Getting Started

Paramount to CE and good job development practice is the habit of writing down information in a thoughtful and organized manner. Such a record of information and exploration allows teams to share information, and to think critically about statements willingly committed to paper. A formal record helps organize and sequence our development and training actions, and it provides the documentation of effort so critical to building a legacy of quality customer service. The CE Management Plan is a tool used to guide job development efforts (see Figure 1.1; a blank version of this form appears in the appendix). (See Figure 1.2 for a sample of a CE plan design.) Note that in the exam-

---

### GRIFFIN-HAMMIS CUSTOMIZED EMPLOYMENT (CE) MANAGEMENT PLAN

Name: James R. Dodge          Date: 4/1/06

Mailing Address: 505 Meadowlark Lane, Hamilton, MT 59844

Phone: (406) 370-0797          E-mail: (father's) rdodge@qwest.com

URL: N/A          Fax: N/A

Gender: Male          Ethnicity: Nez Perce (Native American)

Age (optional): 23          Primary/secondary disability: Developmental disability (DD)/physical disability

#### Ideal conditions of employment (from discovery):
Working in an accessible space within a short driving distance of home (or with a car pool); working during the day rather than at night; learning new things with some assistance available; full-time work is preferred in an uncrowded, small setting, well lighted, with the local radio station playing. The opportunity to learn about car and truck repair and paint and bodywork; the opportunity to learn radio broadcasting (music) (Revised 1/15/06)

#### Where I'm at my best:
Talking with friends about cars; riding around; listening to rock music

#### When and where I need the most support:
Learning new tasks, such as the computer or a CD copier without clear hands-on instruction. "Show me; don't talk to me!" I tend to be shy around new people and do not like crowds of unfamiliar people.

#### People who know me best:
My dad and mom; Ellen, the special education teacher; Uncle Samuel; my best friend, Henry, who I graduated with; Jerry, my counselor at Mountain Vocational Services (MVS)

---

**Figure 1.1.**   Griffin-Hammis customized employment (CE) management plan.

(continued)

**Figure 1.1.**  *(continued)*

## Current CE Team Members

| Name | Affiliation | Phone/E-mail | Expertise |
|---|---|---|---|
| Jerry Adams | Employment specialist | 370-4434 | Job development |
| Trina Lightly | State DD resource coordinator | 370-2430 | Case coordination |
| Roger Dodge | Father | 370-0797 | Parent (retired history teacher) |
| Mary Dodge | Mother | 370-0797 | Parent (high school art teacher) |
| Samuel Dodge | Uncle | 370-2292 | Family (rancher) |
| Henry Cisneros | Best friend | 243-8456 | Friend and college student (former classroom mentor) |

## CE Team Members, Mentors, or Consultants Needed

| Name | Affiliation | Phone/e-mail | Expertise | Who will contact |
|---|---|---|---|---|
| N/A at this time | | | | |
| | | | | |
| | | | | |

## Vocational Profile

**Key interests:**

Live music, cars, working on his uncle's ranch, church

Note: See the discovery summary below for a more thorough review

**Preferred situations/activities:**

Smaller venues without a lot of strangers; enjoys tasks that involve solving problems; likes to use his hands and is somewhat mechanical; enjoys working with animals; does not enjoy computers!

**Situations/activities to avoid:**

Except for reading his car and music magazines, Jim prefers to have work that involves physical activity, assisting other people (e.g., customers), working with animals, or working in an uncrowded setting. Verbal instructions often frustrate Jim; modeling approaches and precision training techniques work best for complex skill acquisition. Jim can get quite frustrated when presented with time-sensitive tasks that are not reinforced with good instruction.

## Methods for Gathering Additional Vocational Profile Information

| | Approach/action | Date(s) of activity | Person responsible | Comments/outcomes |
|---|---|---|---|---|
| 1. | Observed at his last job (of several years) at the feed/farm supply store. Interviewed current employer who was positive about Jim but felt it was not a good situation after several years. | February 2005 | JA | Jim was asking for a new job; has since left this employment. |
| 2. | Interviewed uncle about Jim's activities on the ranch. Uncle lives 45 minutes away and, without Jim driving, hiring on a regular basis is difficult. | February 2006 | JA | Have been pursuing Jim's driver's education possibilities; possible Plan to Achieve Self-Support for a car and adaptive controls; Uncle has some part-time work available and will help with future job development connections (he got Jim his first job lead that resulted in the feed store job). |
| 3. | Interviewed family | February 2006 | JA | Mom and Dad are very supportive; noted Jim's household chores and hobbies (e.g., cooking, cleaning, mowing the lawn, weeding the garden, washing the car [with Dad], reading, fishing, church). Family has many interests and connections: Dad is a Vietnam-era vet and has approached the Legion Hall about employing Jim; they will provide transit within town and prefer daytime hours. They support Jim in his goal of moving out on his own (see discovery summary for more). |
| 4. | Vocational rehabilitation and the One-Stop Center, along with MVS, are supporting on-the-job trainings and discovery | February–June 2006 | JA and team | As noted above |

**Customized Employment (CE) Plan Design**

1. CE design refinement:

    A. Meet with team to determine discovery activities

    B. Plan for on-the-job trainings (OJTs)

    C. Develop a PowerPoint-based portfolio for sales calls (if needed)

    D. Use team member networks to find job leads

    E. Approach new employers by suggesting that Jim is "planning his career and needs information on a possible direction. Can you help?"

    F. Complete benefits analysis to project funding for car and possible resource ownership or small business capitalization

2. Business feasibility study if indicated by discovery (attach instruments as appropriate):

    A. Various business ideas have surfaced, including a freelance concert promoter, hired hand on ranches, and a DJ for parties and public events. To date, Jim has not been excited about running his own business.

3. Business plan if indicated by discovery (attach draft):

    N/A

4. Benefits analysis (attach draft): N/A

5. School transition plan (attach draft):

    N/A

6. Tribal planning activities (attach draft): No connection to Nez Perce tribe; some familial connections to the reservation in Idaho

    1. Other (e.g., specialized training/classes needed):

        A. Investigate adaptive driver's education program in Missoula

        B. Approach One-Stop about Individual Training Account for auto-body technician or mechanic's assistant. (Preliminary call reveals no local training programs, but One-Stop will discuss supplementing employer on-the-job training in a local business)

**Personal Budget**

| Resources | Current $ | Potential $ |
|---|---|---|
| Day program funding | $12,000 | Approximately $5,000 for job development services and coaching (no cash value under current funding structure) |
| Vocational rehabilitation (VR) | $3,000 in services | $3,000 potential for a business |
| Workforce Investment Act (WIA) | $1,500 in services | No cash available directly to job seekers under current funding structure |
| Tribal VR/other tribal | N/A | N/A |
| Social Security/Plan to Achieve Self-Support (PASS) | $0 | Excellent PASS potential; analysis is being performed. Estimated conservatively at $10,188 over 36 months |
| School | N/A | N/A |
| Savings/personal assets | $0 | $0 |
| Family | unknown | unknown |
| Loans/grants | N/A | N/A |
| Other | | |
| Totals | $16,500 | $18,188 |

**Figure 1.2.** Customized employment (CE) plan design.

*(continued)*

**Figure 1.2.** *(continued)*

---

### Specific Roles of Supporting Organizations/Individuals

| | |
|---|---|
| CRP | Job development, PASS development and management, job site coaching, extended employment supports |
| VR | Possible business funding, job development, and coaching |
| WIA | OJT funds |
| Tribal | |
| SCORE | |
| SBA/SBDC/TBIC | |
| School | |
| Individual | Discovery, career interviews, and job tryouts |
| Family | Transportation, networking, work experience on ranch |
| Investors | |
| Partner | |
| Other | Best friend will assist with discovery and career/work experience development |
| Other | |

### Ongoing CE Support Development

| Item/activity | Due date | Persons responsible | Comments |
|---|---|---|---|
| Job development | 7/1/06 | JA | Will have completed discovery, OJTs, and will have begun a new job by July |
| Business plan | | | |
| PASS design/submission | 7/1/06 | JA and state benefits planning assistance and outreach staff | Once career objective is known, PASS will be written for equipment, training, car, etc., as appropriate |
| Worksite support/training | 7/1/06 | JA | As required |
| Financial plan | | | |
| Benefits monitoring | 7/1/06 | JA, family, state resource coordinator | Set up management system for reporting PASS and earnings to SSA |
| Business supports | | | |
| Transportation | 7/1/06 | Family | Long term to assist Jim with personal transit |
| Assistive technology | 7/1/06 | JA/state assistive technology program | Seating evaluation completed; Medicaid may be asked for power chair if work duties require it; possible universal technology needs depending upon job |
| Rehabilitation supports | 7/1/06 | JA | Short-term job coaching mostly to assist the natural training in learning how best to teach and support Jim |
| Other | | | |

---

ple, Jim is someone known well by the provider agency, and therefore the discovery process is abbreviated. A more thorough discovery process and management plan would be required if Jim were not well known to those assisting him, and if he had not already worked for a significant amount of time. Figure 1.3 documents how a job not being considered for Jim arose through discovery and work tryout efforts. (See Figures 1.4 and 1.5 for examples of a Quarter One and Quarter Two CE Development Progress Report as applied to Jim; blank versions of these forms, as well as forms for Quarters Three and Four, appear in the appendix at the end of the book.)

**Date: 4/15/06**

**Field notes (i.e., what's happened to date, who is involved, critical issues, etc.):**

Jim was referred to my caseload after losing his job at Bitterroot Feed and Supply store. Jim was responsible for sweeping floors, cleaning restrooms, and stocking lower shelves. There were problems with new tasks. For example, instructions for running the pricing gun were not explained to him. Jim also made it clear that he does not wish to be a janitor or shelf stocker after almost 3 years of this part-time job.

Jim and I assembled his team and explained discovery would be used to answer the question, "Who is this person?" Once we knew, we could begin to explore job matches. We decided to meet first in the family home where Jim lives. Jim's folks described Jim as someone always wanting to help out. He loves to cook breakfast on the weekends, he likes getting dressed up for church, and he likes to go fishing in the summer with his friend Henry. (There's a new accessible fishing pier on the river in town, but Henry used to help Jim into his raft occasionally, too.) Mom noted that Jim gets frustrated when she tries to teach Jim to draw; he doesn't feel he's talented in this way and doesn't enjoy drawing unless it's a hot rod or another kind of car (which he draws fine already). Dad noted that Jim is not interested in reading, writing, or math, but will read his car and rock-and-roll magazines from cover to cover. Jim especially enjoys visiting his uncle's ranch. He hasn't been able to get on a tractor yet, but he can maneuver throughout the milk barn and feed the cows grain and hay as long as someone pushes the feed cart ahead of him. (Jim uses a manual chair; a motorized chair could solve this problem.) He especially enjoys helping his uncle with painting and uses brushes, rollers, and the paint sprayer. (He has painted the bottom sections of the sheds, the milk barn, and his uncle's house.) He especially enjoys helping his uncle fix the various vehicles around the ranch and has assisted with handing his uncle tools when his uncle changed the clutch in his truck.

Jim has been very vocal about learning to be a mechanic or a paint and body customizer. We are still working on this. Jim is scheduled to do a paid work experience at Hamilton AutoBody for 1 week this month with wages paid by the Workforce Center, and his uncle is planning to have Jim assist with the inoculation of 200 cows in May. We have been unable to explore a work experience at the local radio station (which is located within walking distance of the family home); it is now almost totally automated and uses a downloaded playlist. Jim and Henry are going to check out the bands playing at the Mint Bar over the next couple weekends and will ask them for advice on breaking into the music business. Jim and his dad went to the music department at the local big box store, but were told that their liability policies would not allow for work experiences or internships. (This is doubtful, but it is what the staff there believe.) They were also told that he could fill out an application and go through an interview, but Jim decided he wasn't interested.

**Critical issues:**

Transportation to/from work is an issue (his folks do this now). Jim was making only about $200 a month gross at his last job and cannot afford to move out on his own as he wants to do; his vocational rehabilitation (VR) counselor has suggested that Jim learn to drive through the adaptive driver's education program at the university, but his parents are fearful for his safety.

**Opportunities:**

Jim is receiving a Supplemental Security Income (SSI) check of $300 per month and a Social Security Disability Insurance (SSDI) check of $303 per month. He is a good candidate for a Plan to Achieve Self-Support (PASS). Montana VR services have agreed to purchase job-coaching supports up to 60 hours. The Bitterroot Workforce Center (One-Stop) has agreed to fund up to $1,500 in on-the-job training (OJT) wages. Mountain Vocational Services (MVS) will provide the discovery, job development, worksite instruction, long-term (extended) supports, and auxiliary transportation. Jim's former employer is willing to provide a letter of reference and will make personal phone calls on Jim's behalf to prospective employers and training sites.

**Next steps:**

Follow through on the work experience at the body shop; make sure Jim assists his uncle; get funding offers formalized; follow up on Jim and Henry's visit with musicians.

**Figure 1.3.**   Field notes.

*(continued)*

**Figure 1.3.**  *(continued)*

**Date: 5/15/06**

**Field notes (i.e., what's happened to date, who is involved, critical issues, etc.):**

The musicians were especially helpful, but could not imagine Jim being on their payroll. They saw transportation, accessibility of venues, and physical strength as real liabilities to working on the road with any band. However, they suggested back-office opportunities such as bookings agent, recording engineer, or CD sales on the Internet as promising opportunities. Jim was not especially excited about any of these ideas and repeated that he likes listening to the bands instead; he does not especially even care for recorded music but rather favors watching live music.

The OJT at Hamilton AutoBody went very well. Long-term employment would require some modification of work benches (i.e., lowering to assist Jim with mixing paint) and some job carving of tasks, but overall Jim fit in really well, and the coworkers really seemed to enjoy having Jim there. Jim was introduced to paint mixing using graduated paint cups. While Jim couldn't really understand the numbers of ounces, he immediately picked up on the concept of proportions and ratios of thinner to base coat; all the cups are already marked with standard measures so that anyone can mix the paint with a little practice and instruction. Jim was also taught how to run a jitterbug air sander. At first, the supervisor was concerned since Jim couldn't reach above the fender and quarter panels, but I explained that perhaps someone else could do the sanding on the top surfaces of the vehicles. The supervisor felt they had enough work to keep two people sanding. Jim was also instructed in application of body filler and got to spray a panel with primer. He enjoyed all these activities, and an employment negotiation with the owner of the garage is pending. They currently do not have any positions open, but we will explore some resource ownership options and job creation possibilities in the coming 2 weeks.

While assisting Jim at the body shop and sketching out a job analysis in order to refine the training plan, I got to talking with a customer who was having his car pinstriped and had stopped by to see its progress. His name is Greg, and he owns Engine Rebuilders, adjacent to the county fairgrounds. He noticed Jim and asked about my relationship with him. I said Jim was doing some career exploration: that he really liked cars and that this was a job tryout to see if he liked it. Greg asked Jim how he was doing and Jim noted that the work was "fun so far." After Greg left, I asked Jim if he was interested in pursuing a tour of Engine Rebuilders. I explained that it was a machine shop that did precision engine and transmission work. Jim liked the idea, so we called Greg and asked if we could come over and get some advice on pursuing career options in the automotive field. We went to visit Greg this Monday, and although we'd only asked for 15 minutes of Greg's time, Greg spent over an hour with us showing Jim the specialized tools he uses and the various operations he performs from aligning and boring engine blocks to grinding valves. We noted the backlog of work he has. Jim was really excited about the machine shop and asked me help him apply for a job.

**Next steps:**

Jim and I are meeting next week to discuss what we observed at Engine Rebuilders, and we are also going to outline the job-carving proposal for the body shop.

**Date: 5/22/06**

**Field notes (i.e., what's happened to date, who's involved, critical issues, etc.):**

Jim toured Engine Rebuilders. He really liked the equipment and Greg. We talked afterwards and put together a brief employment proposal for Greg to job carve based on the following tasks that we observed:

A.  Clean (in automated parts cleaner) engine parts disassembled by Greg
B.  Paint engine blocks and heads in paint booth using existing shop equipment
C.  Deburr various metal parts using air grinder
D.  Perform 3-angle valve grinding using existing templated shop equipment
E.  Media blast engine parts (connecting rods, bare heads, blocks) using existing shop equipment
F.  Perform various shop maintenance tasks

I noted to Greg that having Jim perform these routine but critical steps would free up Greg to perform the machinist tasks critical to his business. Greg understood how this would save him time and money and also provide someone to welcome customers and answer the phone when he has to run out for parts, deliveries, or to pick his children up at school.

Greg accepted the proposal and we are working out a training schedule with Greg doing most of the training; I will be onsite most of the first few days to assist Greg with teaching strategies, but I plan a fast fade after that. Jim starts work June 1 and will get paid a starting wage of $7.50, with 1 week paid vacation and 10 paid holidays/personal days. Work hours will be 8:30 a.m. until 3:30 p.m. with a paid 1-hour lunch break. Greg does not offer health or retirement benefits.

Jerry at VR has agreed to buy Jim two adjustable-height steel work benches so that shop equipment (e.g., valve surfacer, industrial grinder, deburring airtools) can be set at Jim's wheelchair height; VR will also purchase a new semi-automated parts washer on modified legs that Jim can access from his chair, as well as $1,000 in new hand tools, and two portable engine stands that Jim can use to hold and steady engine blocks that need to be painted. Total cost to VR for equipment is approximately $2,275:

Work benches: $800.00
Parts washer: $400.00
Hand tools: $1,000.00
Engine stands: $75.00

The Workforce Center will be approached about paying for the adaptive driving lessons since VR is covering the costs of equipment and coaching. Greg has agreed to add a grab bar to the bathroom and was given information on tax credits for accessibility modifications to his shop.

# QUARTER 1 CUSTOMIZED EMPLOYMENT DEVELOPMENT PROGRESS REPORT

Period: _2/1/06–4/30/06_                              Individual: _Jim Dodge_

Average hours worked per week: _0_

Average gross revenue per month: _0_

Average net revenue per month: _0_

Average gross wages per week: _0_

Average net wages per week: _0_

Employment or business refinements/supports needed or of concern:

In discovery at present time; plan to have Jim working by July. See second quarter report.

Success stories:

Next steps:

Comments:

**Figure 1.4.**    Quarter 1 customized employment development progress report.

## QUARTER 2 CUSTOMIZED EMPLOYMENT DEVELOPMENT PROGRESS REPORT

Period: 5/1/06–7/30/06                    Individual: Jim Dodge

Average hours worked per week: 35

Average gross revenue per month:

Average net revenue per month:

Average gross wages per week: 35 × $7.50 = $262.50 × 4.2 weeks per month = $1,102.50

Average net wages per week:

Employment or business refinements/supports needed or of concern:

Initial worksite training is completed! Some further tool and facility modifications may be needed (e.g., lowering air line couplers on wall, lowering air compressor master switch).

Success stories:

Jim got the job at Engine Rebuilders!

Next steps:

Assess use of Plan to Achieve Self-Support for a car; enroll in adaptive driving course on Saturdays or evenings.

Comments:

**Figure 1.5.**    Quarter 2 customized employment development progress report.

## CONCLUSION

Job development for individuals with disabilities is always evolving and adapting, integrating new strategies that reinforce person-centered approaches, capitalize on natural supports, and use resources creatively. CE methods, as described throughout this book, maintain an emphasis on the individual's skills, preferences, and circumstances. CE methods rely heavily on negotiated job tasks that enhance the worker's competencies and replace the hunt for job openings with proactive strategies to match employment candidates with their ideal conditions of employment. Throughout the job development process, attention to the details of discovery, job analysis, and negotiation determine the levels of success achieved.

## REFERENCES

Americans with Disabilities Act of 1990, PL 101-336, 42 U.S.C. §§ 12101 *et seq.*

Balanced Budget Act of 1997, PL 105-33, 111 Stat. 251.

Becker, D., & Drake, R. (2003). *A working life for people with severe mental illness.* New York: Oxford University Press.

Bissonnette, D. (1994). *Beyond traditional job development.* Chatsworth, CA: Milt Wright & Associates.

Boeltzig, H., Gilmore, D., & Butterworth, J. (2006, June). *The National Survey of Community Rehabilitation Providers, FY2004–2005 Report 1: Employment outcomes of people with developmental dis-*

*abilities in integrated employment* (Issue No. 4, 1–6). Boston: Institute for Community Inclusion, Research to Practice.

Bond, G., Becker, D., Drake, R., Rapp, C., Meisler, N., Lehman, A., et al. (2001). Implementing supported employment as an evidence-based practice. *Psychiatric Services, 52*(3), 313–322.

Braddock, D., Hemp, R., Parish, S., & Rizzolo, M. (2002). *The state of the states in developmental disabilities: 2002 study summary.* Boulder: University of Colorado, Coleman Institute for Cognitive Disabilities and Department of Psychiatry.

Braddock, D., Rizzolo, M., & Hemp, R. (2004). Most employment services growth in developmental disabilities during 1988–2002 was in segregated settings. *Mental Retardation, 42*(4), 317–320.

Brooks-Lane, N., Hutcheson, S., & Revell, G. (2005). Supporting consumer directed employment outcomes. *Journal of Vocational Rehabilitation, 23*(2), 123–134.

Brown, L., Branston, M., Hamre-Nietupski, S., Pumpian, I., Certo, N., & Gruenwald, L. (1979). A strategy for developing chronological age-appropriate content for severely handicapped adolescents and young adults. *Journal of Special Education, 13,* 81–90.

Butterworth, J., Gilmore, D., Kiernan, W., & Schalock, R. (1999). *State trends in employment services for people with developmental disabilities.* Boston: Institute for Community Inclusion.

Callahan, M. (2003). *Customized employment Q & A.* Washington, DC: U.S. Department of Labor, Office of Disability and Employment Policy.

Callahan, M. (2004). *Fact sheet on customized employment.* Retrieved November 27, 2006, from http://www.t-tap.org

Callahan, M., & Garner, B. (1997). *Keys to the workplace: Skills and supports for people with disabilities.* Baltimore: Paul H. Brookes Publishing Co.

Callahan, M., & Nisbet, J. (1997). *The vocational profile: An alternative to traditional evaluation.* Gautier, MS: Marc Gold & Associates.

Condeluci, A. (1991). *Interdependence.* St. Augustine, FL: St. Lucie Press.

Condon, C., Gelb, A., & Gould, J. (2005). The 30-day placement plan. *Research to Practice, 21,* 1–4.

Condon, E., & Brown, K. (2005). *It takes a village (or at least several partners) to transition a student from school to work.* Missoula: University of Montana, Rural Institute.

DeLoach, C.P. (1992, January–March). Career outcomes for college graduates with severe physical and sensory disabilities. *Journal of Rehabilitation.* Retrieved December 11, 2005, from http://www.findarticles.com/p/articles/mi_m0825/is_n1_v58/ai_12382057

Donohue, T. (2006). *The state of American business.* Washington, DC: U.S. Chamber of Commerce.

Griffin, C.C. (1994). Organizational natural supports: The role of leadership in facilitating inclusion. *Journal of Vocational Rehabilitation, 4.*

Griffin, C.C., Brooks-Lane, N., Hammis, D., & Crandell, D. (2006). Self-employment: Owning the American dream. In P. Wehman (Ed.), *Real work for real pay: Inclusive employment for people with disabilities.* Baltimore: Paul H. Brookes Publishing Co.

Griffin, C.C., Flaherty, M., Kriskovich, B., Maxson, N., Shelley, R., et al. (1999). *Bringing home the bacon: Inventive self-employment and supported employment in rural America.* Missoula: The University of Montana, Rural Institute.

Griffin, C.C., & Hammis, D. (1996). *StreetWise guide to person-centered career planning.* Denver, CO: Denver Options, Inc.

Griffin, C.C., & Hammis, D. (2003). *Making self-employment work.* Baltimore: Paul H. Brookes Publishing Co.

Griffin, C.C., & Hammis, D. (2005). *The contradictions of leadership: Making customized employment work.* Fact Sheet. Retrieved November 27, 2006, from http://www.t-tap.org

Hatch, J., & Clinton, A. (2000). Job growth in the 1990s: A retrospect. *Monthly Labor Review, 123* (12), 3–18.

Individuals with Disabilities Education Improvement Act of 2004, PL 108-446, 20 U.S.C. §§ 1400 *et seq.*

Kamenetz, A. (2006). *Generation debt.* New York: Riverhead Books.

Kraus, L., Stoddard, S., & Gilmartin, D. (1996). *Chartbook on disability in the United States, 1996.* Washington, DC: U.S. Department of Education, National Institute on Disability and Rehabilitation Research.

Mank, D., Cioffi, A., & Yovanoff, P. (2003). Supported employment outcomes across a decade: Is there evidence of improvement in the quality of implementation? *Mental Retardation, 41*(3), 188–197.

McGaughey, M., Kiernan, W., McNally, L., Gilmore, D., & Keith, G. (1994). *Beyond the workshop: National perspectives on integrated employment.* Boston: Institute for Community Inclusion.

Metzel, D.S., Boeltzig, H., Butterworth, J., Sulewski, J.S., & Gilmore, D.S. (2007). Achieving community membership through community rehabilitation provider services: Are we there yet? *Mental Retardation, 45,* 149–160.

Minnesota Governor's Council on Developmental Disabilities. (2005). *Employer focus research.* Minneapolis, MN: Market Response International.

Office of Disability and Employment Policy Customized Employment Grants Notice, 67 Fed. Reg. 43154–43169 (June 26, 2002) (to be codified at 29 C.F.R. pt. 95).

Olmstead v. L.C., 527 U.S. 581; 119 S.Ct. 2176.

Priebe S., Warner R., Hubschmid, T., & Eckle, I. (1998). Employment, attitudes toward work, and quality of life among people with schizophrenia in three countries. *Schizophrenia Bulletin, 24* (3), 469–477.

Rehabilitation Act Amendments of 1986, PL 99-506, 29 U.S.C. §§ 701 *et seq.*

Rehabilitation Act of 1973, PL 93-112, 29 U.S.C. §§ 701 *et seq.*

Shapiro, J. (1993). *No pity: People with disabilities forging a new civil rights movement.* New York: Times Books.

Thornton, P., & Lunt, N. (1997). *Employment policies for disabled people in eighteen countries: A review.* Ottawa, Canada: Global Applied Disability Research & Information Network.

Trieschmann, R.B. (1987). *Aging with a disability.* New York: Demos.

University of Alabama National Spinal Cord Injury Statistical Center. (2006, June). *Spinal cord injury facts and figures at a glance.* Retrieved November 27, 2006, from http://www.spinal-cord.uab.edu/

U.S. Bureau of the Census. (2001). *Statistical abstract of the United States: 2001.* Retrieved November 27, 2006, from http://www.census.gov

U.S. Department of Health and Human Services, Substance Abuse and Mental Health Services Administration. (2003). *Supported employment: A guide for mental health planning and advisory councils.* Rockville, MD: Author.

Wehman, P. (2006). (Ed.). *Life beyond the classroom: Transition strategies for young people with disabilities* (4th ed.). Baltimore: Paul H. Brookes Publishing Co.

Wehman, P., & Kregel, J. (1998). *More than a job.* Baltimore: Paul H. Brookes Publishing Co.

Workforce Investment Act of 1998, PL 105-220, 29 U.S.C. §§ 794 *et seq.*

# 2

# Discovery

## The Foundation of Job Development

*Michael Callahan and Ellen Condon*

The starting point for job development for persons with significant disabilities has been to determine employers' demands. These demands are most often stated in the openings that employers might have and in the job descriptions and expectations associated with those openings. This chapter offers a new starting point for the employment process—the job seeker. It is common practice to put individuals with disabilities through comprehensive, even rigorous, preemployment preparation and evaluation activities. Rather than comparing and preparing, this approach to employment seeks to answer the most fundamental question regarding job seekers: "Who is this person?" Even though demand for job readiness indicators continues to increase within both the disability field and the generic employment arena, it is more important than ever to discover both the true life complexities that create barriers to many job seekers and the unique contributions they may have to offer. Evaluation procedures that focus solely on identifying deficits almost never get at the critical factors for employment success.

In response to these comparative, exclusionary methods, many in the disabilities field have embraced person-centered planning as an alternative. Person-centered planning has evolved over a generation as a strategy that puts focus on individuals; evoking and honoring their wishes, values, and outcomes as a way to guide job development. However, even this valued approach often misses a critical distinction: the difference between what job seekers say they want and who they are as individuals. In other words, the strategy of person-centered planning frequently gets ahead of itself. Too often, job seekers are simply asked what they want to do before anyone takes the time to fully understand who the person is. If person-centered planning does not embrace discovery as the foundation, the resulting lack of information can create as many problems for employment as do the typical, exclusionary methods person-centered planning was meant to replace. Job seekers with complex lives will be asked what type of work they want to do, with little or no understanding of the complex issues that might emerge to compromise employment efforts.

The solution is to use an employment strategy known as *discovery*. Discovery provides an ideal foundation for any person-centered planning approach that focuses on employment. This activity precedes person-centered planning and explores all relevant facets of the job seeker's life to identify, including a) the conditions necessary for successful employment based on the job seeker's complexities and individual preferences, b) the job seeker's employment interests that provide a direction to specific segments of the labor market, and c) the potential contributions that the job seeker might offer to employers. The activity of discovery is an investment in the individual that builds a foundation of accurate and useful information upon which person-centered employment plans can be based.

In its simplest sense, discovery involves getting to know individuals with disabilities beyond the public face they present as they interact with others such as teachers, service providers, counselors, and other paid staff. The more employment specialists know, the better prepared they are to plan effectively, the clearer the job seeker's strengths, needs, and interests will become, and the better all parties can negotiate and communicate with potential employers regarding possible employment.

## THE CRITICAL IMPORTANCE OF DISCOVERY TO CUSTOMIZED EMPLOYMENT

We feel strongly that by starting with the person's story before engaging employers regarding their needs, employment outcomes for job seekers with disabilities will improve. However, as critical as discovery is, it is possible to overlook a critical variable to success: the need for a newly defined relationship between employers and job seekers with significant disabilities. As supported employment (SE) moved from its early boom phase in the late 1980s to a more stable and mature phase in the mid-1990s, a leveling-off of growth and innovation was observed (Mank, 1995; Wehman & Kregel, 1995). An analysis of these articles indicates that the vocational rehabilitation (VR) and developmental disability (DD) fields had successfully employed many of the "easier" and "more apparently capable" persons in adult services. The future trend for growth was not as optimistic as the first decade of SE. In addition, the effect of employers ensuring that their job descriptions were sufficiently concrete so as to avoid discrimination under the Americans with Disabilities Act of 1990 (PL 101-336) resulted in the unintended exclusion of applicants with more significant disabilities (Callahan & Garner, 1997).

During the 1990s, it became necessary for those representing adults and students with significant disabilities to negotiate the essential responsibilities of a job, as defined by employers, in an individualized manner (Callahan, 2000; Callahan & Garner, 1997; Mast, Sweeney, & West, 2001). When successful, these negotiations allowed individuals with the most significant disabilities to become employed (Eaton, Condon, & Mast, 2001). This approach to employment includes most of the ingredients identified for successful SE—planning, training, supports, inclusive outcomes—but adds the essential factor of customization. Employment is not likely to be successful for job seekers with significant disabilities unless innovative strategies for negotiating customized employment (CE) are added to professional practice.

The evolution from SE to CE has taken an unusual route. Born out of necessity for employing persons with the most significant disabilities, CE can have dramatic effects both in the disability field and beyond, to mainstream employment services. In a series of national demonstration projects that started in 1987 and continued through 2000, targeting persons with significant, multiple disabilities—both physical and intellectual—over 1,800 persons were successfully employed using this customized approach (Callahan, 1990; Callahan, 2000; Mast & West, 1995; Shumpert, 1997). This new approach is different from the more traditional labor market approach in a number of ways (Callahan, 2000).

1. The starting point of employment begins with the individual, rather than with openings in the labor market.

2. The strategy of discovery, rather than comparative testing and evaluation procedures, is used to get to know the job seeker.

3. Person-centered employment planning creates a blueprint for employment, as it takes the place of responding to the existing demands of the workplace.

4. Job seeker contributions are offered as a proposal to employers rather than having job seekers accept arbitrary job descriptions.

5. The applicant often uses representation by an agent, such as a job developer, to communicate the complexity of CE instead of relying solely on self-representation.

6. Effective representation tools such as portfolios are used in place of traditional résumés and applications to help employers understand and appreciate the potential contributions of applicants with significant disabilities.

During the period from 1987 to 2000, questions were raised regarding whether this approach was valid in the context of employer relationships in generic employment for all persons. This concern was allayed early in 2001 when, within a week of her confirmation by Congress as the Secretary of the U.S. Department of Labor (DOL), Elaine Chao, said

> In one sense, the new economy is deconstructing work, with jobs that can't be pigeonholed into a traditional workday or workweek, and corporate structures that, in some cases, are eliminating the need for a workplace altogether. Workers themselves are demanding more autonomy, more freedom, more *customization* [emphasis added] of the terms and conditions of their employment. As we invest in critical job training, we are giving workers the bargaining power they need to *custom-design* [emphasis added] their jobs around their lives—instead of the other way around. (Chao, 2001)

Secretary Chao's remarks indicate that the strategy that had been working for persons with significant disabilities for over a decade does, indeed, have relevance for the broader population. These comments offer an opening for the disability field to partner with, teach, and learn from the generic employment system by referring to disability as one of many forms of life's complexity. This connection can become a powerful tool for broadening the message of CE to a vast array of employers. Indeed, disability is only one of many lenses through which life complexities can be understood:

Disability

Health

Poverty

Homelessness

Family responsibilities

Lack of experience or skills

Low self-esteem

Cultural

Age: youth/maturity

Minority status

Lack of education

Habits/life routines

Even though, conceptually, CE seemed to represent a relevant approach for both persons with disabilities and for the general population, it is fair to say that little had been written or discussed about the strategy on a nationwide basis until the summer of 2001. On July 20, 2001, the *Federal Register* contained a solicitation for projects to implement CE options within DOL-mandated local workforce boards for persons with disabilities who might need such approaches to become successfully employed (Solicitation for Grant Application for CE Program for People with Disabilities, 2001). This initiative resulted in a series of multiyear demonstrations in 20 locations across the country to examine the feasibility of negotiating a customized relationship between job seekers with disabilities and local employers with specific needs. Now in its fifth year, this initiative has clearly shown the benefit of the customized approach (Elinson & Frey, 2005). During the course of the demonstration, it became evident that the process had to begin with the job seeker as the primary information source from which subsequent negotiations would follow.

## The Process of Discovery

While the purpose of this chapter is to link the process of discovery to job development, an overview of the strategies to be utilized will be discussed. For additional information, readers are directed to *Discovery: Charting the Course to Employment* (Callahan, Shumpert, & Condon, in press), *Discovery Is…Vignettes on the Discovery Process* (Callahan, 2001), and *Common Sense and Quality* (Callahan, 1991). These resources offer detailed strategies and stories regarding the process of discovery.

Discovery is a capacity-driven information gathering process: a guide that suggests areas in a person's life that may allow the necessary discovery of significant information about an applicant that guides the search for a customized job. Using discovery, the employment professional uses time spent with the job seeker to form a relationship that provides insight into the fears, concerns, and hopes regarding employment for both the individual and relevant family members. These expectations and concerns have a significant impact on employment outcomes. Meaningful discovery time with a job seeker and family members allows for discussions around possible concerns and provides information to the family regarding Social Security and Medicaid impact. Discovery sometimes reveals the fear that a family member will be exploited, isolated, or unhappy. Defining the dimensions of safe environments and then including these factors in the ideal working conditions identified during the employment planning process can often address these concerns.

Discovery is a form of qualitative research with the job seeker as the primary focus. Discovery uses many of the tools that anthropologists, ethnographers, and social scientists have used for decades:

- Interviews of job seeker, family, friends and professionals who work with the job seeker

- Conversations with job seeker, family, and close friends

- Observations of job seeker in typical activities of life

- Participation with the job seeker in typical and targeted activities

- Review of records that currently exist

In the event that these activities do not yield information necessary for effective planning, we then recommend that additional, more transitional assessment procedures can be implemented.

- Situational assessments in contexts that are consistent with the discovered information

- Targeted evaluations or assessments to answer specific questions

## Who Is Involved in the Discovery Process?

Discovery relies on the perspectives of a variety of people who know the person best and who are the most optimistic about the chances for successful employment. In all cases, the job seeker is the primary source of information, even when the individual has limited ability to communicate effectively. But discovery goes beyond personal reflections to include the perspectives of others, including

- The person of concern
- His or her family and loved ones
- Close and trusted friends
- Neighbors with good relationships
- Community members who have an association with the job seeker
- Professionals who care
- Counselors
- Teachers
- Service providers
- Medical personnel

## Where Is Discovery Conducted?

Discovery operates from the perspective that people behave and perform differently in various situations of life. We believe, too, that people are rarely in their best situation when they participate in the human service employment system. Therefore, it is necessary to get beyond our offices and testing rooms and to engage job seekers in places "where they are most who they are." The following locations are typically used for discovery of persons with disabilities:

- Home
- Neighborhood
- Local community
- Local businesses with whom the job seeker has relationships and contacts
- Church (as appropriate)
- School (as appropriate)
- One-Stop center
- Outdoors/recreational locales

## Steps for Implementing Discovery

There are countless strategies that employment providers might use to gather information about the job seeker during discovery. The following steps offer strategies that work for many individuals.

1. Set a time to visit the job seeker's home, with parents and family available, as appropriate.

2. Before or after the meeting, drive throughout the immediate neighborhood for a radius of about one fourth to one half of a mile, noting relevant dimensions.

3. Meet with the individual and his or her family or representatives at their home. The meeting should last approximately an hour and a half. Permission should be obtained.

4. Return to the individual's home for additional information, unstructured conversation, observation, and interviews.

5. Interview selected staff members that have provided the job seeker with instruction and support.

6. Contact advocates, neighbors, and close friends to gain information concerning the person's social life, skills, preferences, and connections.

7. Have both structured and informal conversations with job seekers to determine their interests, activities, routines, and other essential information.

8. Observe the person in a sample of the activities—school, home, or community—that comprise the majority of his or her day.

9. Accompany the person on planned community activities, both familiar and novel.

10. Accompany the job seeker while he or she participates in organized events; interacts with local merchants and service providers, and in other planned, unique activities.

11. Review all existing records, scrapbooks, photo albums, and other existing documentation on the job seeker, focusing on positive perspectives.

12. Record, narratively and photographically, all the activities of discovery, with permission from the job seeker (Callahan et al., in press).

## The Need for Tools to Guide Job Development

Even though employment has been a critical focus of adult state DD and VR services for over a generation, there continues to be little focus on improving job development techniques and tools. This contradiction is undoubtedly responsible for a portion of the unemployment experienced by persons with disabilities. A review of professional literature from the 1990s to the early 2000s indicates few references to techniques for tailoring employment presentations.

Instead of focusing on effective individualized employment strategies and tools, employment services have relied almost exclusively on preparation of job seekers (Wehman, 2006) to ensure access to employment. CE requires a focused "picture of the job seeker" and strategic planning that enables detailed negotiation with employers to tailor a job match. Without CE, an essential ingredient is missing from the mix. The authors believe that employment personnel need to add CE, based on discovery, to the array of strategies offered to job seekers. And they need the tools and strategies necessary to make the job match and to negotiate with employers. The discovery process, described below, will offer employment professionals new and useful tools to confidently approach employers and negotiate customized outcomes.

## The Effectiveness of Discovery and Profiles: A Person-Centered Planning Process

In the early 1980s, the ecological inventory strategy for assisting people with disabilities in vocational settings was just beginning to gain importance (Brown et al., 1986). In place of traditional assessments to assist people with disabilities, this strategy was used to identify employment and life needs. Early implementation experiences of discovery indicated that the more significant a person's disability, the greater the need for an individualized approach to employment (Callahan & Nisbet, 1987). They also found that traditional assessments indicated primarily what a person was not able to do. Even the ecological strategies were not focused enough to result in positive employment outcomes for people with the most significant disabilities. By using a discovery approach to uncover the strategic information that guides employment, Callahan and Nisbet took the ecological inventory process one step further in developing the *vocational profile* and the *employment plan.*

Discovery is an open-ended approach to gathering useful information. The vocational profile and the employment plan were designed to capture that information. These two strategies linked information about an individual with information about potential jobs for the individual. CE approaches were used extensively by United Cerebral Palsy (UCP) associations in several federally funded demonstration projects from 1987 to 2000, which demonstrated that people with severe physical disabilities could successfully be employed (Callahan, 1991, 2000; Mast & West, 1995; Shumpert, 1997).

And yet, years later, people with the most significant disabilities are, too often, not the people who are getting jobs through SE. When UCP looked at this issue and worked with provider agencies that used the vocational profile strategy, the method of implementing the discovery process came into question. Many job developers were merely completing a profile form and missing the way information on job seekers needed to be gathered and utilized through discovery. We found that job developers needed examples of situations where job seekers were at their best. They needed to know what supports should be in place and what conditions in the environment, such as the location of work, inside/outside tasks, the number of customers in the area, and so forth, make things work successfully. This type of open-ended discovery requires taking the time to focus on how people get things done in their lives.

## Time: The Essential Ingredient to Address Complexity

The information mined during discovery is the raw material for employment planning from which the job developer can create a picture of ideal working environments. Discovery can identify other critical information, such as potential contributions of an individual with significant disabilities. The discovery interaction may be as simple as observing the person put personal belongings in order or noticing that the job seeker does component pieces of larger tasks of everyday life. Discovery allows employment staff to communicate with, interview, observe, and participate with prospective employees in an array of environments and situations as a strategy for identifying competent performance. This type of information is unlikely to be learned with traditional assessments. But doing this effectively will require spending time with the job seeker. Too often, professionals are encouraged to "hot box," or hurry the time spent with individuals as a way to save money and increase efficiency. When job seekers with significant disabilities, or other major life complexities, are processed in this manner, the typical result is exclusion and continuing unemployment.

Beyond identifying competencies and contributions, another critical piece that must be known to direct employment effort is what motivates a person to work. If job seekers are not motivated by the need for money, employment specialists must find a job that interests them enough for them to want to go to work. Ideal working conditions, competencies, contributions, and interests must all be discovered to direct meaningful employment for persons with significant disabilities.

Many employment professionals have raised concerns that time is the one ingredient in short supply in both the disability and the typical employment systems. However, by embracing the offering of time to job seekers, we are not implying an open-ended, never-ending process. Indeed the data from thousands of discovery inter-actions brings the time required into a time frame similar to many more traditional evaluation processes. The average time required for discovery is about 20 hours, with a range of 15–25 hours. The time frame for discovery averages 4 weeks, with a range of 3–5 weeks from start to completion (Callahan, 1990; Mast & West, 1995; Shumpert, 1997). When employment professionals share the time load with others who have responsibility for funding and services, the time demand becomes far more reasonable.

More important, discovery is not recommended for all job seekers, either within disability services or in the generic workforce system. Discovery that is intensively facilitated by employment professionals is recommended primarily for those for whom traditional services have not been effective. Therefore, discovery becomes an invest-ment in our commitment to offer employment to all job seekers, including those with the most significant life complexities. Job seekers with less complex needs might bene-fit from small group discovery classes or self-discovery reflection.

## Tasks and Skills

In order to effectively negotiate a customized job, we must address clear needs of employers. CE avoids predetermined job descriptions, but it cannot avoid the necessity of meeting employer needs. This need is met through the current skills and potential job tasks offered by the job seeker. Discovery is an ideal strategy to identify these essential ingredients of negotiation. For purposes of CE, current skills refer to any work-related performance activity that the individual can currently perform, without support or with support, as described. Whereas skills relate to a job seeker's current capacity, potential job tasks, on the other hand, refer to any work-related performance activity that the indi-vidual should reasonably be expected to perform at work (based on current skills), with training, supports, and accommodations as necessary. This category represents the potential capacity that a job seeker might develop and it sends the clear message to employers that all new employees have tasks that they must first learn to perform. It is critically important for employers to understand that a job seeker's current skills are not representative of all potential workplace contributions.

Traditionally, the disability field has used comparative testing and evaluation pro-cedures to determine the current skills and potential job tasks of job seekers with dis-abilities. This approach has placed many individuals in a conflicting situation because the more significant their disabilities are, the less likely they will compete effectively against the performance of others. Instead, discovery uses a descriptive, observational strategy that relies on activities of everyday life, present and past, as the indicator of one's current skills. In this way, there is no pass/fail associated with discovery, only information. If necessary information is not available in one context, it will be necessary to dig deeper, change contexts, and discover more.

## The Value of Positive Information

How many of us have ever heard of a job seeker putting all of the negative information of life in their résumé? There would not be a very good chance of getting any job by using this type of approach. Oddly enough, most of the information on job seekers with disabilities available to job developers is based on a negative slant that results from eval-uations, standardized tests, and other comparative procedures. There is a desperate need for positive, useful information that describes job seekers at their best, referencing the employment contexts, tasks, social conditions, and other aspects of the individual that offers employers an optimistic view of each applicant. During the discovery process, it is essential that job developers look for situations and experiences that pro-vide a positive slant to the information and reputation that describes the job seeker.

## Descriptiveness

Embracing descriptiveness is a fundamental aspect of discovery. Descriptiveness removes the professional's opinion, the job seeker's reputation, and the assessments of others from our knowledge of the person. When human service professionals describe, rather than evaluate, the job seeker's life becomes available to us as useful information. But this is often a challenging concept for human service professionals. They are socialized to have evaluative opinions about the individuals they serve. They use evaluative jargon as a way of communicating both positive and negative information, such as, "Andy is a wonderful young man who is friendly and outgoing" or "Julie is a spitter." These characterizations are simply opinions about specific behaviors people have seen or heard about. When positively stated, they are often banal, becoming little more than fluff terms that mean different things to different people. When the labels are negative, they become destructive and isolating for job seekers, evoking fear or concern on the part of others.

Instead, descriptiveness allows human service professionals to address both positive and negative aspects of job seekers in a way that allows each person who hears or reads about the person to determine their own views of the behavior. If the characterization of Andy was stated descriptively, it could have been noticed that "when Andy enters his classroom each morning, he rolls up to each student, smiles, and says 'Good morning.'" Imagine the relative effectiveness of relating to an employer the description of Andy's behavior instead of expressing an opinion in terms of a fluff label. Conversely, Julie's spitting might be described as, "When Julie is surprised, fatigued, or angered, she often grabs the arm of the person closest to her and spits once in the person's face." While this behavior is clearly disgusting, it is now known the conditions under which Julie spits and what others might be able to do to avoid being spat upon.

Discovery and descriptiveness go hand in hand. The time spent in getting to know the job seeker allows human service professionals to consider how we might describe the various aspects of the person's life. What we are actually doing is preparing for job development by offering clear, opinion-free information about who the job seeker is to potential employers.

## Imagery

As an often-quoted proverb suggests, "A picture is worth a thousand words." If this is true, imagery offers a powerful form of description for the job seeker. Too often, potential employers of people with disabilities perceive those with disabilities as something less than contributing employees. Effective imagery can help to bridge the gap between perception and reality. For that reason, we recommend that job developers use a visual representational tool known as a portfolio or visual résumé. This strategy is compatible with traditional sales approaches and, with the use of available desktop technology such as PowerPoint and ink jet printers, can be produced by job developers and other employment professionals with little training at a reasonable cost. The portfolio uses digital photos and a succinct narrative to promote and describe the job seeker to potential employers much the way a traditional written résumé does. By carefully selecting imagery that communicates competence and contribution, employers can look past their presumptions about disability and see the job seeker as a potential employee.

Discovery provides an excellent opportunity for employment professionals to find existing imagery and to take new pictures that can be used in the development of a presentational portfolio. We recommend that permission be obtained from the job seeker early in discovery and that job developers use this time period to capture images that illustrate the competence of the job seeker.

## Relationships and Sharing

Since discovery involves a person allowing others access to personal, often private aspects of his or her life, it is necessary for professionals to shift the tone and manner of the traditional professional relationship. Employment staff are trained to maintain a purposeful distance from those who receive services so that they do not become too emotionally involved or send confusing signals regarding the limits of the relationship. Whereas we do not suggest that professional distance be eliminated, the process of discovery requires that human service professionals find ways to humanize the employment process and to minimize that distance. It is unlikely that job seekers and their families will be willing to open their lives to anyone unwilling to do the same, at least to some degree.

One easy way to accomplish this is to engage job seekers with a conversational tone at various times during the process. Within conversation, employment professionals have opportunities to relate their own perspectives, emotions, concerns, and uncertainties. Again, we are not recommending full disclosure, but simply a shift towards a balanced, reciprocal relationship. Another strategy is to use mealtime as a venue for discovery and interaction. Sharing meals is a universal means of connecting with one another.

## Documenting Discovery

As we come to know the job seeker through discovery, it is necessary to shift from learning about the individual to considering how to use the gathered information for customized planning and job development. At this point, we also need to consider how the information learned during discovery can be documented for future use. Instead of having the bits and pieces of information—the various pieces of the puzzle that is the job seeker—sitting in the pockets of all those with information to share, we strongly recommend that those pieces be assembled into a coherent and comprehensive picture that tells each individual's story. There are a number of options that might be used to assemble the information learned during the discovery process—written profiles, vignettes, scrapbooks, graphic representations, and narrative/image computer presentations, to name a few. Regardless of the strategy that is selected, we recommend that all written information reflect a set of values that enhance the job seeker's competence (Shumpert et al., in press). We suggest documentation that is:

*Narrative:* using complete sentences to describe the person

*Comprehensive:* covering all relevant areas of the person's life relating to employment

*Optimistic:* focusing on the best of who people are rather than on difficulties or shortcomings

*Respectful:* treating carefully the intimate information which is developed

*Noncompetitive:* not requiring comparison against any arbitrary norm, skill, or other person

*Robust:* fully developing aspects of the person's life so that contributions and qualities can be translated to employers

*Descriptive:* describing the individual while carefully avoiding any evaluative or opinion-based statements

## SUMMARY

The use of discovery as the starting point for employment is perhaps the clearest indicator that human service professionals are embracing a customized approach to employment by starting with the job seeker before dealing with the demands of the labor market. Discovery provides a powerful, essential picture of the strengths, needs, and interests within the complex life of each job seeker, especially those with significant disabilities. The concept also allows the use of recognized qualitative research procedures to be used, one person at a time, while avoiding the traditional evaluation and testing tools that so often exclude persons with significant disabilities. Using this approach, human service professionals are able to get beyond the surface level responses and behaviors that are often relied upon to describe the interaction between job seekers and employment professionals. Discovery allows human service professionals to know their customers before job development efforts begin.

# REFERENCES

Americans with Disabilities Act of 1990, PL 101-336, 42 U.S.C. §§ 12101 *et seq.*

Brown, L., Shiraga, B., Ford, A., Nisbet, J., Vandeventer, P., Sweet, M., et al. (1986). Teaching severely handicapped students to perform meaningful work in nonsheltered vocational environments. In R. Morris & B. Blatt (Eds.), *Special education: Research and trends* (pp. 131–189). New York: Pergamon Press.

Callahan, M. (1990). *Final report of the national demonstration project on supported employment.* Washington, DC: United Cerebral Palsy.

Callahan, M. (1991). Common sense and quality: Meaningful employment outcomes for persons with severe physical disabilities. *Journal of Vocational Rehabilitation, 1*(2), 21–28.

Callahan, M. (2000). *Final report of the choice access project.* (A national project funded by the Rehabilitation Services Administration, H235D30067). Washington, DC: United Cerebral Palsy.

Callahan, M. (2001). *Discovery is...: Vignettes on the discovery process.* St. Paul, MN: Minnesota Development Disabilities Council.

Callahan, M., & Garner, J.B. (1997). *Keys to the workplace: Skills and supports for persons with severe disabilities.* Baltimore: Paul H. Brookes Publishing Co.

Callahan, M., & Nisbet, J. (1987). *The vocational profile: An alternative to traditional assessment.* Gautier, MS: Marc Gold & Associates.

Callahan, M., Shumpert, N., & Condon, E. (in press). *Discovery: Charting the course to employment.* Gautier, MS: Marc Gold & Associates.

Eaton, B., Condon, E., & Mast, M. (2001). Making employment a reality. *The Journal of Vocational Rehabilitation,16,* 9–13.

Elinson, L., & Frey, W. (2005). *Evaluation of disability employment policy demonstration projects: Interim report.* Rockville, MD: WESTAT.

Mank, D. (1995). The underachievement of supported employment. *The Journal of Disability Policy Studies, 5*(2), 1–24.

Mast, M., Sweeney, J., & West, M. (2001). Using presentation portfolios for effective job representation of individuals with disabilities. *The Journal of Vocational Rehabilitation, 16,* 135–140.

Mast, M., & West, M. (1995). *Research and demonstration on supported employment for individuals with severe physical disabilities.* Final report to Rehabilitation Service Administration. Award #H133A20026–93. Washington, DC: Rehabilitation Service Administration.

Shumpert, N. (1997). *Final report on UCP/PWI employment project.* Washington, DC: United Cerebral Palsy.

Shumpert, N., Callahan, M., & Condon, E. (in press). *Profiles: Capturing the information of discovery.* Gautier, MS: Marc Gold & Associates.

Solicitation for Grant Application for Customized Employment Program for People with Disabilities, 66 Fed. Reg. 38,001 (July 20, 2001).

Wehman, P. (2006). *Life beyond the classroom: Transition strategies for young people with disabilities* (4th ed.). Baltimore: Paul H. Brookes Publishing Co.

Wehman, P., & Kregel, J. (1995). At the crossroads: Supported employment a decade later. *The Journal of the Association for Persons with Severe Disabilities, 20,* 4.

# 3

# Job Matching and Analysis

## Exploring Worksite Ecology and Seeking Goodness of Fit

*Cary Griffin, David Hammis, and Tammara Geary*

Discovery, the resulting vocational profile, and other person-centered approaches to assessment and planning provide a map for individualized job development. Goodness of fit occurs when well-prepared job developers and job seekers match preferred work tasks and environments, thereby increasing job retention (Callahan & Garner, 1997; Mank, Cioffi, & Yovanoff, 1998).

The job match is a critical survival tool for this journey and serves to formalize this difficult process by aligning the talents and desires of the job seeker with the needs of the employer. Job match is often short-changed in the real-world lives of employment specialists and job developers. Administrative focus is often on quick placements that keep billable hours to their maximum, and the short-range payment mechanisms, such as the 90-day closures known to the public vocational rehabilitation (VR) system, reinforce speed and inaccuracy, which contributes to the high rate of job loss for people with significant disabilities (Callahan & Garner, 1997). In over 200 nationally located employment development and demonstration sites that the authors have supported, the reluctance by community rehabilitation program (CRP) workers to spend time recording and analyzing potential worksite operations and developing written and formal training plans is obvious and troubling. Job analysis and matching is a pay now or pay later technology: Failure to record, interpret, prioritize, and share information on worksite ecology and goodness of fit for a potential employment opportunity results in

Low rates of consumer job retention because matching the person to a desired job did not occur

Loss of confidence by job seekers with disabilities who suffer the same feelings of failure or rejection as anyone who loses a job

35

A preponderance of easy-to-get high-turnover and stereotypical jobs because the depth of the job search is minimized by budget and time constrictions

A focus on individuals who appear easiest to place and support (known as "creaming") because job seekers with more complex disabilities are often considered poor risks

Greater costs per placement caused by 1) ineffective jobsite training that must be reperformed and 2) constant job losses that injure employer and funder relationships, thereby creating a negative image of human service agencies

Employers report that such inattention to detail makes employment specialists and job developers appear naive about business operations, aloof or disconnected from the commercial fabric of their communities, and unreliable as sources of quality employment supports (Kregel & Unger, 1993; Locklin, 1997; Luecking, Fabian, & Tilson, 2004). Combating these outcomes is clearly necessary for achieving long-term employment success for people with significant disabilities. Still, there has been some concern expressed in the rehabilitation field over how formal and intrusive a process job analysis should be (Hagner, 2000; Nisbet & Hagner, 1988). It is clear that with proper negotiation and communication among the job seeker, the employer and co-workers, and the employment specialist, a process augmenting the image of people with disabilities and respectful of a business's operations can be forged (Griffin, 1992; Luecking et al., 2004).

## JOB MATCHING AND CUSTOMIZED EMPLOYMENT

The hallmark of customized employment (CE), as noted in Chapter 1, is its emphasis on creating employment that matches the best possible working conditions for an individual. This matching process demands serious attention to detail and therefore must be written down using templates such as the Job Analysis Record (JAR). (See Figure 3.1; a blank version of this form appears in the appendix.) Guessing at a proper match can sometimes be successful, but organizing training sequences, critically analyzing support strategies, and thinking through the process of engaging co-workers to support the new employee are all done more efficaciously when the detailed steps of worksite training are ordered and written. Creating a competent image for the rehabilitation agency, the employment specialist, and the job seeker demands a written, defensible, logical, and revisable document that can be shared as needed with the various stakeholders. Failure to construct a job analysis matching the individual to the proper worksite and assistive training represents malfeasance in the rehabilitation field.

Examples of eyeballing placements and the resulting problems are universal. In one case, a young man named "Toby," who had just left high school, was assigned to a fledgling employment specialist's caseload. After meeting with Toby, the employment specialist reviewed his special education file and noted that he had completed an unpaid work experience at an express-mail and packaging shop. She asked Toby if he enjoyed the work, and Toby quietly said that he did. Toby was very shy, quiet, and complacent; he seldom spoke out or disagreed with what anyone requested of him, and when he said he enjoyed packaging work, he had little other work experience to draw upon. Had the specialist dug a bit deeper into Toby's preferences, interests, and talents, she would have discovered an individual seeking work on a college campus, an environment he frequently referenced in discussion.

The employment specialist developed a job for Toby, based solely on the school records available to her, at a new packaging company she had noticed on her way to work. Following her agency's standard procedures, she completed no job analysis. She simply asked the employer if he needed any help, and he agreed to hire Toby. Toby's job was to package all types of manufactured products, gift items, and candies on a short production line where he used an overhead hopper to fill boxes with Styrofoam peanuts. All day long he aimed the chute and squeezed the trigger on the machine. The training took 3 days, just to make sure Toby was working fast enough and fitting in with the others at work.

However, the presence of the employment specialist had caused the others on the assembly line to behave in a deferential and polite manner, thus masking the true workplace culture. Because the men on the line all spoke to the employment specialist, she assumed that once she left they would accept Toby and engage him in their conversations as well. Unfortunately this did not occur, and Toby found himself stuck in a boring job, surrounded by people who did not talk to him or respect him. The employer had been on his best behavior around the employment specialist as well, because as soon as she faded from the workplace (as Toby later reported), the boss circled the assembly line throughout the day threatening the workers, cursing at them, and calling them lazy. The business owner was a former city police officer who had been relieved

---

## JOB ANALYSIS RECORD

■■■■ ■ ■■■■ ■ ■■■■ ■ ■■■■ ■ ■■■■ ■ ■■■■ ■ ■■■■ ■ ■■■■ ■ ■■■■ ■ ■■■■

Instructions: This form is used to capture the major task steps of each job or project. The recorder should pay particular attention to how the tasks are typically performed and note any accommodations, technology, or specialized training strategies that should be employed with the new employee. The task sets are to be recorded as projects so that a discrete training format can be established for each.

Name of worker: James Dodge       Date initiated/date completed: 5/15/06, 5/22/06, 5/23/06

Company: Engine Rebuilders

Contact person/supervisor: Greg       Phone/e-mail: 370-5532

Person completing Job Analysis Record (JAR): Jerry Adams

Proposed job title: Assistant machinist

Major tasks or projects: Grind valves, deburr parts, sandblast components, clean parts, paint parts

Proposed work hours/days per week: 8:30 a.m.–3:30 p.m. M–F

Anticipated pay rate/benefits: $7.50/hour plus 10 paid holidays

Comments/considerations: Will need modified tables, Plan to Achieve Self-Support (PASS) approval for tools and equipment; training plan with task analyses needs to be completed prior to start date

### Culture of the company:

Record observations regarding the rites and rituals of the company (e.g., dress code, commonly used language and slang that may be helpful to understand, work hours, break times and lunch behavior, initiation rituals for new hires, social interactions, car pooling)

Notes from observation and conversation: Worksite is relaxed, with only one other person (owner, Greg) on site. Customers come and go throughout the day and interrupt Greg, who always appears happy and loves to talk! Some jobs are rush orders, but if the current workload is too much, Greg will nicely refuse work in order to maintain honesty with his customers (many local garages send their machining work to Greg). Dress is coveralls. Greg brings his lunch, as should Jim. Greg often leaves at about 3:30 or 4:00 p.m. to get his kids from preschool.

The shop can be pretty noisy when grinding equipment is operating. Radio plays rock-and-roll throughout the day. There are four distinct areas in this building: the customer counter and computer workspace/cash register; hot tank room where large, heavy items are degreased; the clean room for precision assembly; and the large general work area (where Jim will be stationed most of the day), which includes a parts washer, sand blaster, and paint booth.

Overall the worksite is clean and relaxed, with tools in their places (boxes and wall boards), and is somewhat noisy at times.

**Figure 3.1.** Job analysis record.

(continued)

**Figure 3.1.** *(continued)*

## *Project one description:* Valve grinding

Task steps:
Match valve to template found in grinder rack.
Install template.
Fit valve into grinder.
Turn on grinder.
Slowly move guide wheel clockwise, forcing valve into cutting wheel.
Slowly add pressure with guide wheel until sparks stop.
Turn guide wheel counterclockwise.
Turn off grinder.
Remove valve to finish rack.
Fit next valve into grinder.

Quality measures: Valve mating surface is clean and smooth.

Tools required: Grinder and attachments

Speed and accuracy considerations: Accuracy is much more important than speed, though the grinder and template make this an easily mastered job. Training attention will need to be given to selecting the proper template by matching it to the particular intake or exhaust valve.

Natural instructors/supervision: Greg understands the importance of teaching this task himself since it is core to Jim's job. Job coach should only offer more powerful strategies should Jim have difficulty with task acquisition.

Task duration: Takes about an hour for a standard set of V-8 engine valves (16 valves total). Greg mentioned that they recondition an average of 10–20 sets of heads a week.

Task acquisition concerns: Matching template to valve may be a start-up issue.

## *Project two description:* Sand blasting small parts

Task steps:
Degrease part in parts washer (otherwise the blast media will just adhere to it).
Insert part. (Make sure there is only one part in the blast cabinet at time! Very important!)
Fill blast cabinet hopper with media using scoop. (100-pound bags of silica are kept leaning against the back of the blast cabinet.)
Attach air hose to coupling.
Insert arms into black cabinet gloves.
Grasp spray gun.
Blast item until clean.
Move item as needed to access all sides for blasting.
Remove arms from gloves and remove piece from cabinet.
Inspect and reblast if not clean of debris, rust, and paint.
Empty spent media tray and dispose of in trash barrel.
Disconnect air line when done.
Refill blast cabinet hopper with media (if below one half full).

Quality measures: Blast cabinet hopper is one half full of media; clean up any spilled media (sand in a machine shop work area is NOT GOOD!); degrease/clean items and dry them with compressed air before blasting; parts should be totally bare metal upon completion.

Tools required: Parts washer; blast cabinet

Speed and accuracy considerations: Work rate varies from piece to piece; cleanliness more important than speed, but Greg will often be waiting for the piece in order to finish an assembly, so teaching should include attention to speed.

Natural instructors/supervision: Greg will demonstrate; job coaching should take very little time. Jim really enjoyed this activity during his work trial.

Task duration: Varies. Greg estimated that Jim might be blasting parts for about 1–2 hours per day.

Task acquisition concerns: As noted above

***Project three description:*** Parts washing. Greg will set parts in a staging area in plastic milk crate or work trays. Any part over about 10 pounds will be cleaned by Greg in the hot tank area, so lifting is not a concern for Jim. Generally these parts are small and include pistons, rods, valve springs, transmission valve bodies, transmission gears and synchronizers, oil pumps, etc.

## Task steps:
Put on face mask and solvent-proof gloves.
Turn on exhaust hood and washer pump.
Place part, or several smaller parts, into parts washer.
Depending on amount of dirt/grease, allow to soak.
Use wire brush or bristle brush to remove grease and dirt.
Rinse repeatedly and scrub until part is clean (or ready for blasting if Greg has indicated).
Remove parts as cleaned and store in milk crate or specific project tray.
Close lid on parts washer and turn off pump.
Greg will check cleaning fluid regularly and will change it as needed.

## Quality measures: Parts are clean and ready for reassembly or media blasting.

## Tools required: Parts washer, brushes, putty knives for scraping

## Speed and accuracy considerations: Depends on the job; cleanliness is most important aspect

## Natural instructors/supervision: Greg will instruct with assistance from job coach.

## Task duration: Varies from job to job. Greg estimates Jim will spend several hours a week cleaning parts. Many parts, though, are cleaned in the hot tank which Greg operates.

## Task acquisition concerns: Speed may be a concern; make certain parts are thoroughly degreased before going to media blasting! (If greasy part is placed in blast cabinet, then it creates a mess and the cabinet may have to be disassembled and cleaned!)

***Project four description:*** Painting engines and component parts (Note: In the beginning, Greg has indicated he'll mix the paints and solvents/reducers but will add this to Jim's job as he masters the painting process.)

## Task steps:
Mask off intake/exhaust openings, fuel pump canal, and lifter valleys on each engine.
Attach chain hoist to engine stand.
Lift engine, using hoist pump, to eye level. (Do not get under engine block under any circumstances!)
Turn on exhaust fan.
Wipe down engine with Metal Ready treatment to remove any grease or oil.
Mix paint and add to spray gun (Greg).
Attach compressed air line to spray gun (slip-on fitting).
Set air pressure gauge on spray gun to 45 lbs/ft.
Put on air respirator and protective hat and gloves.
Start at top of engine on one side and spray across evenly, move down, spray across, etc., until one side is covered with first thin coat.
Move to front of engine and spray across and down as before.
Move to other side of engine and spray across and down.
Spray oil pan and bellhousing flange last.
Wait 10 minutes and apply second coat.
Clean paint gun with lacquer thinner, spraying out excess.
Remove air hose.
Disassemble gun and place spray diffuser in bottle of thinner.
Stow gun on shelf.
Turn off exhaust fan.

## Quality measures: No drips or runs; correct color applied; surface was prepared accordingly so that paint adheres evenly, safety precautions followed, two coats applied; clean up done thoroughly.

## Tools required: Spray gun, engine hoist, engine stand

## Speed and accuracy considerations: Paint coverage must be complete (10 minutes between coats helps with self-managing time).

## Natural instructors/supervision: Greg will instruct and assist.

## Task duration: Approximately 60 minutes per engine or major component part due to setup and cleanup time. Actual paint application time is less than 15 minutes generally.

## Task acquisition concerns: Mixing paint should not be an issue with the use of graduated mixing cups, but this task will be introduced later. Greg and coach will instruct on proper spray gun paint application techniques.

*(continued)*

**Figure 3.1.** *(continued)*

---

### Notes and recommendations for onsite trainer, resource ownership, universal/assistive technology, further job modification, etc.:

There will be various other tasks added to Jim's work routine, but these are the core duties that require the most intensive teaching strategies. Greg and the employment specialist will consult with Jim on best teaching methods, job modifications needed, and any possible universal technologies.

Jim will be bringing various resource ownership components into the job: adjustable-height work benches, engine stands (these make the painting much easier for Jim), new parts washer that is wheelchair accessible, and various hand tools that Jim can use rather than borrowing Greg's.

It is critical that the employment specialist emphasize to Greg that Jim is "your new employee" and that Greg knows best how to perform the tasks. Employment specialist is there to offer more powerful teaching strategies or job modifications.

---

of his duties following an investigation and accusations of brutality. When he began his business, he used his connections in the criminal justice system to hire parolees. To maintain order in the shop, he threatened to call each employee's parole officer with false accusations of violations.

Whenever the boss came around, venting and cajoling, the workers waited for him to turn and leave the area, and then in unison they would raise their middle fingers to his back and laugh among themselves at their defiance. Toby had lived a sheltered life and did not fully appreciate the gesture or the circumstance, and he had no one to explain it to him. After watching this for almost 2 weeks, he was anxious to fit in, so when the boss approached one morning, cursing and complaining, Toby raised his middle finger to the owner's face and smiled. The boss fired him immediately and called the employment specialist to come get him.

A formal, written job match and analysis could have prevented this situation in several ways. First, if Toby's talents and desires had been discovered through a functional assessment, he would never have been considered for this job. Second, by observing the worksite on a more regular basis, particularly if unannounced, the employment specialist might have anticipated and bridged the conversational gulf on the assembly line, or realized that the nature of the employee backgrounds was such that Toby did not fit well in this particular environment. Third, had Toby experienced the worksite before being hired, he may have offered insight into the support he would need to fit in. And fourth, had the employer met Toby beforehand instead of relying solely on the recommendation of the employment specialist, he may have realized that Toby was not a good match. This placement so discouraged the employment specialist that she soon quit her job. Toby was labeled unready to work and was placed in a sheltered workshop. And the employer and employees of the packaging company may believe that people with disabilities are socially incompetent.

## JOB ANALYSIS IS CRITICAL FOR DEVELOPING QUALITY EMPLOYER RELATIONSHIPS

Job analysis is the act of systematically studying and recording the tasks, interactions, and methods involved in performing a job. The negotiation for mutual benefit is a critical element in CE because it recognizes that job analysis identifies essential tasks needing completion. The acts of job carving and creation, detailed in Chapter 8, reinforce these employer priorities while blending them with support and teaching processes that best complement the new employee's skills. Throughout the job analysis, it is necessary to recognize the importance of natural supports and a quality fit within the corporate culture or work place environment. Corporate culture herein refers to the formal and informal rules, rites, and rituals of a work place (Griffin, 1999). Employment specialists should practice recognition of unique cultural attributes by recording their observations as they tour potential places of employment. They should ask questions about the natural interplay of supervisors and co-workers as tasks are mastered or routinely performed. However, the degree to which co-workers routinely assist one another could go unobserved in short interviews. In some situations, observing and recording on site and asking for clarifications later may be the most effective method of gaining information about work place culture.

Videotaping work routines, discrete tasks, and general operations at a prospective employer's site is also recommended for several reasons.

1. Taping allows the employment specialist and team members to review the tasks studiously and repeatedly in order to break down teaching tasks and to hypothesize about assistive technology, teaching strategies, worksite accommodations, or co-worker supports.

2. Taping allows the prospective employee an opportunity to study the tasks, ask questions, and become familiar with various work processes.

3. Taping allows for at least a partial observation of the worksite cultural milieu, including such ingredients as dress code, language, humor, and official and unofficial power.

4. Taping allows family members to observe a worksite, to offer their accumulated advice on best possible teaching strategies, to identify additional tasks the job seeker may be interested in learning, and to voice any safety and security concerns they may have.

Regardless of the methods used to record worksite data, analysis of co-worker supports and corporate culture are critical to successful skill attainment and job retention. Throughout the job analysis, reference should be made to the observation of naturally occurring worksite teaching or support, and to critical cultural issues. All aspects of corporate culture are not easily observed, so some discussion of support and worksite rituals and rules is necessary, and will probably be driven by the individual needs of the employer and the prospective employee (Griffin, 1992). For example, a few common points of observation or discussion of opportunities with members of the current work force might include:

1. Is there a formal orientation for all new workers?
   *Why this is important:* Smooth integration of any worker often depends upon using natural means to fit in and learn. Support attendance of the new hire at this orientation in order to promote inclusion and normalcy.

2. Is there a formal training plan for each new employee? What is the best and least intrusive method for the employment specialist to join in?
   *Why this is important:* Should formal training already exist, it is best to use the existing system of staff development and to offer training strategies and supports to the natural trainer as needed in order to aid inclusiveness and ecological fit. Avoid the temptation to replace the natural trainer or co-worker support.

3. Are initiation rituals commonplace? If so, how can these be facilitated?
   *Why this is important:* Many workplaces welcome new employees by playing tricks on them or by having them perform a disagreeable task, such as cleaning a bathroom, even though this is not in their job description. Initiation rituals are rites of passage that test a person's sense of humor and help establish the new worker as "one of the guys." Some rituals are subtle and some are more outlandish. One common initiation ritual is going out for drinks after work. The new hire is invited along. After several rounds, the team members slowly fade away from the table to "go to the bathroom," "make a quick phone call," or "go outside for a smoke." Slowly it dawns on the new hire left at the table that no one is returning, except the server

with the bill for the drinks. Never allow a new hire to be put in a humiliating or dangerous situation. Some rituals can be anticipated and adapted to, if it is appropriate to do so.

4. Do employees share the same equipment and tools?

   *Why this is important:* Sharing tools, and workspace as well, signals a need to make certain the new hire understands that tools must be returned to their proper place, and protocol must be followed when scheduling the use of certain equipment and maintaining proper cleanliness of equipment and space. Knowing the standards before a conflict arises is critical to job security. The employee should know to ask for training assistance and support from others who know the routines and best methods of tool operation.

5. Is there a dress code?

   *Why this is important:* Clothing can help one fit in or stand out. Make certain the new hire is properly dressed. Clothing should not compromise safety. If uniforms are worn, the new hire should wear one.

6. Do employees engage in social conversations?

   *Why this is important:* Talking while others are concentrating can lead to dismissal or inhibit acceptance on the job. But conversation can also be a useful means of fitting in and gaining acceptance. Employment specialists should observe and encourage proper behavior as a means of smoothing worksite acceptance.

7. Do co-workers carpool? Does the employer participate in a transit program?

   *Why this is important:* Transportation is a critical element to any job match. A job that one cannot get to is a bad job. To augment the natural relationships in worksites and to speed the exit of the employment specialist, access these transportation resources, or common transit options such as public buses, or use of a Plan to Achieve Self-Support (PASS) for purchasing one's own car.

8. Are there regularly scheduled staff meetings or in-service training events?

   *Why this is important:* Make sure the new hire can participate. Provide some role playing while off site, or better yet, seek out a co-worker to assist the individual with participation during the meeting or training. Too often workers with significant disabilities are not actively engaged in these events, especially if verbal language is an issue, and this situation can contribute to a lack of status or the assumption of incompetence by co-workers.

9. Are there shared work tasks?

   *Why this is important:* Shared tasks are a prime avenue for engaging co-workers. Almost any time two or more workers collaborate to perform a task is an opportunity to socially bond through shared experience, natural training, and mutual achievement. Fitting in is the result of sharing the same environments and activities over time (Oldenburg, 1989); therefore, improving the likelihood of job retention can be achieved naturally by recognizing and utilizing shared tasks.

10. Is career advancement encouraged in this company?

    *Why this is important:* So often people with disabilities are placed in high-turnover positions. This circumstance exists because these jobs are abundant, they tend to be easily taught and learned, and they satisfy the general assumption that all workers begin at the bottom and work their way up the career ladder (Fitzgerald, 2006).

Unfortunately, the data are clear that people with disabilities do not climb the ladder; they instead are subjected to dead-end, high-turnover jobs, which reinforces the indifference of employers and other more upwardly mobile co-workers towards the plight of the expendable laborer (Braddock, Hemp, Rizzolo, Parish, & Pomeranz, 2002).

Employment specialists enhance consumer lives by noticing career building opportunities and helping to facilitate those by reinforcing the notion that job growth is just as important to their new hire as to any other employee (Griffin et al., 2006).

## JOB ANALYSIS RECORD

One way to facilitate entry into the worksite is through completion of an initial JAR. This form is used to capture information critical to the job training, modification, and accommodation process. This book does not cover worksite teaching strategies, such as systematic instruction, largely because resources are abundant in this content area (Brooke, Inge, Armstrong, & Wehman, 1997; Callahan & Garner, 1997; Gold, 1980). Almost every major university rehabilitation program, federally funded Rehabilitation Continuing Education Program, and various disability and employment training organizations have seminars and materials available in this content area. This book is more concerned with the process leading up to worksite training, and job analysis sets the stage for successful skill acquisition through quality worksite supports and teaching strategies.

Poor job retention rates have been directly tied to the lack of proper job analysis and job match (Brooke et al., 1997). The discovery process, coupled with a vocational profile or JAR, is used to direct the job development process to match the job seeker's desires and talents. The JAR is a written process of confirming that prospective employment situations mesh with those talents and desires. It helps detail the exact tasks and possible training strategies and supports available or needed in the worksite. One important feature of this format is that it ignores the more traditional job description and instead focuses on the particular jobs within a job.

CE seeks to match the worker within the best possible conditions of employment and often that means creating or carving new positions not reflected in any single job description. Since CE works especially well in smaller businesses, the existence of job descriptions may be moot. Many created or carved jobs do not have a smooth transition from one event to another. Often in smaller businesses, an employee will work in one work space to complete a particular task, then move to another area and work on a different task. This is also true for individuals who own their own businesses, where tasks vary throughout the day or week depending on production cycles or customer needs. This is why the JAR is designed around projects. Each job within a job is considered a discrete event, with perhaps a distinct set of tasks, tools, and quality measures, as well as differing quality standards, time or speed considerations, co-workers, and supervisors.

For example, one job at a car dealership was created to match the skills and desires of a particular young man. Each day at work was a little different, and the supervisors changed depending on the assigned task. In the morning of one particular day, the worker was expected to mop the showroom floor before customers and sales staff arrived. At 9:00 a.m. when the public doors opened, the floor was expected to be dry, and the worker moved on to the body shop to wet sand a car. This particular car on this particular day was not a rush, so the supervisor (the body shop foreman) kept the young man working at a relaxed pace for the rest of the day. The following morning, and every day thereafter, a new list of jobs and supervisors was assigned. Many of the jobs, of course, were repeated week after week, but their order and importance varied from department to department.

Completing the JAR requires the job developer or employment specialist to pay particular attention to the requirements of the job seeker as derived from the discovery process and the unique qualities and ecological conditions of the worksite. This form seeks to capture the negotiated tasks of a new position to guide worksite skill acquisition and natural support identification. Critical aspects of the analysis are the identification of natural supports that can be engaged in order to highlight the new employee's talents; the need for the same, although perhaps more intensive, training and support that any new hire requires; and the existence of shared tasks and work space that enable enhanced skill acquisition and social acceptance.

Natural supports are abundant in most employment settings. These are the typical resources, methods, and processes available to all workers. During the job analysis, the employment specialist seeks to capitalize on these resources as training supplements and cues for behavior. A clock on the wall is a natural support, or stimulus, that tells employees when it is break time. If a new hire does not tell time, then the employment specialist knows to cue that person by teaching him or her to watch others headed to the break room, gets the person a programmable alarm watch, or perhaps asks a co-worker to give the employee an inconspicuous signal. In terms of skill acquisition, most businesses have natural trainers, often a supervisor or co-worker, who show all new hires the proper methods for completing tasks. The employment specialist's job is to employ these same natural trainers and anticipate when more powerful teaching strategies, adaptations, or technology may be needed to bridge a performance gap. The job of the employment specialist is not to take over the natural process. When this occurs, it can often unfortunately result in the employer and the new employee becoming dependent on the presence of the employment specialist, which makes assimilation into the work force more difficult.

One useful approach to maximize the impact of natural supports is to identify shared or overlapping work tasks during the job analysis, and to preserve these circumstances, or to carve them in, during the job development and training negotiations (Griffin & Sherron, 2001). For example, Melinda, a transition-age female with little verbal communication and a developmental disability, began a discovery process that revealed a mixed bag of interests and preferred working conditions. Melinda wanted

To work alone sometimes

To work with others sometimes

To work indoors sometimes

To work outdoors at other times

To do clerical work sometimes

To work with plants sometimes

To be around people who are wealthy

To travel the world

Discussing this profile with Melinda revealed that gardening intrigued her but that it held her attention for only short periods. She also did not want to work outside when it was cold, and she wanted also to be considered an office worker. She further explained that though she wanted to travel, she was too poor to afford plane tickets, but that if she was around wealthy people, she was sure she would make friends and they would invite her on their trips.

Having this information allowed the job developer to seek out a job, or combination of jobs, to meet her needs. Of course no job description existed for such a list of contradictory requirements. However, a work setting did exist that presented the potential for creating this job. The city's botanical gardens offered indoor and outdoor work; a host of gardening, maintenance, clerical, retail, and educational tasks; wealthy patrons who volunteered in the gift store; ecotourism; and botany lectures. Using his social and professional network, the job developer got Melinda an appointment with a friend-of-a-friend who worked at the gardens, and he and Melinda toured the site together, wrote up a laundry list of all the job tasks they observed, and negotiated a floater position with the employer. After 2 weeks, the new job description was approved by several department heads at the gardens who shared tasks from Melinda's position and agreed to split the costs of employing her. Melinda's new job included

Working alone, weeding plant beds indoors and out

Working in the woodshop with a team of people building displays and cutting plant stakes

Working on the watering and plant relocation teams

Assisting in the mail room with bulk mail jobs and assembling fliers and training materials

Stocking shelves in the gift store and assisting at the reception desk giving out daily programs and maps of the grounds

The subsequent training plan capitalized on a host of shared and overlapping tasks. For instance, moving plants required at least two people. The employment specialist, assigned to guide Melinda through the first couple weeks of on-site work, simply shadowed the co-worker and Melinda as they moved plants and offered assistance only as required, allowing the natural training to occur uninterrupted. This strategy was also used in the other settings, including the mailroom, where the employment specialist built a simple folding jig to assist her in preparing papers neatly and quickly but otherwise removed himself from the situation. In the tiny wood shop where a team of four to five people worked, the employment specialist could not physically remain, so the training proceeded as it would for any new hire. Melinda exhibited several excessive behaviors that were exacerbated by the presence of authority figures, and her paucity of verbal language contributed to her sometimes violent frustration with being told what to do. Working as part of a team or even with another co-worker of equal status significantly reduced this anxiety. Without a job analysis and significant conversation with her parents, Melinda's opportunities are likely to have gone unrecognized. Melinda could then have suffered the stigma associated with job coaching, as a wall of services would isolate her from natural conversation and learning, and possibly increase her challenging behavior and complicate worksite assimilation.

## EMPLOYMENT-RELATED SUPPORTS

In previous employment situations, considerations such as transportation, medication management, and personal care issues have been left for others, such as the family, resource or case managers, or residential services, to address. While these various stakeholders play a role, adding in the considerations *after* the job is secured or seriously considered may inhibit job success. An employee without reliable transportation is doomed to unemployment, and someone without assistance with managing their diabetes or seizures may suffer even greater consequences. During the discovery process, which often includes short-term work experiences, issues of employment-related supports (e.g., quality improvement, supervision and communication methods, bathroom assistance) reveal themselves. Throughout the job analysis process, the employment specialist or job developer should meld personal health, behavioral, and transportation-related needs with the natural or purchased accommodations available. Examples of modifications and employment-related support appear throughout these chapters, but it bears emphasizing that the job analysis process must reveal these needs and prompt the plans for their provision in the least intrusive manner.

Transportation, accessibility modifications, and personal care remain among the most serious ongoing employment-related support needs (Hammis & Griffin, 2002; Young, 2003). Formal job analysis using the JAR makes the case for such accommodations and provides a brainstorming tool for team problem solving. The document also professionally presents factual information useful during funding negotiations with such entities as VR, the local workforce center, or the state mental health authority; when applying for a Plan to Achieve Self-Support (PASS) or utilizing an Impairment Related Work Expense (IRWE) from the Social Security Administration; or when investigating the use of Medicaid for communication devices or mobility aids such as wheelchairs (see Chapter 9). In the example of Jim Dodge, the job analysis revealed several worksite accommodation issues which were addressed by simple and inexpensive equipment purchases, but which may have remained obstacles had the available resources not been known and accessed (see Figure 3.1; a blank version of this form appears in the appendix). Unfortunately, many consumers, employment specialists, job developers, families, and other stakeholders do not know of, understand, or utilize these resources; a circumstance that probably contributes to the maintenance of the high unemployment rate for people with disabilities (Flippo, Inge, & Barcus, 1995; Wehman & Kregel, 1998).

## CONCLUSION

Job analysis provides the platform for considering the best support strategies for both the employee and the employer. Without detailed information regarding the individual through the discovery process and the JAR, the job match is compromised. This lack of information exacerbates the intrusiveness of corrective jobsite training and impedes the acquisition of typical worker status. Quality job matching will challenge quick assumptions by minimizing guesswork and by providing concrete evidence for making job development decisions. It is a formal, written process, which when done correctly, blends the realities of work life and employer profitability with the generous spirit often found in corporate cultures. Job analysis presents an opportunity for job seekers, the professionals around them, employers and co-workers, and family members to innovate and problem-solve in the spirit of both improving lives and the world of work.

## REFERENCES

Braddock, D., Hemp, R., Rizzolo, M., Parish, S., & Pomeranz, A. (2002). *The state of the states in developmental disabilities: 2002 study summary.* Boulder: University of Colorado, Coleman Institute for Cognitive Disabilities and Department of Psychiatry.

Brooke, V., Inge, K., Armstrong, A., & Wehman, P. (Eds.). (1997). *Supported employment handbook: A customer-driven approach for persons with significant disabilities.* Richmond, VA: Virginia Commonwealth University, Rehabilitation Research and Training Center.

Callahan, M., & Garner, B. (1997). *Keys to the workplace: Skills and supports for people with disabilities.* Baltimore: Paul H. Brookes Publishing Co.

Fitzgerald, J. (2006). *Moving up in the new economy: Career ladders for U.S. workers.* Ithaca, NY: ILR Press.

Flippo, K., Inge, K., & Barcus, M. (1995). *Assistive technology: A resource for school, work and community.* Baltimore: Paul H. Brookes Publishing Co.

Gold, M. (1980). *Try another way training manual.* Champaign, IL: Research Press.

Griffin, C.C. (1992). Typical, generic, in vivo, in situ, granola, voodoo, normal, informal (a.k.a., natural) supports. *The Advance, 3*(2).

Griffin, C.C. (1999). *Working better, working smarter: Building responsive rehabilitation programs.* St. Augustine, FL: TRN Press.

Griffin, C.C., Brooks-Lane, N., Hammis, D., & Crandell, D. (2006). Self-employment: Owning the American dream. In P. Wehman, K.J. Inge, W.G. Revell, & V.A. Brooke (Eds.), *Real work for real pay: Inclusive employment for people with disabilities.* Baltimore: Paul H. Brookes Publishing Co.

Griffin, C.C., & Sherron, P. (2001). Finding jobs for young people with disabilities. In P. Wehman (Ed.), *Life beyond the classroom.* (3rd ed.) Baltimore: Paul H. Brookes Publishing Co.

Hagner, D. (2000). *Coffee breaks and birthday cakes: Evaluating workplace cultures to develop natural supports for employees with disabilities.* St. Augustine, FL: TRN Press.

Hammis, D., & Griffin, C.C. (2002). *Social Security considerations for entrepreneurs with significant disabilities.* Florence, MT: Griffin-Hammis Associates, LLC.

Kregel, J., & Unger, D. (1993). Employer perceptions of the work potential of individuals with disabilities. *Journal of Vocational Rehabilitation, 3,* 17–25.

Locklin, D. (1997). *Community exchange.* Knoxville, TN: Community Rehabilitation Program–Rehabilitation for Continuing Education Program.

Luecking, R., Fabian, E., & Tilson, G. (2004). *Working relationships: Creating career opportunities for job seekers with disabilities through employer partnerships.* Baltimore: Paul H. Brookes Publishing Co.

Mank, D.M., Cioffi, A., & Yovanoff, P. (1998). Employment outcomes for people with severe disabilities: Opportunities for improvement. *Mental Retardation, 36,* 205–216.

Nisbet, J., & Hagner, D. (1988). Natural supports in the workplace: A reexamination of supported employment. *Journal of the Association for Persons with Severe Handicaps, 13,* 260–267.

Oldenburg, R. (1989). *The great good place: Cafes, coffee shops, bookstores, hair salons, bars, and other neighborhood hangouts at the heart of a community.* New York: Marlowe & Company.

Wehman, P., & Kregel, J. (1998). *More than a job.* Baltimore: Paul H. Brookes Publishing Co.

Young, T. (2003). The evolution of personal assistance services as a workplace support. *Journal of Vocational Rehabilitation, 18*(2), 73–80.

# 4

# Person-Centered Job Development Strategy

## Finding the Jobs Behind the Jobs

*Cary Griffin, David Hammis, and Tammara Geary*

The past decade witnessed the evolution of best practice job development approaches away from a sales-based strategy to a person-centered model (Bissonnette, 1994; Griffin & Hammis, 1998; Griffin & Sherron, 2001; Hoff, Gandolfo, Gold, & Jordan, 2000; Luecking, Fabian, & Tilson, 2004). Previously, the availability of jobs often guided the selections developed for the job seeker, but person-centered job development begins by determining the individual's interests and preferences and seeks out negotiated work opportunities within companies. This shift is critical in understanding the potential impact of customized employment (CE) on the day-to-day activities of adult rehabilitation and school-to-work transition employment specialists, job seekers, and supportive family members. The recognition that job development today represents an interest-based, relationship-building effort has transformed the art and science of securing employment from one of salesmanship to one of engineering mutually beneficial relationships between job seekers and employers. Accomplishing this mind shift requires job developers to recognize the potential contributions of individuals with significant disabilities and, simultaneously, the needs and motivations of employers as the job development process's starting point. The concept of employability fills the research journals of the past decades, but CE refutes the historic cornerstone ideas of job readiness and realistic career objectives with the notion that everyone possesses personal genius of value in the marketplace. Making the profitability of an individual's personal genius visible to an employer, as well as to various funders and family members, is the task of the modern job developer (Callahan & Garner, 1997; Griffin, Brooks-Lane, Hammis, & Crandell, 2006; Griffin & Hammis, 2003).

## JOBS BEHIND THE JOBS

This chapter presents strategies for developing jobs that respect an individual's career goals while recognizing that many of these jobs simply do not exist in the traditional format and that they must be identified piecemeal and then constructed through negotiations with the employer. Because CE's hallmark is the negotiated job, the tasks are often assembled from disparate locations or activities within a particular company, or they are carved from existing jobs hidden from the eyes of the general public, common customers, or job developers performing perfunctory analyses. These jobs behind jobs can require specialized skills or equipment, union membership, or simply a unique bundling of duties previously performed haphazardly or only when absolutely necessary.

For example, a job might be developed as a seamstress assistant in a sewing factory following observations that reveal seamstresses leaving their work areas for the store room to get thread to replace their empty spools. In addition, the new job might include entering data on inventory each time thread is removed. In the past, the seamstresses were responsible for these tasks, but the immediacy of sewing led to their neglecting to record data, and downtime for trips to the supply closet led to reduced production quotas. Creating this job required an individual who had interests in sewing, data, and being helpful with supplies, and an employer who was willing to consider the job development proposal from the employment specialist.

In this example, the employment specialist created a job that resided unseen behind other jobs. In the authors' experience, these types of jobs, when 1) properly matched to a job seeker, 2) designed to solve a production or service delivery problem for the employer, and 3) negotiated to satisfy the interests of the primary stakeholders (e.g., employer, co-workers, job seeker), can garner higher wages than other entry-level positions. In addition, they present more stable and lower turnover employment. They represent positions that become integral to the work of others within the company because their primary tasks are complementary to the core duties of the workforce. These jobs behind jobs are less obvious; sometimes they are more complicated to learn, teach, and perform, but they can be more meaningful due to their built-in uniqueness.

## SALES TRAINING

Sales training remains an important aspect of the employment specialist's arsenal. Employment specialists must know how to manage their time, understand the technical aspects of their services, and represent their constituents in a professional manner. However, overemphasizing selling misses the point of CE. CE's bedrock is the melding of personal contribution with the needs of the workplace. It is not, as sales approaches sometimes imply, the coercion of customers.

## HIGHLIGHTING PERSONAL CONTRIBUTION

Highlighting personal contribution is indeed the job developer's first job. Most employment for people with disabilities is based on this principle. However, for many individuals, the potential personal contribution of individuals with complex disabilities is difficult for employers (and professionals as well) to discern. *Resource ownership,* an approach pioneered by the authors (Griffin & Hammis, 2003; Hammis & Griffin, 1998), and discussed in more detail in Chapter 6, addresses this issue and illustrates mutually beneficial relationship-building and job creation from a person-centered/business-centered standpoint. Resource ownership is the process of acquiring materials, equipment, or skills that, when matched to a job seeker's interests and customer needs, generates profits for the employer. For instance, many people spend $50,000 or more on a college degree and that degree is a symbol of exploitable knowledge. As mentioned in Chapter 1, employers reason that they can profit from a graduate's intellect; therefore, job seekers with degrees get hired. In essence, the graduate uses the degree as a bargaining chip with the employer in return for wages. The same occurs when a truck driver who owns a tractor-trailer applies for a hauling job. Without the trucking equipment, the trucker possibly faces unemployment, or a less satisfactory, lower paying trucking job. In order to secure good jobs, job seekers must have exploitable resources; such resources, when placed in the hands of people with disabilities, lends to an increase in their job options and makes them more employable (Griffin et al., 2006). Certainly sales skills are involved, but the discovery of personal genius, coupled with job exploration and analysis, create a logical path, again of mutual benefit, that reduces the traditional reliance on sales and the negative stereotypes associated with selling (Cathcart, 1990; Underhill, 1999).

Adopting a CE approach means that the rehabilitation organization or school transition program embraces a more adventurous culture of entrepreneurship and abandons the dependence culture of human services. Typically, the world of business moves a bit faster than the nonprofit or public realm, is more focused on outcomes than processes, and rewards those who accomplish company goals. Policy and practice may necessitate changes that allow teachers to leave classrooms for job development and networking activities, and that encourage employment specialists to make quick decisions and commitments while networking in the community. Comparing the two models illustrates the significant difference in world views (see Table 4.1). Each model has its necessary place in the world, but traditional approaches to job development often sought to extend the human services model into the business realm by selling employees with disabilities based on a charitable approach (DiLeo & Langton, 1993; Mank, 1996). Instead, human services should adopt the business model in recognition of the employer as an essential customer.

## NETWORKING

A good deal of job development involves employer prospecting. In CE, knowing the employer base before beginning a job search is preferred but is not always possible. Therefore, methods of warming up prospecting calls are utilized. Networking is the generally accepted strategy of introduction (Bolles, 2003; Granovetter, 1974; Hoff et al., 2000; Luecking et al., 2004). Numerous studies reveal that networking strategies are used by over 50% of successful employment seekers and that the more diverse the members of that network are; the greater are the number of opportunities created (Fesko & Temelini, 1997; Gladwell, 1999).

A critical issue in rehabilitation, however, is that human services personnel and job seeker networks remain shallow due to numerous factors.

1. Human services are charitable in nature and not expected nor typically invited to participate in the business activities of the community.

2. Frontline staff, such as job developers and employment specialists, are often relatively new employees and do not have personal resources or agency money available to wine and dine clients, or to join and participate actively in civic clubs.

3. People with disabilities lack resources and the mobility necessary to access community activities.

**Table 4.1.**   Comparison of entrepreneurial and human service models

| Entrepreneurial: abundance-adventure model | Human services: scarcity-dependence model |
| --- | --- |
| Identify a profitable product or service to satisfy a need | Identify public or government resources to address a problem |
| Research and development | Assessment of the individual in need |
| Develop a functional business proposal | Develop a plan |
| Market | Service delivery |
| Provide service after the sale | Serve the next consumer |
| Profit | Cost |

*Source:* Luecking, Martin-Luecking, and Steckel (2004).

4. Human services, and therefore those served by human services, are typically isolated physically and psychologically from the mainstream community.

Breaking the cycle of isolation and creating networks is relatively easy. The key to any of these measures is active participation. Passive attendance at a chamber of commerce luncheon does not engage others in the cause of employment for people with disabilities. Management must measure the effectiveness of each strategy and hire and train employment specialists to engage community members in meaningful ways. Strategies that increase community networks include

1. Providing frontline staff with the time and budget to join service clubs (e.g., Kiwanis, chamber of commerce, Rotary) or to participate in community intramural sports, or other such regular activities that match their personal interests and provide the potential for meeting employers. Agencies adopting this approach should measure the increase in job development successes stemming from the connection to these groups.

2. Provide a small expense account for employment specialists to take potential employers to lunch.

3. Refine the organizational image to emphasize employment and community building as the number one outcome, and eliminate stereotypical messages about people with disabilities, such as charity drives based on pity.

Another easy strategy to implement is *relationship charting*. A key component of discovery and person-centered planning is the listing of stakeholder relationships. For instance, each member of a person-centered planning team, chosen by the job seeker, draws up a list of every one known to them, from acquaintances, to best friends, to family members. Since most people are employed, their jobs are listed. The team searches the list for job associations related to the job seeker's preferences, talents, and needs. Any matches are further refined to determine if this person is the point of contact for a job development call. Or perhaps that individual might know someone within their company, or their supplier and customer chains, who, with an introduction, could be tapped as an employment source. Generally networks can be mined to reveal layer upon layer of potential connections.

Another suggested activity is having every employee of the rehabilitation agency or school complete a relationship chart and then pledge to use these personal contacts to introduce job seekers and job developers. A sample relationship chart is included in Figure 4.1 for listing names, relationships, career, trade, or personal interest areas, and contact information. A database of completed forms is kept by the employment specialist and used to match job seekers to people known in the community with similar connections or interests.

## Organizational Networking

An underutilized source of employment opportunity is organizational connections. All agencies purchase diverse goods and services throughout their communities, and in many small towns, these are themselves among the top employers. Because these organizations are nonprofits, they also have boards of directors or school boards in the case of local educational agencies, and numerous city and county relationships. Seldom are these relationships exploited to their fullest.

Agencies should add to their board members' job descriptions an active role in hiring and promoting the employment of people with disabilities within their own businesses or work places and throughout their personal and professional networks. School board members should be expected to do likewise. And job matches should be considered within the supplier chain of any organization.

| Name | Relationship to Me (e.g., friend, family, acquaintance, customer) | Career/Trade/Interest | Contact Information |
|------|------|------|------|
|  |  |  |  |
|  |  |  |  |
|  |  |  |  |
|  |  |  |  |
|  |  |  |  |
|  |  |  |  |
|  |  |  |  |
|  |  |  |  |
|  |  |  |  |
|  |  |  |  |
|  |  |  |  |
|  |  |  |  |

**Figure 4.1.**   Relationship chart.

For instance, even a small rehabilitation agency brings millions of dollars into the community over time, placing it in a position of power to leverage its patronage of local enterprises in exchange for assistance with satisfying its mission (in this case, the acquiring of jobs for individuals with significant disabilities). The organization's bank should be chosen based on their hiring practices and their dedication to assisting with the mission of hiring people with disabilities. Most agencies buy gasoline, have their vehicles serviced, call repair technicians for computers and office equipment, purchase clerical and custodial supplies, buy food for their residential programs, utilize local medical services, and purchase a host of other goods and services. These vendors should welcome employment specialists and job seekers alike; if not, the agency should actively recruit suppliers willing to assist in the mission of community employment. That participation may not always be supplying jobs, but certainly every vendor can assist in building the network, providing work experiences and mentoring, and publicly declaring their support.

Networking remains the single most effective means of finding job leads (Hoff et al., 2000). The methods of network development presented here are basic and certainly not exhaustive. Even though the literature addressing networking is plentiful, basic connections are often overlooked in the day-to-day flurry of rehabilitation.

For example, one of the chapter authors attended a job development meeting for a young woman living in a large metropolitan area. In his role as consultant, he listened to the staffing team discuss the fact that they could not come up with any ideas regarding a job for this young woman. She was unmotivated in the sheltered workshop and did not have verbal language to express her interests. She was, however, wearing a hat with the word *Corvette* above the brim. She wore this hat to work every day. No one had ever asked her if she liked Corvettes. It turns out that she did. And, on that very team was a woman whose parents were organizers of the largest classic Corvette show on the

East Coast. Attending the Corvette show was the first step in determining if her interest was a vocational clue or simply something she enjoyed but did not prefer to pursue for employment. Sometimes the clues and the networks are right there in front of us.

## THE DREAM JOB TRAP

The person-centered/business-centered job development strategy adopts an *abundance–adventure* model philosophy. In other words, the job market is forever expanding through the creation of products and services that meet evolving needs or solve emerging problems. Just as entrepreneurs create business, job developers can create jobs.

Beginning, as always, with the job seeker's profile developed from discovery, the best possible conditions of employment are sought. Matching the potential contributions of the job seeker with an employment situation, without regard to existing job descriptions, is the key feature. The savvy employment specialist, or self-directed job seeker, is out to create employment, not to react to what is available as revealed through want-ads or employment postings at the local workforce center.

Reacting to the paucity of employment options offered by the job market results in a profusion of entry-level, stereotypical, and high-turnover, low-paying jobs for people with the most significant disabilities. Correcting this situation by matching people's individual talents and aspirations to adaptive work situations is the employment specialist's cause. This effort requires ingenuity and imagination; a rethinking of how the job development process should work.

Person-centered planning approaches emphasized the accumulation of the dreams of people with disabilities (Griffin & Hammis, 1998; Mount, 1987). An unintended consequence of this vital planning method was the development of the *dream job*. Person-centered planning is still an important technique, but chasing after a dream job is a noble gesture that in the long run too often ends in failure. Although the authors have promoted the dream job approach themselves, they can still suggest several reasons why this approach may be problematic.

First, dream jobs are often one of a kind. For example, a young man decides he wants to be the manager of the Philadelphia Phillies. There is no reason to think he cannot do this; however, only one such position exists and without experience in the major leagues it is highly doubtful that even exhaustive efforts will result in the dream's attainment. Chances are the manager's position was the most visible and desirable job to the individual. However, should he be prompted to explore this interest in baseball, he could uncover opportunities to create employment related to baseball precisely, or in the general sports field. Perhaps by exploring what a baseball manager does, the young man would discover that the act of being in charge is a factor that motivates him, thereby opening up opportunities in supervisory positions in a number of fields. Or, perhaps management positions offer a symbolic respite from a life of clienthood where control is vested, not in the individual, but rather in programs and professionals. The baseball theme deserves exploration, and with an open mind and some imagination, a wondrous number of possibilities may arise.

Also, dream jobs assume only one vocational interest. Many people with significant disabilities have little life experience. Discovery, coupled with various work experiences as a youth in school and perhaps later as an adult, expands interests and choice making. Too often, staff close to the individual—with the best of intentions—suggest jobs based on their limited knowledge of the person. Because some people with significant disabilities acquiesce to those in charge, or perhaps because they are highly prone to suggestion, the dream job identified is not a choice, but rather represents a decision to work or not to work.

Often, dream jobs suggest a one-time career placement, instead of the growth and change expected from typical workers, who, in the United States, change jobs and careers multiple times (Hoff et al., 2000). This reinforces the rehabilitation system's emphasis on quick closures, regardless of historical data showing the initial job as often short-lived.

Dream jobs are often governed by the experience and talents of the rehabilitation professionals. Stereotypical jobs for people with significant disabilities exist because the rehabilitation field has limited skills in teaching complex job tasks. Because our social and professional networks are limited to others in this or similar fields, new ideas do not arise unless new people with unique experiences are engaged in the process.

Finally, dream jobs suggest that people with significant disabilities are one-dimensional. Job developers should adopt a philosophy that recognizes the complexity and potential of all human beings. Through significant experience all people learn, adapt, and grow new interests. Looking only at one exhibited preference fails to acknowledge and appreciate multiple, and perhaps unlimited, interests.

The CE process suggests that discovery and work experience present an array of employment opportunities awaiting exploitation. The job developer, armed with all this evaluative information, can locate or create money-making opportunities using inventive and imaginative strategies. Instead of making sales calls to likely business prospects, the employment specialist should seek to capture the essence of a workplace by touring, arranging for paid work experiences, and getting past the ubiquitous entry-level positions to find the career opportunities often hidden from the view of the general public: the jobs behind the jobs.

Entry-level jobs serve a number of important functions in the life's work of any person. We learn critical work and social skills, we learn how to manage our money between paychecks, we discover growth opportunities through exposure to other operations within a company, and we also hone our talents and recognize our employment-culture preferences. Closer scrutiny of entry-level job histories, however, often reveals personal preferences and themes, and not simply the acceptance of jobs solely because they existed. Anecdotal research by the authors, in discussion with a small sampling of about 130 adults in several states, reveals that the majority of jobs they held as teens were indeed related to personal interests and also allowed them to be close to friends. Those entry-level jobs also represented a mere starting point in their careers and were meant to be short term, serving as stepping stones to better jobs, higher earnings, and increased professional satisfaction. When jobs for people with disabilities represent limited growth potential, attempts by the worker to move on to better jobs is often greeted as a sign of noncompliance or failure (Griffin & Hammis, 2001; Griffin & Sweeney, 1994; Noble, Honberg, Hall, & Flynn, 1997). There are over 20 million businesses in the United States; opportunities for upward and lateral movement in career exploration abound and growth should to be encouraged and expected.

## NAÏVE JOB DEVELOPMENT: THE ANTIDOTE TO SALES CALLS

As illustrated in Chapters 1 and 3 through the example of Jim Dodge, casual or naïve job development represents a subtle and effective means of creating employment. Naïve job development replaces the traditional sales call that prompts the familiar employer reply: "I'm sorry; we're not hiring right now." The process of naïve job development is individualized and highly variable, but follows a logical design pattern. During, and sometimes following discovery, a series of informational interviews are arranged with the employer. The information gathered will be compared with that emerging from discovery of the job seeker's interests and talents. Because information, and not employment, is being sought, the pressure on the individual, the employment specialist, and the employer is minor. Included in this section is a sample script for approaching an employer once a vocational interest has been uncovered. The employment specialist may call or stop by to see a particular employer, or arrange to be in attendance at a social or professional gathering where they can chat, and where the idea of an informational interview and tour can be broached.

For example, Jason's assessment process revealed that he had interests in the areas of farming, horses, computers, and machinery. He also enjoyed being around people and was intent on helping others. Jason also liked lifting weights and demonstrating how strong he was. In the small town where he lived, east of the foothills of the Rocky Mountains, there was not much commerce, and no one seemed to be hiring. Still, the employment specialist made an appointment to visit the manager at the local grain elevator. She explained that she was a career counselor for the high school, that Jason was a hometown boy, set to graduate in the spring, and that he was exploring various career options. She asked if it would be possible to bring Jason by for a brief 30-minute discussion and maybe a tour of the business, simply to get some advice on choosing a career path in the agricultural sector.

In this job development strategy, the employment specialist did not ask for a job or even work experience. She did not pressure the potential employer. Instead, she intuitively understood that employers care about their communities and the next generation of citizens. She also understood that most people enjoy giving advice to others; being a mentor and consultant; and being recognized for their experience, success, and knowledge. As such, the employer scheduled a time to talk with Jason.

Numerous experiences with this approach revealed a pattern that held true in Jason's case as well. Jason was coached by the employment specialist using a short role-playing exercise. The employment specialist coached Jason to ask the potential employer some key questions about the operation, including

What does the future hold for the grain business?

Are there other competitors challenging your market?

What technological advances are on the horizon?

Do you have challenges in finding and training new employees?

Are there products or services that you are not providing, because you cannot afford the investment in personnel or equipment, but that you believe your customers desire?

These queries were intended to prompt further conversation with the potential employer. The queries were presented conversationally and interspersed with the follow-up questions from Jason. In general, an interview should never sound like an interrogation, and employment specialists and job seekers alike should also practice gathering information without the use of aggressive questioning. Making simple and leading statements generally elicits open-ended responses, rather than the *yes* or *no* answers one gets when going through a checklist.

For instance, the exchange may have resembled the following:

|  |  |
|---|---|
| Jason: | This looks like a big operation. |
| Manager: | Well, yes, it is. We have 14 employees, and we handle the feed and grain demands for most of the valley's ranches and farms. |
| Jason: | I've always enjoyed the little bit of work I did around horses and on a ranch where I worked after school for one semester. I think we bought our grain and silage from you. |
| Manager: | It's very likely you did. Six of our staff pick up loads and also deliver the processed grain that's not grown locally. |
| Employment Specialist: | Is there much competition in this business? |
| Manager: | In the past there hasn't been, but with online Internet services ranchers can shop around and have their feed delivered via train or truck to the depot here. It's not a big deal yet, but those big agri-businesses can afford to sell more cheaply than we can. |
| Jason: | Would you say this is a good business to be in? |

| Manager: | Sure. I enjoy it, and I get to know lots of folks in the community. It's a real community business and everyone here gets along. Of course, agriculture is a tough enterprise these days, but then it always has been. Many of the local kids don't stay here anymore. They move to the western part of the state, or they go away to college. |
|---|---|
| Employment Specialist: | I'll bet that makes it hard to find good employees. |
| Manager: | We've been lucky, I guess. We've got a good crew. |
| Jason: | Can you show us around while we talk? |

As the tour proceeded, new questions arose and conversation continued. The employment specialist noticed a host of small jobs and asked for some clarification of processes. Jason noted that there were several computers in the office and adjacent to the loading dock. These computers were used to enter sales, to read the truck scales, and to manage inventory. There was also a radio system to monitor delivery drivers and a number of other tasks not seen by the typical customer being greeted at the front counter.

The informational interview and tour are critical to getting a good sense of the hidden or backroom operations of business. In competitive employment the emphasis has been on responding to a job description, whereas in CE the detective work of uncovering the true operations of a company reveal job creation opportunities.

Both Jason and the employment specialist made mental notes of the tasks Jason found interesting. After a week, the employment specialist called the manager and asked for some additional advice:

| Employment Specialist: | Thanks again for helping us clarify some of the questions Jason and I had about your business. Jason has been talking a lot about the tour and the insights you gave into the agricultural supply business. I was hoping you could give me some recommendations on other businesses we could visit that would help us design his career plan, and I'm wondering if he might do a short internship with your company. |
|---|---|

After some further discussion, the manager accepted the work experience proposal. Jason fit in, with just a bit of coaching, and the next semester and throughout the summer, Jason worked after school and Saturdays as a part-time, paid employee. His job included loading bags of grain into customer trucks, entering inventory data on the computer, as well as a variety of other tasks. No real selling occurred. Instead, the process of engaging an employer in conversation with someone with similar interests allowed opportunities to occur. Of course, the employment specialist managed the situation somewhat, pointed out opportunities to all parties as they arose, and gently pulled Jason and the employer together. Closing the deal is still a critical ingredient in the job development process.

## INFORMATIONAL INTERVIEWS

Informational interviewing is a great way to develop work experience settings, to build a job placement network, to discover new kinds of jobs, to introduce yourself and your services to employers, and to build the mental database that all of us rely on for employment ideas when beginning a job search with someone.

Getting an appointment for an informational interview is usually much easier than setting up a job development meeting. A casual conversation with a prospective employer at the monthly chamber of commerce "Business After Hours" social or at a service club meeting (e.g., Kiwanis, Rotary, Lions club) can lead to a probe such as, "I've never seen your operation before. Would you mind if I called you to set up a time for a tour and a bit of a chat?" Most folks love to talk about their business and since you are not pressing them, setting up a phone call is considered low risk. Make sure to follow up soon, before the conversation is forgotten, and to illustrate commitment.

A request for 15–30 minutes works well because it signals respect for the person's time, and it indicates that you are busy as well. In our experience, 15 minutes always becomes 30–60 minutes once the discussion and tour begins.

On site, the job developer or employment specialist is seeking information about the company, its hiring practices, what opportunities exist to create or carve jobs, and company culture. The general format of an informational interview is

1. *Brief discussion*

    The employment specialist can ask something to the effect of: "Before we tour, can you tell me a bit about the history of the business, the products and services, and how the business is evolving?" People want to know that you care, so give them a chance to talk about themselves.

2. *Tour*

    Ask questions at appropriate times.

3. *Wrap-up*

    Thank the person for the tour, indicating that you may have someone interested in this field as a career or possibly in working there now or later. Make your exit and promise to stay in touch.

Throughout the process, opportunities to ask questions conversationally exist. Since this is not a job development visit, it is not necessary to press someone for a job. That comes later in the relationship. For now, the tour is about answering questions regarding the varying tasks and duties people perform, the values and culture of the company, and the needs the business has that your organization or workers can address.

The tour provides an opportunity to witness, for instance, the level of natural support that may be available to someone with a disability. Keen observation reveals whether co-workers and supervisors help each other out during a typical day; it reveals who does the training and how an employment specialist might structure the initiation period so that the employer takes significant responsibility for supervision and training right from the start; it reveals what is valued on the worksite, such as muscle, brains, humor, attendance, speed, quality, or other worker traits. These are important considerations when designing a job match that minimizes on-site training and consultation.

The interviewing process reveals opportunities, or red flags if the place of employment does not provide a good working environment, as well. Some standard questions for an informational interview, asked in a conversational and not in an interrogative tone, include

1. *Where do you find or recruit employees?*

    This question is asked to determine whether you now need to refer to a job service (which does all the hiring searches for this particular employer), to identify your competition, and to create an opportunity to discuss the service you provide.

2. *How are people trained in their jobs?*

    The answer will provide information about natural training means and methods that can be sculpted into a job match and training plan—especially one that recognizes that most businesses already train employees and that the support you offer is customizing their training, not replacing it.

3. *What are the prerequisites for working here?*

    The answer should point out the various qualifications, certifications, and other preparation that might be needed.

4. *How or where do your employees gain the experience required to work here?*

   The answer will clarify qualifications and give the job developer a list of other similar companies.

5. *What personal characteristics do you look for in employees?*

   The answer, while giving insight into the kind of candidate the employer seeks, will point out what to highlight in a résumé or interview. It will also afford a glimpse inside the culture of the company regarding the most valued skills and attributes.

6. *When employees leave, what other industries or businesses do they go to?*

   The answer can reveal issues of staff turnover, with low turnover indicating a great place to work and high turnover indicating poor management. It can also provide the job developer with information on related industries and possible opportunities for someone interested in similar work.

7. *What are the pay and benefit rates?*

   The answer clarifies the status of the job, allows for benefits planning considering the impact of wages on Social Security, and helps to clarify expectations of both parties so that there are no surprises later.

8. *What are the work hours? Is there shift work? Does the company allow for flex time or other job accommodations?*

   The answer gives the employment specialist insight into the flexibility of management and the company's policies on work hours and expected work effort.

9. *What impact is technology having on the industry?*

   The answer addresses a common concern for most businesses today and provides an opportunity for the job developer using resource ownership strategies to propose a job for someone who can use, or bring with them, a piece of essential technology that can be purchased through a Plan to Achieve Self-Support (PASS) plan or through vocational rehabilitation.

10. *What are the current forces for change in this industry?*

    The answer often starts a lively discussion of how the market is changing, how personnel preparation and training is evolving, and how the competitive market is adapting.

All these questions and their answers breed add-on questions and discussion points that provide opportunities to solve labor problems or to innovate in the face of emerging trends in hiring. Informational interviews are a low-tech, high-touch option that provides insight into the inner workings of business. Knowing what goes on in a given company gives the employment specialist or job developer an added advantage when creating employment or responding to an employer need.

## WORK EXPERIENCE

Work experience remains an important tool in job development. Work experience should be paid at commensurate wages and should last long enough for the individual to get a good sense of the tasks and the trade. Depending upon the person, work experiences range from a few hours to multiple weeks.

The role that wages play is important. Without pay, some people might assume work is punishment or that work has little benefit to them when compared to others who do get paid. The absence of pay also stigmatizes people. Whereas in some cases it is argued that an individual may not understand money, certainly those around that person understand its value and see the absence of pay as another indictor of the person's lack of worth. Finally, the lack of pay suggests that the person is volunteering. Most of us volunteer after our financial needs are met, and not before. In the rehabilitation field, we often hear that volunteer work leads to employment, but after years of consulting and running employment agencies, we have no evidence to support that assertion, and we would speculate that volunteering actually weakens an individual's case for pay by devaluing their labor in the first place. Further, if the work experience or tryout is in a nonprofit or government setting, volunteer work may have some legitimacy, but for-profit businesses do not have volunteers. In fact, voluntary labor, or work without pay, is generally recognized as illegal in the United States.

The U.S. Department of Labor enforces the Fair Labor Standards Act (FLSA) of 1938 (PL 75-718). This law stipulates minimum wage and overtime rules throughout the country, and it also details the conditions for work experience. These conditions are

There has been no displacement of employees, vacant positions have not been filled, employees have not been relieved of assigned duties, and the individuals are not performing services that, although not ordinarily performed by employees, clearly are of benefit to the business.

The individuals are under the continued and direct supervision by either representatives of the rehabilitation program or by employees of the business. Such placements are made according to the requirements of a formal (written) training plan and not to meet the needs of the business.

The periods of time spent by the individual at any site or in any clearly distinguishable job classification are specifically limited by the formal training plan.

Individuals are not entitled to employment at the business at the conclusion of the work experience; however, once an individual becomes an employee, the person cannot be considered a trainee at that particular community-based placement unless in a clearly distinguishable occupation.

The sure way to avoid violating the law is to pay the individual for the work. Otherwise, unpaid tryouts of three principal types are governed, again by the FLSA, as not exceeding the following totals.

Vocational exploration: 5 hours per job experienced

Vocational assessment: 90 hours per job experienced

Vocational training: 120 hours per job experienced

Pay for work experiences can be covered by redirecting classroom funds from the authorized daily rate paid to a school district for a student or from the daily rate paid to a mental health or developmental disability program in cases of adults with those disabilities. State vocational rehabilitation and workforce development centers (One-Stops) can also cover these expenses, as can a PASS through the Social Security Administration (Hammis & Griffin, 2002). Of course, working at part-time paid jobs, such as the ones most people get before their real career lives begin, is a most natural way to enter the world of work, to determine a possible career path, to meet new people and make friends, and to earn some spending money.

## Go Where the Career Makes Sense

Networking is just one method of job prospecting. When no obvious connection to a vocational interest is available through known networks, go where the career makes sense. In other words, seek out people in the same or a related business and ask them to advise the job seeker on steps to getting employed, or exploring the field further. This approach couples perfectly with the informational interview. As with any job development strategy, it is not guaranteed to result in an offer of employment, but the information gathered builds the foundation of the job search.

One example of this technique involves Errol, a young man expelled from school due to his disruptive behavior. Errol was 18 years old, labeled with both a developmental and a psychiatric disability, and he was adamant that he own a car detailing business. He did not want to work for anyone else, did not want to take orders from anyone else, and did not want to be bothered with working his way up the ladder. Acknowledging and accepting all career goals as valid is a critical first step in building a trusting relationship with a job seeker, so even though Errol had no car wash experience and no start-up funds for his business, he and his team began collecting data on what it takes to start such an operation.

The research revealed start-up costs well out of reach of Errol's savings or resources, and a referral to the state's VR program resulted in a denial for self-employment funding. Still, the research was not over. The team knew that other members of this community had started successful car detailing businesses and that there must be a way. So they went where the career made sense by contacting several car washes to make appointments for tours and informational interviews. The news was not good, however. The managers largely discouraged Errol and advised him to get a job in a car wash first in order to learn the business and save some money for his own business. Errol was not convinced and insisted that development work continue.

At this point another owner was contacted who agreed to advise Errol and the team. During the 15-minute meeting this employer also suggested that Errol get a job as a car detailer. A team member asked if the employer had any openings, and he said no. But, another team member asked if the enterprise was able to offer their customers all the services they requested. The owner responded that no, he could not yet provide carpet cleaning services because his cash flow would not allow for the purchase of a $2000 shampooer. Within 5 minutes, with Errol's permission, a deal was made for him to begin work as lead shampooer for the company and to receive training in all aspects of the business's operations, and in return, Errol, through the agency's funding, would purchase and use a carpet shampooer of the employer's choice within the business. Errol was excited by the job offer; he still wants to some day own his own car wash, but when opportunity knocked, he responded.

By meeting with others, getting advice on how to start Errol's business, and then using sales strategies to close the deal, the team secured employment for Errol. And even when this method does not result directly in a job, the advice given is often crucial for the job seeker's decision making, and for leading from one contact to another. The employment specialist is not looking for a specific job title or description. The search is for the best working conditions that will match the individual's potential contribution to the business. Someone interested in raising dogs would prompt visits and informational interviews with veterinarians, pet stores, dog kennels, dog breeders, and pet food manufacturers. And each of these visits should reveal unseen back office operations as well as other related industry sectors not obvious at first.

Job developers should know that many first-time job seekers suggest that they want jobs in companies, based on a very limited experiential base. This is why discovery is crucial for serving individuals who have little or no work, or life, experience. People often want to work at a hamburger or ice cream stand because they envision a friendly place where good food is available all through the shift. In reality, these jobs are tough and failure often ensues, resulting in loss of pride and status for the job seeker, and costing the agency hundreds of dollars in improper effort and a damaged reputation as a quality organization.

Thousands of people do earn a living making ice cream, however. Visiting the headquarters for Blue Bunny Ice Cream near Sioux Center, Iowa, one quickly realizes that most of the people there probably enjoy ice cream, but their motivation in applying for work was their interest in the computers that manage inventory, or in driving the trucks that deliver their product, or in performing the accounting functions they studied in college by working in the financial services department. Going where the career makes sense helps to refine the interests of the job seeker, builds the network, and reveals the many operations performed even in the smallest companies.

Revealing such back-office tasks is often the cornerstone of inventive job creation. Acknowledging someone's interest in ice cream, or hamburgers, or bagging groceries, or animals is important, and many good first jobs have been developed following these clues. However, these first jobs tend to be high-turnover positions that can be weak in the provision of natural supports, and lacking in advancement potential. Since most people with significant disabilities only get one or two chances to get a good job, strenuous efforts should be made. The job developer is advised to dig deeper than surface expressions of interest in jobs involving, say, animals, ice cream, shaking hands, or music. Liking these things is a human characteristic, as almost every human being enjoys them. That does not mean, however, that people should make their living through these preferences. Stereotypical jobs arise from concentrating on such obvious human enjoyments; good jobs are more difficult to discern than this.

True, some people really do want to work in these fields, but rigorously digging into the operations of a company reveals options of better quality and higher interest: the jobs behind the jobs. Most job developers see only the most obvious positions in a company, the tip of the iceberg. These jobs are abundant, but they are often high-turnover, entry-level, and without much social status. The jobs hidden from public view are rich in their variety, require more sustained training, and provide better wages than more obvious jobs. Figure 4.2 illustrates the Iceberg Effect: entry-level jobs abound, but employment with career opportunities, complexity, and better pay require research and good job matching to attain.

There are many operations in even the most basic businesses that are not seen from either the human resources office or the front sales counter. Many auto parts stores have machine shops in the back that perform countless services; almost any business of any size has a computer room or performs numerous computer functions; many businesses have sophisticated information management, inventory, and clerical departments; public recreation programs have laundries, equipment repair workshops, and snack bars; supermarkets perform produce waxing, meat cutting, and prepared food packaging out of sight of the customers. A well-developed network and going where the career makes sense reveals countless tasks performed in the most mundane companies. These tasks can often be isolated or carved into new jobs that match the requirements of the job seeker.

## SALES SKILLS AND MARKETING MATERIALS

Though sales is not the leading technique utilized in CE, skills in this discipline are essential. In particular, understanding negotiation and problem-solving strategies (see Chapter 7), handling objections, and personal management are critical. Being seen as solidly competent is requisite and requires the agency to invest in sufficient training and development specific to one's duties. Job developers must present themselves in a professional manner that illustrates confidence and the ability to solve problems efficaciously, to speak for the agency, and to represent the job seeker in a respectful manner.

Ensuring that job developers or employment specialists have adequate time and support to create quality employment requires first that their employer bring the proper structure and resources to bear. Caseloads must be reconfigured in many agencies to fos-

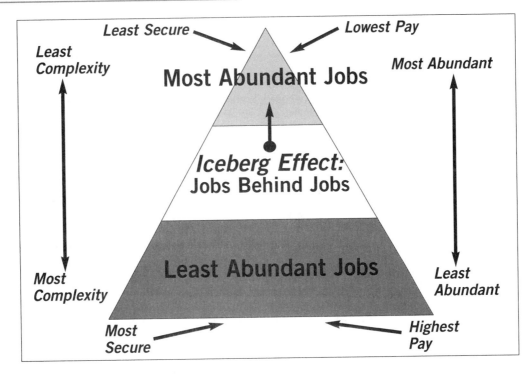

**Figure 4.2.**  The Iceberg Effect.

ter lasting employment. An employment specialist assigned to a dozen people has fewer than 3.5 hours a week to create good jobs for each. Caseloads of three to five individuals actually speed up placements over time, increase funding because of higher quality service delivery, and result in improved agency income from increased referrals and hourly rates. Well-trained staff are more successful, resulting in lowered turnover and improved morale. Happy staff serve their customers better, networks grow through customer referrals, and the circle is complete (Brooks-Lane, Hutcheson, & Revell, 2005; Catlette & Hadden, 2001; Griffin, 1999; Henton, Melville, & Walesh, 1997; Kohn, 1993).

Investing in staff development that teaches job developers what to say in any sales situation is an important organizational investment as well. Concise, honest language, free of human services jargon, should be used when assisting a job seeker. Clarity of purpose is critical to natural supports development as well, and using terms such as *your new employee* when describing the hiring of an individual makes the subtle point that the employment specialist's role is to support both the employer and new hire in worksite assimilation. It should be pointed out that the employment specialist's role is to support the natural training and supervision process by providing additional and more powerful teaching strategies as needed, but not to replace or radically modify typical processes (Callahan & Garner, 1997). Having the technical skills to provide assistance to both employer and employee is critical to sales success and customer service; without these tools, good jobs for people with complex lives are difficult to design and support (Griffin et al., 2006).

## Features and Benefits Table

One handy tool for developing a casual script when job prospecting is creating a features and benefits table (see Table 4.2). Completing this table as an employment specialist team activity brings consistency to the message that everyone representing the

**Table 4.2**　Features and benefits table

| Feature | Benefit |
|---|---|
| Job match | Only qualified job seekers are presented for employment. |
| Job analysis | We analyze your processes in order to offer efficient training and supervision assistance. |
| Job coaching | We assist you and your new employee with training and adaptations as needed. |
| Ongoing support | We stand ready to assist in the future as job duties are expanded. |
| High quality | Local employers we work with include Nebraska Light and Power, Bellview Ford, Pier Two, Cattleman's Pub, Magic City Welding, Independent Grocer, Lighthouse Computers, Douglas County Library, and so forth. |

agency will spread. Still, it is vitally important that this message not overshadow the individual; this is a customer service dialogue aid and not a sales tool for the CE program. Employers do not hire programs, they hire individuals, and the emphasis should always be placed on one distinct individual, matched to one distinct employer.

Completing the features and benefits table is easy. Simply list the features of the CE service in one column and determine at least one benefit to the employer of that feature. Completion of the table provides each employment specialist with a script explaining his or her role in the process.

Now, when the employment specialist is explaining his job at a civic club meeting, or in a face-to-face meeting with an employer, the rehearsed, but casual, conversation can flow naturally. For example, a job developer may tell a new acquaintance—upon being asked the ubiquitous, "What do you do for a living?"—that he is a "career counselor for OmahaWorks. We match job seekers to appropriate employers and use a systematic support strategy in assisting employers as they orient and train their new employees. What do you do?"

## Leave-Behind Materials

Sales calls generally require a leave-behind, such as business cards; a brochure or fact sheet; and, for specific job development, a professional looking résumé or a visual portfolio highlighting the contribution potential and the experience of the job seeker. All language used in such tools should be person-first and respectful, and be devoid of program language and jargon. Using the services of a qualified marketing firm or graphic artist may be too expensive for some programs, but quality and eye appeal does matter in promotional materials. Networking may reveal such services for free or at a significant discount, so using the relationship charting process may reveal talent within reach of the agency.

A review of job development brochures collected throughout the country over the years revealed some terrific, straightforward messages that emphasize job match, assistance with training, follow-up, and attention to customer care. A couple in the authors' collections revealed common mistakes that could perhaps send damaging messages. One read, "We address your entry-level employment needs." This sends the message that people with disabilities can only work in starter or low-skill jobs and hints that people with disabilities do not possess the capacity to grow and learn. Another brochure read, "We know you are not hiring now, but when you do, consider us." The message is clear: "Sorry to bother you; we are not worthy; if you have any leftover jobs, maybe you could call us."

### Brochures

Brochures, while sometimes a good idea, raise many issues. Good ones are expensive and time consuming to produce. They generally require several layers of approval and may be outdated before they reach the streets. Agencies have to live with mistakes until the next budget allows for updating and reprinting. Also, the brochure may overemphasize the organization or service and overshadow the job seeker. Fact sheets are an efficacious compromise for employment specialists who desire this sort of leave-behind.

## Fact Sheet

A fact sheet augments job development efforts while freeing up limited capital. A fact sheet is prepared with word processing software, using large, eye-catching type, and printed on one side using a laser printer or professional print shop. Good quality, light-colored stationery is recommended. Print only as many as are needed for the next few sales calls. Without a great deal in inventory, changing the fact sheet in response to consumer demand is practically painless. Keeping the fact sheet neat, easy to read, and professional looking increases the possibility that it will be read following your departure from a sales call.

The fact sheet should contain a few brief statements regarding your service and approach to satisfying employer needs. It makes sense to produce fact sheets for specific industries (e.g., electronics assembly, agriculture, gasoline stations) if, and only if, consumer interest aligns with these vocational areas. The low cost of producing a fact sheet makes updates and target marketing possible.

The next section should list local businesses with which the agency works. Be certain to have permission before adding their names. When targeting a particular industry, list related businesses here. The narrower the focus, the more relevance an employer will see to his or her operation. For instance, if the agency has successfully supported individuals in a number of grocery stores, a fact sheet with a section listing half a dozen of those stores will impress a potential employer in the grocery business. Furthermore, the fact sheet can be more direct and personally focused by listing a specific job seeker's talents and experience. A personalized fact sheet is a perfect accompaniment to a graphic résumé or portfolio that uses pictures to represent a job seeker's experience and talents.

A few employer testimonials in the next section of the fact sheet will help sell the service. Sales research indicates that employers want to hear what others think of a product or service (Cathcart, 1990; Underhill, 1999). Their endorsement gives you credibility in the marketplace, and provides prospective employers comfort in knowing that their competitors trust your service and practice hiring people with disabilities.

Finally, list the name of a contact person on the fact sheet, preferably the same person making the job development call. The addition of a home phone number signals your commitment to working with the employer and may be just the reassurance a business owner needs when weighing hiring options.

Do not take up space with incidental information regarding an explanation of service delivery. Employers do not generally understand the variety of employment strategies utilized today, and no employer hires a program, they hire individuals. Employers probably do not care that you have a supported employment program. Giving such information only serves to muddy the waters. And, while utilizing tax credits and other incentives may be helpful, no mention of them here is warranted. These incentives might sweeten the deal later, but bringing them up in the initial stages of job development devalues individuals with disabilities by suggesting to employers that rebates are provided upon hiring.

## Personal Portfolio

Another successful marketing tool is the personal portfolio. As noted in Chapter 2, discovery and the job exploration process create a résumé of job interests and experiences that can be captured in a portfolio typically displayed through a PowerPoint presentation. The portfolio is especially effective because it makes the job seeker the focus of the process and not the employment specialist or the community rehabilitation program. Portfolios are also designed with and for the consumer, highlighting the match to a particular field of interest or to a specific employee. They are easily modified through the software, and can be narrated for playback if the job seeker so desires due to the anticipation of nervousness or because of a paucity of verbal language (Callahan & Garner, 1997; Koch & Rumrill, 1999).

Picture books are a forerunner of the computerized portfolio. These can be hardcopy, set up on a laptop computer, or copied onto a CD for employer viewing. Making a picture book is straightforward. Usually, job seekers have some work history, or have work experiences, or in the case of transition-age youth, have had in-school or afterschool jobs. A picture book is made up of a series of pictures of the individual at work. The pictures show the individual interacting with co-workers, running equipment or using tools, and otherwise looking as competent as anyone else. Sometimes pictures of the prospective employee using a job modification or assistive device are a good way of answering the employer's unspoken questions about how a worker with significant disabilities might need to be accommodated.

The job seeker should review the photos, and all confidentiality issues should be discussed and documented prior to public disclosure. The picture book becomes a visual résumé that highlights the individual's strengths. Pictures help employers visualize supervising and training an individual with disabilities and provide concrete evidence of productivity and competence.

If the job seeker has had only one or two jobs or work experiences, use five or six pictures from each location. Each photo should be specific, clear, and shot with the purpose of helping anyone viewing the book identify the basic task or situation pictured. The action or competence of the employee should be obvious. For instance, if the job seeker ran a band saw, then a picture of the individual running this equipment should be featured, instead of a picture of the individual standing next to a band saw. Showcasing action and skill mastery is extremely important.

Also included on the back of each series of photos should be a letter from the employer or work experience site manager. The letter should be on original letterhead (do not use copies for marketing materials). Job developers might offer assistance to the employer in writing the letter. Inadvertently, employers sometimes make wellintentioned statements that reinforce stereotypes about disability. For instance, a letter that states, "John is always on time for work, always happy, and a joy to be around," is less impressive than the statement, "John worked hard, learned new tasks, and contributed to our bottom line." The second statement is more believable than the first. After all, few of us are always happy, on time, or a joy to be around.

The prospective employee with a rich job history may want to showcase a few of their best experiences, or the ones that best fit with their current career goals. In this case, two or three representative pictures from a few settings, also accompanied by employer letters of recommendation, make a nice visual résumé. If no pictures exist from previous jobs, stage some shots, but make certain to point out during the job development call that these are recreated. Further, make certain the recreated photos reinforce the content of the employer's accompanying letter.

The pictures in the book should be of high quality. Someone with photographic talent can develop high contrast black and white shots that are visually impressive, but generally good color shots are fine. Put the photos in a high quality portfolio, along with contact information and a nicely designed résumé.

Although digital photos can be displayed on a laptop computer and make résumé revisions easy, hard copy photo albums do have advantages. For one, the book is a high touch item. The employer can see and touch this marketing tool; it is real and hard to argue with. A properly designed picture book anticipates employer fears and questions; it silently answers those unspoken questions about safety, communication, and supervision that too often go unaddressed and result in employer ambivalence and job seeker rejection. The picture book can also be left behind. When the employer then peruses it at her leisure, the selling continues even in the absence of the job developer and job seeker. This tangible book allows an employer who is new to disability time to grow comfortable with hiring. And, of course, the employment specialist or the job seeker needs to return to get the book. So, a second job development call is almost ensured.

Finally, one nice feature of the picture book is that the job seeker can use it to personally guide the employer through the résumé. This creates a unique circumstance that is impressive in content and circumstance, and it allows the individual to detail and exhibit their competence. If the job seeker needs support, the job developer might be along to assist. Regardless, the picture book is a low-tech, low-cost, unique, person-centered, and high-touch tool for job seekers and job developers alike.

## HANDLING OBJECTIONS

Perhaps the most difficult aspect of any employment specialist's life is the rejection that occurs on a regular basis. The high unemployment rate for people with disabilities is certainly influenced by the fragile systems of supports the rehabilitation industry provides and the images it uses to raise funds and promote services. Employers are the mirror held up to our faces, reflecting the sometimes patronizing stereotypes emanating from our profession. For employers, hiring someone with a significant disability represents a risk, and risks often result in lost profits, and lost profits mean their children may not be able to afford college. All job developers need to understand that hiring anyone is a tough decision, and that hiring a person with a disability demands circumspection by employers.

Wisely, many employment specialists do not interpret objections or hesitations of employers as disregard for people with disabilities. In fact, the vast majority of businesses donate to charities and community projects for those considered disadvantaged. Instead, competent job developers understand that objections are actually a symptom of the need for more clarity and information.

There are many tactics for handling objections (Cathcart, 1990), but two in particular help prepare the employment specialist and anticipate the most common concerns. The first strategy is called a Left Hand/Right Hand Analysis (see Figure 4.3) and was developed by Harvard Business School professor Chris Argyris (Argyris, 2004). The tool is simple, concise, and very effective; it can be used alone, or used to frame a role play with the job seeker or other members of the employment team. Using the Left Hand/Right Hand Analysis simply involves dividing a piece of paper, or a computer screen, into two columns. In the left column the key phrases of the upcoming job development discussion are listed, and for each point, the employment specialist writes out in the right-hand column the possible objections a specific employer may have. This process makes the job developer think about the future, anticipate objections, and even construct a causal script that anticipates concerns before they have had time to solidify in the employer's mind. Preparation in sales is critical, and this process instrument provides an eloquent framework for forecasting issues and rehearsing effective responses.

Another tactic for handling objections from employers is known as Feel, Felt, Found. The power of Feel, Felt, Found is that it acknowledges the employer's viewpoint, and calmly, carefully provides a sound response. For instance, suppose an employer complains that worker's compensation or liability insurance will increase if an employee with a disability is hired. One response might be:

> I understand how you *feel*. No one would want harm to come to anyone, and we would not recommend Beth for the job if we *felt* there were major safety concerns. Still, when I started working with companies, helping solve their recruitment and training problems, I *felt* these concerns needed investigation and serious

| | | | |
|---|---|---|---|
| 1. | What did you think of the job carving proposal for Samantha? | 1. | I liked it. I think she'd be good at it. I am concerned that the regional manager will not accept another modification to a job description. |
| 2. | Perhaps I could provide you with some samples of other job carves we've done in other companies to show your boss? I would also be happy to sketch out a new job description using your format. | 2. | That would be great! Another issue though is with the work table. We can't modify it; it's secured to the wall, and other people need to use it as well. We're a small operation and I really can't justify a new adjustable work table for a part-time employee. |
| 3. | I understand your concern about the table. We have possible funding through the state, and I checked into a hydraulic table that Samantha can adjust depending on the particular tasks she's performing. It will be good to have as you add other duties to her job, such as the wrapping of processed fruits and nuts, as we discussed. | 3. | Sounds good. I'll get with the regional manager and iron this out. |
| 4. | How about we shoot for a start date of Monday, the 5th? | 4. | If the regional manager approves. |
| 5. | I'll call you Thursday and see how your meeting went, and if you'd like me to be here, I'll be happy to attend. | 5. | Sounds good. |

**Figure 4.3.**    Left Hand/Right Hand Analysis. *Source:* Argyris (2004).

consideration. What I and our many customers *found* is that worker's comp rates and liability insurance premiums do not increase. In fact, safety records for people with disabilities, according to several studies conducted by companies such as the DuPont Corporation, are actually as good as or better than those for people without disabilities.

Consider another all-too-typical job development scenario. The employer raises a concern during the interview that their entire operation will now have to be made wheelchair accessible or that outrageous expense will be incurred due to accommodations. The response might unfold in a conversational tone that iterates the following:

> I understand how you *feel* about the potential costs of accessibility. In fact, some smaller companies, and those not open to the buying public are not actually required to be fully accessible. Many retailers I have worked with, for instance, *felt* that with the passage of the Americans with Disabilities Act, their profits would suffer. But, what they have *found* is that with minor expense, some of which can be offset with tax credits that I can help you with, revenues increased. This is because of the number of new customers now able to access their stores. Let's face it, most of us are going to live long enough to require a walker or a wheelchair, and that means that millions of other folks, potential customers or star employees, are waiting to benefit from your business. And, actually, the cost of most accessibility measures or job accommodations is relatively small compared to the benefits. Why don't we investigate what it would take to make these changes possible?

Certainly, no approach fits all circumstances. But, having a few rational negotiation devices ready helps the job developer organize her thoughts, remain calm, and present a cogent and logical counter to common objections. Job development does not need to be a brutal series of rejections. Instead, finding the common interests of all parties and logically addressing concerns with honesty and the facts gets consistently good results.

## SALES SKILLS SUMMARY

Every circumstance is different; therefore, job development approaches must be customized to complement the development of the relationship between employer and/employee. CE is focused on creating relationships, and some general guidelines for sales conduct are important.

1. Preparation is crucial. Anyone developing jobs must know the job seeker's personal characteristics and be able to synchronize these with the employment marketplace.

2. Selling is personal. Customers want to know you care. This is not about intimacy but rather about listening before helping the customer solve a problem.

3. Listening is more important than talking. If the employment specialist is not hearing what the customers need, the wrong placement scenario is liable to be offered, thereby injuring the opportunity for a lasting relationship.

4. Prospecting is an ongoing process. Building a network of friends, suppliers, and business associates is crucial to finding new employers.

5. Initial contacts can make or break a customer relationship. Job developers should be aware of interfering. Cold calls or job development calls made without prior contact are seldom appreciated. Instead, a warm call approach is generally greeted more favorably. A call is warmed up by sending out a letter of introduction or meeting a prospect at a professional or social gathering and then following up with a phone call.

6. Use leave-behinds. Each individual served should have representative materials such as portfolios or résumés, and each job developer should use business cards or other items that illustrate credibility.

7. Be prepared to handle objections. Employers new to hiring people with disabilities may doubt the viability of such an effort. Listen respectfully, but anticipate concerns and respond professionally.

8. Allow the employer to say no. Sometimes a business just does not need or want a new employee. Be respectful and polite. By walking away promising to be in touch later, the customer is relieved from making a decision they wish to avoid, and they may remember the job developer's graciousness later.

9. Stay in touch. Job development and even hiring is never final. Show customers, employers, and job seekers alike that their satisfaction is important.

10. Follow up. If an employer or job seeker asks questions the job developer does not know the answers to, getting back in touch with that customer with the answers will maintain the relationship.

11. Be a gracious guest. Job development calls are typically on someone else's turf. Act like a good guest. Arrive promptly. Be sociable but professional.

12. Be concise. Friendly talk is important to loosen up the situation. Comment on a picture in the office or ask about the employer's family, but keep it short and sweet. People are busy, and employment specialists should respect that.

13. Be aware of personal behavior. Employment specialists dress respectfully and appropriately. When developing a job at a bank, dress as the bankers do; when developing employment in the auto parts trade, dress like those behind the counter or a little better, but not in a three-piece suit. Be neat and clean; do not smoke, drink alcohol, or tell dirty jokes; do not overstay the set meeting time unless the employer makes it clear they want to hear more; do not talk politics or religion.

14. Ask for a referral. Whether an employment situation is secured or not, ask the employer for the name of someone else in a similar business or someone they believe might be interested in knowing about the individual job seeker.

15. Be kind. Do not attempt to develop employment by complaining about, slandering, or attacking another competing service agency or employer. Resorting to

attacks in an effort to secure a particular employer offends and frightens. Focus on the qualities of the individual seeking employment and the match to this specific business.

16.  Pay attention to time management. Keep appointments, write up job analyses immediately, manage time, and do not miss deadlines.

17.  Think in terms of high-quality customer service. See that promises are kept, appointments are honored, training occurs as negotiated, and support is conveniently accessed by employer and job seeker alike. Make sure that people answering the phones at agency headquarters are informed and courteous; make certain that promises are honored with a minimum of customer frustration. Do not promise what the agency cannot deliver.

18.  Get busy. Job prospecting is hard and demanding work. Design an individualized job development plan with each consumer, outline the employers to be contacted, target broadening personal networks to expand employment possibilities, document the efforts, and work with a team to provide support and advice (Bivins, 1994; Griffin & Hammis, 2003; Griffin et al., 2001; Underhill, 1999; Zyman, 1999).

## DISCLOSURE

The very presence of a job developer signals to the employer the existence of a disability or some other uniqueness about the employment candidate. In the case of both obvious significant disability and hidden disability, confidentiality is critical, with the consumer having the ultimate say in how much information is provided. In CE, the job search process is consumer directed, and employment support is provided at the pleasure of the job seeker.

When job developers are prospecting and meeting new people through networking efforts, referring to oneself as a *career counselor* is a proven approach, vague enough to invite additional conversation. The subject of disability, though, should not be equivocal. Being upfront and honest is a key to building a solid reputation. When in conversation, the professional approach is to speak respectfully about disability, focus on skills and talents, and respect specific individuals by guarding their identities. Speak instead of successes, and perhaps some of the businesses successfully employing people with disabilities.

Because CE is a consumer-directed process, job development involves having the job seeker along when meeting prospects. This eliminates surprises later on in the process, and it affords the consumer an opportunity to survey a workplace for its feel and fit. In designing and detailing résumés, portfolios, and other personal job search materials, the consumer is again in charge, and chooses then, with the informed advice of the employment specialist, how much and what should be revealed.

Disclosure and presentation guidelines are recommended for both the job developer and seeker.

•  Describe skills, talents, potential contribution, and qualifications.

•  Emphasize work experiences and any solid references.

•  Do not volunteer more information than necessary, and rehearse for a professional presentation.

•  Use visuals including portfolios and picture books to focus the employer on positive images.

•  Avoid using medical or programmatic terms; instead, when disability is discussed put the symptoms or effects in conversational terms (e.g., *sadness* versus *depression*).

- Emphasize interest in this particular line of work and discuss present capabilities, adaptations, and successes (i.e., do not dwell on past issues) (Hoff et al., 2000).

Following the suggestions presented throughout this chapter, there should be only rare times when a formal interview is the first occasion that the job seeker and the employer meet. Because CE does not react to or chase job openings, the competitive scene of 50 applicants awaiting their turn to present résumés is eliminated. Still, confidentiality and disclosure are essential topics for discussion before the job search begins.

## CONCLUSION

One study of employment specialists revealed that only 4%–8% of an employment specialist's time was spent on job development tasks (Gold, Van Gelder, & Schalock, 1999). CE redirects the professional's role away from the emphasis on jobsite training to focus on accurate job matching, thereby producing the best ecological fit between worker and environment. The result of this shift away from long-term rehabilitation staff presence on the job is a less invasive and more consultative role aimed at augmenting the natural trainers and supervisors found in businesses everywhere. In this circumstance, job development and job matching become far more critical than in past practice, as the need for long-term job coaching is reduced and job seekers are effectively matched with work and business cultures that enhance their contribution and personal genius.

## REFERENCES

Argyris, C. (2004). *Reasons and rationalizations: The limits to organization knowledge.* New York: Oxford University Press.

Bissonnette, D. (1994). *Beyond traditional job development.* Chatsworth, CA: Milt Wright & Associates.

Bivins, B. (1994). *Operating a really small business: An owner's guide.* Menlo Park, CA: Crisp Publications.

Bolles, R. (2003). *What color is your parachute?* Berkeley, CA: Ten Speed Press.

Brooks-Lane, N., Hutcheson, S., & Revell, G. (2005). Supporting consumer directed employment outcomes. *Journal of Vocational Rehabilitation, 23*(2), 123–134.

Callahan, M., & Garner, B. (1997). *Keys to the workplace: Skills and supports for people with disabilities.* Baltimore: Paul H. Brookes Publishing Co.

Cathcart, J. (1990). *Relationship selling.* New York: Putnam.

Catlette, B., & Hadden, R. (2001). *Contented cows give better milk: The plain truth about employee relations and your bottom line.* Germantown, TN: Saltillo Press.

DiLeo, D., & Langton, D. (1993). *Get the marketing edge! A job developer's toolkit for people with disabilities.* St. Augustine, FL: TRN, Inc.

Fair Labor Standards Act of 1938, PL 75-718, 29 U.S.C. §§ 203 *et seq.*

Fesko, S., & Temelini, D. (1997). What consumers and staff tell us about effective job search strategies. In W. Kiernan & R. Schalock (Eds.), *Integrated employment* (pp. 67–81). Washington, DC: American Association on Mental Retardation.

Gladwell, M. (1999, January 11). Six degrees of Lois Weisberg. *The New Yorker,* 52–63.

Gold, M., Van Gelder, M., & Schalock, R. (1999). A behavioral approach to understanding and managing organizational change: Moving from workshops to community employment. *Journal of Rehabilitation Administration, 22*(3), 191–207.

Granovetter, M. (1974). *Getting a job.* Chicago: The University of Chicago Press.

Griffin, C.C. (1999). *Working better, working smarter: Building responsive rehabilitation programs.* St. Augustine, FL: TRN, Inc.

Griffin, C.C., Brooks-Lane, N., Hammis, D., & Crandell, D. (2006). Self-employment: Owning the American dream. In P. Wehman (Ed.), *Real work for real pay: Inclusive employment for people with disabilities.* Baltimore: Paul H. Brookes Publishing Co.

Griffin, C.C., Flaherty, M., Hammis, D., Katz, M., Maxson, N., & Shelley, R. (2001). *People who own themselves: Emerging trends in rural rehabilitation.* Missoula: The University of Montana, Rural Institute.

Griffin, C.C., & Hammis, D. (1998). *Streetwise career planning.* Denver, CO: CTAT.

Griffin, C.C., & Hammis, D. (2001). What comes after what comes next: Self-employment as the logical descendant of supported employment. In P. Wehman (Ed.), *Supported employment in business.* St Augustine, FL: TRN, Inc.

Griffin, C.C., & Hammis, D. (2003). *Making self-employment work for people with disabilities.* Baltimore: Paul H. Brookes Publishing Co.

Griffin, C.C., & Sherron, P. (2001). Finding jobs for young people with disabilities. In P. Wehman (Ed.), *Life beyond the classroom.* (3rd ed.). Baltimore: Paul H. Brookes Publishing Co.

Griffin, C. C., & Sweeney, J. (1994). Approaching zero exclusion: The role of positive behavioral approaches in community employment. *American Rehabilitation, 20*(2), 32–37.

Hammis, D., & Griffin, C.C. (1998). Employment for anyone, anywhere, anytime: Creating new employment options through supported employment and supported self-employment. *The Advance, 9,* 2.

Hammis, D., & Griffin, C.C. (2002). *Social security considerations for entrepreneurs with significant disabilities.* Florence, MT: Griffin-Hammis Associates, LLC.

Henton, D., Melville, J., & Walesh, K. (1997). *Grassroots leaders for a new economy: How civic entrepreneurs are building prosperous communities.* San Francisco: Jossey-Bass Publishers.

Hoff, D., Gandolfo, C., Gold, M., & Jordan, M. (2000). *Demystifying job development: Field-based approaches to job development for people with disabilities.* St. Augustine, FL: TRN, Inc.

Koch, L., & Rumrill, P. (1999). The career portfolio as a job placement and retention tool for people with disabilities. *Journal of Vocational Rehabilitation, 13*(3), 141–142.

Kohn, A. (1993). *Punished by rewards.* New York: Houghton Mifflin Company.

Luecking, R., Fabian, E., & Tilson, G. (2004). *Working relationships: Creating career opportunities for job seekers with disabilities through employer partnerships.* Baltimore: Paul H. Brookes Publishing Co.

Luecking, R., Martin-Luecking, D., & Steckel, A. (2004). Effective employer relations. In P. Wehman, V. Brooke, & H. Green (Eds.), *Public/private partnerships: A model for success.* Richmond: Virginia Commonwealth University Research & Training Center.

Mank, D. (1996). Evolving roles for employers and support personnel in the employment of people with disabilities. *Journal of Vocational Rehabilitation, 6,* 83–88.

Mount, B. (1987). *Personal futures planning: Finding directions for change.* Unpublished doctoral dissertation, University of Georgia, Athens.

Noble, J., Honberg, R., Hall, L., & Flynn, L.M. (1997). *A legacy of failure: The inability of the federal-state vocational rehabilitation system to serve people with severe mental illness.* Arlington, VA: National Alliance for the Mentally Ill.

Underhill, P. (1999). *Why we buy: The science of shopping.* New York: Simon and Schuster.

Zyman, S. (1999). *The end of marketing as we know it.* New York: Harpers Books.

# 5

# Active Employer Councils

## Leveraging the Networking Power of the Community

*Cary Griffin, David Hammis, and Tammara Geary*

Enlisting employers in the identification of work opportunities is essential to the success of any customized employment (CE) venture. A variety of employer advisory groups have been implemented over the years to bridge the gap between the nonprofit and the for-profit worlds, to find a link within human resources networks, to get up-to-date information on employment trends, and to get leads on new businesses coming to a community. The most common employer assemblages are Business Advisory Councils (BACs) and Business Leadership Networks (BLNs).

The U.S. Department of Education's Rehabilitation Services Administration (RSA) institutionalized the BAC by requiring that one be established by every recipient of a Projects With Industry (PWI) grant. PWIs are federally funded job placement programs initiated in 1968 (U.S. Department of Education, 2006). Overall, the success of the BAC has been checkered. In some urban areas, they have become a masterful mix of local movers and shakers who offer their advice on employment approaches and programs and lend credibility to program legitimacy, and sometimes, fund-raising efforts. In many rural communities, they offer the business community a glimpse into the challenges of job development and career exploration for neighbors with disabilities. In far too many cases, however, BACs become monthly social gatherings that are long on agendas of despair over the state of hiring, that are maintained solely to meet an accreditation standard, and whose members shy away from challenging expectations. While some BACs generate solid employment leads for the projects, others languish (Griffin, 1999; Griffin & Hammis, 2002; Housman, 1992).

The BLN movement has spawned over 43 chapters in 32 states in the last decade. A BLN typically operates statewide, is managed by a human services agency representative or team, and recruits its board members from both small and large employers. The national BLN (USBLN) is tied closely to numerous large corporations and, according to its web site (http://www.usbln.com), enjoys the support and endorsement of the U.S. Chamber of Commerce and the U.S. Department of Labor. The mission of the USBLN and its many chapters is educating employers about hiring people with disabilities. At present, the USBLN does not set employment goals but believes that by delivering critical information on disability awareness, the Americans with Disabilities Act (ADA; 1990), and various hiring approaches, the marketplace will respond through hiring.

## ACTIVE EMPLOYER COUNCILS

The BLN movement can be traced to its 1994 prototype, the Active Employer Council (AEC). The AEC was designed to combat the passive nature of the ubiquitous employment boards. The model detailed herein is based on a pilot project developed in Colorado by authors Cary Griffin and David Hammis while working for the Center for Technical Assistance and Training (CTAT) at the University of Northern Colorado. The AEC was originally a partnership program funded through the Colorado Division of Vocational Rehabilitation (VR) Expansion and Innovation funds, and involved colocation of the AEC director and job developer, within the Greeley, Colorado, VR office. Working in daily collaboration with the individual VR counselors granted David Hammis, as a job developer, leverage in counselor funding decisions, and allowed for the development of strong professional relationships between the job developer and the counselors, fostered by proximity, a shared mission, and mutual success. Within a year of implementation, the project generated over 50 successful VR closures of individuals with significant disabilities into employment in this somewhat rural community of 50,000 people. This success was soon reinforced by federal funding replicating key components of the project in several communities in the region (Griffin & Hammis, 2002).

The AEC, as with the subsequent BLNs, sponsored a series of public programs on the then-newly legislated ADA. One nationally prominent speaker sponsored by the AEC was Rick Douglas, the director of the President's Committee on Employment of People with Disabilities. Rick Douglas was warmly received by the local employer community due to his eloquent and humorous speeches, his personal experience with disability, his leadership capabilities as the former VR director in Vermont, and his business experience as vice president of marketing for British Airways. Rick Douglas visited the Greeley community several times during the first year of the project and used the design to launch the BLN program sponsored by the U.S. Department of Labor. Over the years, however, largely due to his early death, the direct employment function of the AEC was lost, and the educational role took prominence as BLNs grew from this prototype.

The AEC model, discussed here, reestablishes the job development function, redirects efforts to single communities, and is best organized by a single rehabilitation agency. BLNs capitalize on the power of large rehabilitation networks and capture the attention of diverse employers regionally or statewide using the primary goal of disability awareness with a minimized emphasis on person-centered job development. AECs are best conceptualized as employment programs managed by a single community rehabilitation program (CRP) focused on customizing jobs, building the employer network within a town, and fostering careers for local individuals with significant disabilities.

## DESIGNING AN ACTIVE EMPLOYER COUNCIL

The key to establishing a successful AEC is staying focused on the most important outcome: employment. Most advisory boards fail because they have ill-defined missions, passive members, and little or no budget supporting the efforts. Operating an effective AEC entails committing organizational resources to the effort. An effective AEC board will

1. Focus attention on an exacting mission. A functional and inspiring mission must first be controlled, in large part, by those charged with accomplishing the mission.

Therefore, the member employers are selected based on their ability to leverage power and influence within the employer community.

2. Make the AEC accountable for measurable outcomes. AEC staff and board members are expected to measure their outcomes against the target(s) established by the mission. For instance, if an AEC decides it will contribute to the employment of 20 people in one year, monthly measures serve as points of correction and reinforcement as efforts occur. Changes in budgets, personnel, and tactics are adjusted based on accomplishments.

3. Build the status of member employers through public and private recognition.

Public relations and marketing are key elements of the AEC and are undertaken by the board, primarily. Members voluntarily promote the efforts of AEC and its accomplishments in their discussions at work, within their social networks, and through such formal channels as public speaking, press releases, and educational events enlisting potential employers and future board members (see Table 5.1). These activities are tied back to a management plan, driven by the strong mission statement.

The basic duties of the AEC include meeting one or two job seekers at the monthly board meeting; listening to and reviewing their career plans, portfolio, or résumé; and brainstorming employment recommendations. Generally the job seeker is prepped by the AEC staff and assisted in making the presentation.

Once possible scenarios for job exploration are briefly outlined, the board members with the best connections to the desired worksites are enlisted to introduce both the job seeker and the job developer or employment specialist, as needed, to the potential employer. The job developer schedules further meetings or informational sessions with the board member and the job seeker to refine the search and to design a step-by-step plan for networking.

As the professional networks of the job seekers, employment specialists, and board members expand, so do local career opportunities. The natural competition and camaraderie of the board is reinforced by monthly reviews of consumer success and members' efforts towards AEC goals, which open every meeting. Each AEC meeting highlights the past month's accomplishments and recognizes individuals and the group for its efforts.

Though AECs can be implemented in as many ways as there are communities they serve, employment specialists have found that there are eleven essential steps toward establishing functional AECs. Using these suggestions as a framework for accomplishment, an AEC can flourish and create its own unique flavor.

## 1. Assign a Budget and Lead Active Employer Council Manager

A successful AEC is not an add-on duty for the director of community employment services. It is a team effort benefiting every consumer and employment specialist in an agency. AECs work best when a manager, director, or coordinator is delegated responsibility and a major portion of salary is committed to the program. Undoubtedly, the languid outcomes of BACs can be in part ascribed to the passive nature of board management.

The AEC manager, on the other hand, has a singular focus: Make the AEC successful. Whereas goals are achieved through teamwork, the team must have oversight by the AEC manager, who is in charge and responsible for the outcomes. The manager's duties include

a. Recruitment and training of board members

b. Coordination and delivery of public educational and disability awareness events

c. Negotiation with VR, One-Stops, schools, and other partners and funding agencies

**Table 5.1.**    Year one Active Employer Council (AEC) marketing plan

| Date | Activity | Location | Persons responsible | Notes |
|---|---|---|---|---|
| 1/15 | Press release about AEC start-up | All local media; chamber newsletter | Manager; reviewed by board | Mention all employers represented; submit to business editor and reporters. This is NOT a human-interest story! |
| 2/12 | Press release about upcoming training on Americans with Disabilities Act (ADA) for small businesses | All local media; chamber newsletter; invitations at luncheon | Manager; each board member distributes 50 fliers within their networks | Drive-time radio interviews by manager and board member E. Tyson of HHS, Inc. |
| 3/15 | Press release about AEC mission and first job development successes. Relate story to national and local unemployment statistics | All local media; follow-up mailed release with phone calls to editors | Manager and assistant | Ask for a 10-second quote for local radio and TV news by AEC manager or AEC board chair |
| 4/8 | ADA seminar | PSC Auditorium | Manager and staff | Invite local reporters to cover event and provide them with fact sheet. Training packets include success profiles, mission, and goals of AEC, list of members, funder thank-yous, and contact information |
| 4/9 | ADA seminar follow-up | All local media | Manager and assistant | Contact each reporter attending and provide attendance data, anticipated impacts, importance of ADA to profitability, positive reaction of those attending, next event anticipated |
| 5/1 | Approach local National Public Radio (NPR) affiliate about interview on disability and employment | NPR station | Manager, Ken, board chair | Propose a story on the AEC and employment for NPR's local weekly 30-minute news feature |
| 6/6 | Tape local NPR news feature | NPR station | Manager, Ken, board chair | Rehearse main points prior to taping; maintain adherence to confidentiality rules |
| 8/15 | Develop 800-word article on school-to-work transition | All local media; City Council's Future Workforce Committee; school board | Manager and assistant | Follow-up call to editors and news directors to offer clarity and possible sound bites for evening news |
| 8/30 | Press release about upcoming training on job accommodations and effective job descriptions | All local media; chamber newsletter; invitations at luncheon | Manager; each board member distributes 50 fliers within their networks | Drive-time radio interviews by manager and board member J. Kelley, from Dyna Corp. |
| 10/5 | Job accommodation seminar | Dyna Corp. Auditorium | Manager and staff | Invite local reporters to cover event and provide them with fact sheet; training packets include success profiles, mission and goals of AEC, list of members, funder thank-yous, and contact information |
| 10/6 | ADA seminar follow-up | All local media | Manager and assistant | Contact each reporter attending and provide attendance data, anticipated impacts, importance of topic to profitability, positive reaction of those attending, next event anticipated |

| Date | Activity | Location | Persons responsible | Notes |
|------|----------|----------|---------------------|-------|
| 11/16 | Press release annual accomplishments | All local media | Manager and assistant | Follow-up call to editors and news directors to offer clarity and possible sound bites for evening news; board chair assists with calls and sound bites |
| 12/10 | Holiday greetings from the AEC display ad placed in local paper and newsletters | Morning Herald; chamber; Kiwanis; Rotary Club; Lions; newsletters | Manager | Ad features the names and companies of all board members, and the total jobs created by the AEC this year |
| 12/15 | Develop a graphic presentation featuring 10 success stories | Service clubs; chamber luncheons; annual CRP board meeting; family; self-advocacy meetings next year | Manager and AEC assistant | Get quotes from both employers and their new employees, from the board, families, and funders about the impact the AEC has had on the community and individual lives |

d.  Assignment of staff to carry out AEC functions related to employer development, job development tasks, and design for portfolios, picture books, and résumés

e.  Management of monthly board meetings

f.  Follow-through on board recommendations and networking efforts

g.  Developing formal monthly reports to the board and funders on outcomes, events, and issues pertinent to job development

h.  Public relations and marketing of the AEC, its members, and success stories to the local community and media

i.  Active networking within area service clubs and business groups

j.  Development and management of financial and personnel resources, ensuring the AEC of a lasting legacy

k.  Generating at least 50% of AEC manager's salary from a billable caseload, or other sources

An AEC can start slowly and generate interest and revenue progressively. However, an agency making the commitment to an AEC soon finds that it really is an all-or-nothing effort. Amalgamating funding from various sources is possible and includes an allotment from the CRP's general fund, a percentage of salaries drawn from fee-for-service job development and placement efforts, seat sales for employer training events, various grants from collaborating agencies such as the state VR office or workforce development agency; the state's Developmental Disability Council; the local city or county office managing the Community Development Block Grant (CDBG) program that supports local economic development activities; the state Department of Commerce, and others. Asking the board members for financial support from their companies is a proven strategy and has been used successfully by the BLN network nationwide. The AEC budget is no small item, but the potential in goodwill, networking, education, and job creation far outweighs the initial investment (Luecking, Fabian, & Tilson, 2004).

Budget development for the AEC includes allocations for

• Personnel (AEC manager, who also carries a caseload; clerical support; job developers or employment specialists)

• Board meetings (refreshments, clerical supplies, computer equipment, software)

- Printing and postage (publicizing employer education events, marketing materials, portfolios and résumés, business cards)

- Entertainment and networking (service club and community business group memberships, buying lunches for prospective employers)

- Travel (attending staff development trainings, bringing in speakers for employer events, mileage for home visits with consumers, networking and job development)

- Events, speakers and consultants (staff development, employer education events, awards ceremonies recognizing exemplary employers)

A sample budget during a start-up year might resemble Figure 5.1.

| Personnel | | |
|---|---|---|
| **Name** | **% of time on project** | **AEC salary from general fund** |
| Brian Keith, AEC Manager | 50% | $20,000 |
| Jane Brickett, Employment Specialist and AEC Assistant | 50% | $17,500 |
| **Total:** | | **$37,500** |

| Fringe benefits | | |
|---|---|---|
| **Name** | **Type of benefits** | **Amount** |
| Brian Keith | Vacation/FICA/Health/Life/401k | $8,000 |
| Jane Brickett | Vacation/FICA/Health/Life/401k | $7,000 |
| **Total:** | | **$15,000** |

| | |
|---|---|
| **Office supplies** (paper, software, etc.) | $500 |
| **Travel** (unreimbursed mileage for job development and related business, speaker's travel, etc.) | $2,000 |
| **Contracted services** (speaker's fees for employer education events) | $3,000 |
| **Instructional materials** (books, manuals, videos, etc.) | $500 |
| **Communications** (phone, Internet) | $500 |
| **Printing and copying** (portfolios, résumés, training handouts, etc.) | $1,000 |
| **Postage** | $300 |
| **Miscellaneous** (business lunches, service club dues, etc.) | $600 |
| **Total expense** | **$60,900** |
| **Income offsets:** | |
| Seat sales from two training events (100 seats @ $50) | $5,000 |
| CDBG funds | $15,000 |
| DD Council mini-grant | $5,000 |
| VR Innovation and Expansion Grant | $8,000 |
| Independent Grocers Community Foundation Grant | $5,000 |
| **Total income year one** | **$38,000** |
| **Net year one cost for AEC** | **$22,900** |

**Figure 5.1.** Year 1 Active Employer Council (AEC) budget.

## 2. Develop a Job Description for Active Employer Council Board Members

The recruitment efforts of the AEC manager are aided by a concrete job description that details the expectations for board members. AECs are generally managed by a strict meeting attendance policy and an exacting mission focused on employment outcomes, which reinforces the need for active members. Setting expectations right from the start of recruitment and keeping surprises such as fund-raising requirements to a minimum are key to establishing a high-performance team. Critical elements for the board member job description include

a. Attend 80% of all monthly meetings.

b. Assist (between meetings) with employer educational events.

c. Attend 80% of all educational events (generally 2 or 3 events annually.)

d. Meet job seekers at monthly board meetings and advocate for their employment using personal networking for at least four individuals annually.

e. Assist the AEC in recruiting other board members as needed.

f. Work to fulfill the mission of the AEC by mentoring job seekers, by publicly encouraging other employers to hire people with disabilities, and by advocating the hiring of people with disabilities within your organization.

## 3. Recruit a Solid Core of Local Business Leaders

AEC members should represent the wide spectrum of large and small businesses found in most communities and can range from insurance agents to car dealers, from corporate managers to local restaurateurs. Members bring both community connections and influence within their business networks. It is this influence that is used by the CRP to gain access to informational interviews, paid work experiences, and good jobs. Be careful to stay away from board sitters who are fulfilling their corporate duty but plan to do little work. By selecting a solid core of movers and shakers known for their business acumen, and having them identify additional members, this circumstance is minimized. AECs need working members, not résumé builders. An AEC should be composed of members who make hiring decisions where they work, because members are expected to lead by example by hiring people with disabilities and by speaking from experience to other potential employers.

Recruitment of AEC members is a surgical undertaking. Many nonprofit organizations recruit board members as if serving is a punishment. The AEC should make membership on the board difficult to attain. The traditional model of board member identification highlights the movers and shakers in a community, but settles for less in many instances. The AEC board meets job seekers monthly and advocates for employment; therefore, the function is not the traditional procedural paradigm of the nonprofit establishment. By crafting a meaningful and challenging mission, by precisely measuring job development outcomes, and by making membership difficult to attain on this 10–12 person board, the AEC creates energy and high status for its membership. The best run boards pull great potential members in, while typical boards push the community for members.

Membership should include a representative range of employer types, including government and nonprofit, but be dominated by the private sector. Small, locally owned enterprises should be represented by their owners or top-level managers. Regional vice presidents, operations managers, and various critical decision makers of local corporate operations should be recruited too. Traditionally, human resources staff predominate on employment advisory boards, but individuals closer to production management and customer service are preferred for their understanding of the technical operations of the businesses. Human resources can be a largely symbolic and bureaucratic function, which is not always tied closely to the hiring decision maker.

In replication of the AEC model, the authors have found that identifying two or three board pillars is a good way of starting recruitment. For instance, visiting the local chamber of commerce or small business development center (SBDC) may be the first step in organizing the AEC board. Ask the directors of these agencies who they consider to be the best and brightest business people in the community and have them help set up a quick meeting with each of two or three of these leaders. These will be busy people, but busy people get things done and fit the preferred profile of board membership exactly. At these meetings, explain the AEC concept and ask for their support, such as use of their company's name as an early adopter, and ask if they or another person with hiring authority and organizational status will serve on the board. Once a core group of two or three board members is assembled, have them design a personal recruitment campaign to get other movers and shakers on the board. Set a reasonable time limit for full board assembly (perhaps 4 weeks), make membership by invitation only, and seek diversity of industry type and size. Recruitment efforts should also include the identification of business people with disabilities, or with immediate family with disabilities. Seek ethnic and gender diversity as well.

If a member of the sponsoring CRP board of directors with strong business ties to the local economy will take the lead by joining the AEC board, he or she can become the first AEC chairperson and use his or her personal network to initiate member recruitment. This individual provides a critical natural link to the CRP board and strengthens the understanding of, and governance commitment to, employment outcomes.

## 4.  Set Up an Exacting Mission or Purpose

Once the board is assembled, their first job as a team is to set a monthly meeting schedule and design a functional and stimulating mission. This mission is hopeful and challenging and is established after a preliminary meeting where a general orientation of members to community employment and the various issues of rehabilitation are presented. One example of a successful AEC mission is: Equalize the employment rates of people with disabilities and people without disabilities in the community. This represents a solid, driving target. Another less lofty but precisely drawn guidepost is to create no fewer than 30 jobs this year through the efforts of the AEC.

While mission statements have become clichéd over the past decade, the development of this guiding vision is critical to energize the AEC and its home community, to focus energies on employment outcomes, and to provide a directional beacon when the work gets hard and yielding to simpler tasks tempts the group. All mission statements should follow these basic rules.

a.  The mission is accomplishment driven. That is, there are stated outcomes that result from the board's efforts.

b.  The mission is controlled by those who do the work. Board members, staff, and consumers perform the difficult tasks and take many risks; therefore, they are active participants in designing and performing the work.

c.  The mission guides goals and objectives that are compatible and consistent with the organization's values. A values statement typically accompanies a mission and outlines acceptable practices and beliefs. In CE, for instance, emphasis is on each unique individual job seeker's profile, on commensurate wages, and on job creation. Therefore, an AEC would not seek to develop an employment program placing multiple people into an industry simply because there were jobs available.

d.  Mission accomplishments can be measured through one or more means. Measurable success includes outcomes such as: more individuals working in jobs of their choosing; more job creation examples; more local businesses making their facilities accessible; more people elevated above poverty; increased use of Social Security work incentives; higher customer satisfaction (e.g., job seekers, funders such as VR); increased employer requests for information and applicants; and increased participation by business in promoting education, such as disability awareness events (Griffin, 1999).

Accomplishments and milestones should be briefly reviewed at each meeting and compared to the direction established by the mission statement. Numeric targets can be set either in the mission itself or in the management plan of the AEC. If the mission adopted, for example, calls for 20 jobs, then a quick measure would be 2.5 jobs secured monthly. Actions directly accountable for producing results can be stepped up if the goals lag, and early successes can be leveraged for public relations and as proof of highly qualified board and staff members.

## 5.  Significantly Engage CRP Employment Staff with the Active Employer Council

While at first perhaps only a couple of employment staff members are assigned to the AEC part time, other staff should assist in its operation as a part of their overall jobs. Generally it is assumed that all employment staff will make referrals to the AEC, either to showcase a job seeker during the monthly meetings, or to introduce him or her to individual board members between meetings to enlist support in career exploration. The CRP employment staff support the AEC and make certain that actions such as suggestions and referrals prescribed at meetings are followed up immediately. Not all staff, but a representative sample of staff and referral agents (e.g., VR counselor, Workforce Disability Navigator), should attend AEC meetings to ensure that job seekers and employers remain the focus of activity.

## 6.  Set a Standard Meeting Time in a Community Setting

Employment is a community issue and not simply a rehabilitation issue. The symbolism of having a public meeting with a prominent AEC membership is important. Approach the CRP's bank, for instance, and reserve its conference room. Perhaps ask them to sponsor refreshments for each meeting. City hall and county government buildings, One-Stops, and other public facilities are also good choices. Limit most meetings to less than 1.5 hours using a highly structured meeting agenda. Make certain the board chairperson is skilled at moving the meeting forward. Busy people do not want their time wasted. Be the model of efficiency.

## 7.  Develop the Meeting Agenda for the Next Meeting Before Leaving the Current Meeting

The meeting flow should follow a format that allows a few minutes for introductions; a report back on achievements since the last meeting; new jobs created; new leads being explored; new business; and adjournment. A sample monthly agenda (see Figure 5.2) reveals the business-like approach so important to staying on task.

## 8.  Get Referrals

At the beginning of each meeting, AEC board members bring names and phone numbers of potential employers to the CRP staff. These referrals are used to explore possi-

| 7:30 A.M. | Call to order by board chair |
| | Review of last month's minutes |
| 7:35 A.M. | Report on job development activities, AEC manager |
| | 1. R. Perl has two paid work experiences scheduled (referred by AEC board member J. Kelley) |
| | 2. A. Augustine has an informational interview scheduled (referred by AEC board member G. Rutgers) |
| | 3. S. Iverson started work at BNI (referred by AEC board member N. Gracie) |
| | 4. L. Newman starts work at Molly's Flowers this Thursday (referred by AEC board member C. Barkley) |
| | 5. Assisted J. Smith and K. Crofts with portfolio development (AEC manager and AEC board member D. Johnston) |
| | 6. Board member distribution of monthly referrals and networking opportunities to job development staff |
| 8:00 A.M. | Review of assignments from last month and results, AEC manager and individual members |
| | 1. Secured speaker for April Americans with Disabilities ACT Seminar (AEC Manager) |
| | 2. Secured space for event at Montana Electric Cooperative auditorium (board member S. Childress) |
| | 3. New board member nominations/recruitment (board members N. Gracie and E. Tyson) |
| 8:15 A.M. | Meet job seeker C. Hobbs |
| | Meet job seeker K. Alverez |
| | Review résumés and portfolios; assign mentors from AEC board; make networking assignments and leads |
| 8:45 A.M. | Develop next month's agenda (February 15; National Bank board room) |
| | Review assignments |
| 8:50 A.M. | Adjourn |

**Figure 5.2.**    Monthly Active Employer Council (AEC) meeting agenda.

ble leads and to expand the relationship network. Each member is required to bring at least one referral monthly, preferably related to a job seeker presentation or for use as a possible informational interview source. If possible or necessary, the AEC board member should arrange a face-to-face meeting or lunch between the AEC manager, or an employment specialist, and the prospective employer.

## 9.  Get to Know the Job Seekers

Perhaps the most important function of the AEC is putting job seekers in front of the board and enlisting its help in the job development process. At each meeting, one or two individuals seeking employment are introduced to the council. (These people are not the only people seeking employment, but the AEC will be overwhelmed if 10 people present their résumés every month.) Staff prepare job seekers for a short 5- to 15-minute presentation on their work of choice and distribute a nicely prepared résumé or show the portfolio. Discussion of possible approaches and potential employers follows and an AEC board member agrees to work with the CRP staff and the job seeker in developing employment. The details are worked out later during a short follow-up meeting in order to comply with the agenda and to keep the rest of the AEC engaged. Because the AEC board member is likely quite busy, CRP staff should be prepared to follow up on referrals and suggestions quickly. AEC board members are expected to use their social and professional networks to find job opportunities, to get appointments with decision makers within their supply and customer chains, or to make a few contacts to open up work exploration avenues.

## 10. Receive Training in Best Practices in Community Employment

Training is necessary to fulfill the mission of the AEC, and in order for board members to speak truthfully and supportively of the CRP's capabilities. Training and ongoing technical assistance in employment is crucial and is often available free or at low cost through these and other sources: the regional Rehabilitation Continuing Education Programs (RCEPs) (http://www.rehabeducators.org) funded by the U.S. Department of Education; the Association for Persons in Supported Employment (APSE) (http://www.apse.org); the Disability and Business Technical Assistance Centers (DBTACs) (http://www.adata.org). Other sources include the University Centers for Excellence (UCEs) (http://www.aucd.org) funded by the U.S. Administration on Developmental Disabilities (http://www.acf.hhs.gov/programs/add/index.html) in all states; the National Collaboratives on Workforce and Disability (http://www.ncwd-youth.info and http://www.onestops.info); and the Training and Technical Assistance for Providers programs (http://www.t-tap.org) at the Institute for Community Inclusion and the Rehabilitation Research & Training Center on Job Supports and Workplace Retention at Virginia Commonwealth University funded by the U.S. Department of Labor (http://www.dol.gov).

Topics including job development, natural supports, systematic worksite instruction, the ADA, Social Security work incentives, resource ownership, small business ownership options, job analysis and job match, job carving and creation, sales and marketing, interest-based negotiation, positive behavioral supports, and assistive technology are just a few essential competency concerns. AEC members may be able to provide some of the training, especially related to sales, marketing, and small business options, and the donation of such services is essential to continued expansion of job development networks.

## 11. Make the Active Employer Council Visible

Marketing the AEC through the local chamber newsletter, by sponsoring and attending local events, by buying advertising or running public service announcements, and other means, keeps the AEC in the community's mind. Offer occasional press releases profiling the members and their companies to show how they work to change lives and promote local economic development by actively engaging people with disabilities in the workforce.

All AECs should develop a simple marketing schedule that systematically spreads the word about employment. Public relations activities should be synchronized with AEC activities and reinforce local media coverage of events. Such coordination of efforts will minimize distraction away from job one, which is employment development.

For instance, if the AEC sponsors two communitywide employer events annually, press releases pertaining to the events and display ads can be placed in local newspapers and highlighted on community calendars on radio and television. The AEC website should display an annual calendar of events as well. Radio and television talk shows featuring local interest stories should be scheduled for the AEC manager and various board members. Consumer and employer success stories should be submitted to the local chamber newsletter and to all local news outlets.

Creativity and an on-point message of employment guide this low-cost approach to community outreach and information dissemination. The AEC manager should develop a schedule of marketing activities and review progress at each board meeting, all the time enlisting the assistance of the best-suited board members and successful job seekers. A sample marketing plan reveals the many outlets found even in the smallest communities across the country.

## CONCLUSION

Facilitating an AEC is not an easy undertaking. The "eleven essentials" framework for accomplishment is merely the foundation. Building the capacity is a local effort that requires smart people, dedicated employers, a range of job seekers, willing funders, and community rehabilitation leadership that puts employment first in the mind of the community. Attempting to operate an AEC in the same manner as any ordinary advisory board will end disastrously. This is a high performance model that requires constant tune-ups, ample resources and creativity, and conspicuous talent for engaging local business leaders in the singular mission of creating economic opportunity in the form of good careers. AECs represent a long-term investment, not a short-term solution.

## REFERENCES

Americans with Disabilities Act of 1990, PL 101-336, 42 U.S.C. §§ 12101 *et seq.*

Griffin, C.C. (1999). *Working better, working smarter: Building responsive rehabilitation programs.* St. Augustine, FL: TRN Press.

Griffin, C.C., & Hammis, D. (2002). Revitalizing your business advisory council. In C.C. Griffin and D. Hammis, *The training connection series for employment specialists.* Missoula: The Rural Institute, University of Montana.

Housman, R.Y. (1992). *Business advisory councils in the rehabilitation process.* Retrieved January 24, 2006, from http://www.findarticles.com/p/articles/mi_m0842/is_n4_v18/ai_13715347

Luecking, R., Fabian, E., & Tilson, G. (2004). *Working relationships: Creating career opportunities for job seekers with disabilities through employer partnerships.* Baltimore: Paul H. Brookes Publishing Co.

U.S. Department of Education. (2006). *Projects with Industry Final Regulations,* 34 C.F.R. Pt. 379.

# 6

# Resource Ownership

## Self-Determined Economic Development

*Cary Griffin, David Hammis, Doug Crandell, Tammara Geary, and Nancy Brooks-Lane*

A longitudinal study of the Rehabilitation Services Administration (RSA) of the U.S. Department of Education reports that individuals with various disabilities referred to sheltered workshops work approximately 28 hours per week and earn an average of $2.53 per hour, or $3,400 per year (Braddock, Hemp, Rizzolo, Parish, & Pomeranz, 2002; Hayward, 1998). Today, as sheltered work enrollments increase, a full year's employment still generates similar earnings (Metzel, Boeltzig, Butterworth, Sulewski, & Gilmore, 2007). The world's wealthiest and most costly disability programs are operated in the United States. Yet, our approaches, at least for those with the most significant disabilities, result in earnings much less than the federal poverty level and contradict the very premise and promise of rehabilitation.

One representative scenario reveals an individual working on a supported employment mobile crew in an eastern state earning less than $2,000 in annual wages but generating $9,100 in state developmental disability day program funds for the community rehabilitation program (CRP). Supervision costs for this individual on the crew run $3,400, transportation adds another $1,000, and administrative overhead eats up the remaining $4,700 (Nerney, 2001). The most surprising aspect of this scenario is that the supported employee is considered a success within both the community rehabilitation system and the state and federal policy/funding structure, and that over an estimated 30-year lifetime of working, with no funding increases, this person will earn $60,000 in wages and remain in clienthood but will generate $273,000 in revenue to the CRP.

The advent of self-determination, however, has changed this scenario and realigned priorities in a majority of states. Self-determination, launched in great measure through the efforts of the Center for Self-Determination (http://www.self-determination.com) and funded through a series of state systems change projects in the late 1990s (Human Services Research Institute [HRSI], 2001), places the locus of control back in the hands of the individual and is framed by these basic principles:

- *Freedom*: The opportunity to choose where and with whom one lives, as well as how one organizes all important aspects of one's life with freely chosen assistance as needed

- *Authority*: the ability to control some targeted amount of public dollars

- *Support*: the ability to organize that support in ways that are unique to the individual

- *Responsibility*: the obligation to use public dollars wisely and to contribute to one's community (Nerney, 2004)

Customized employment (CE) assimilates the principles of self-determination and applies them to the world of work. As noted earlier, CE is a one-person-at-a-time approach that uses mutually beneficial job development approaches that engage job seeker and employer alike and exudes an entrepreneurial sensibility to create opportunities. One way that CE can truly empower job seekers with disabilities is through the method of resource ownership, which was mentioned briefly in Chapter 1. This technique evolved through the authors' work in the late 1980s, growing from the use of assistive technology as a means of accommodating workers with disabilities and evolving into an approach for enhancing productivity and contribution in the workplace. Resource ownership represents a vital and inventive method for assuring enhanced earnings, work status, and individually driven job development.

## SELF-DETERMINATION EXPLOITATION

Resource ownership is a mutually beneficial process whereby job seekers can acquire materials, equipment, or skills matched to their interests and customer needs. The use of these materials, when combined with placement in a business, can generate profits for the employer and competitive wages for the employee. For instance, a mechanic who owns his own tools is more likely to be employed than another mechanic without tools. Without the tools, the mechanic faces unemployment, or a less satisfactory, lower paying job. People must have exploitable resources to get good jobs, and putting the means of production in the hands of people with disabilities makes them more employable (Griffin, Brooks-Lane, Hammis, & Crandell, 2006; Griffin & Hammis, 2003).

People with the most significant disabilities are not recognized for their gifts and talents, hence their high unemployment rate. Resource ownership counteracts the effects of a disability's stigma by creating a shared risk between the worker and the employer (and perhaps the funding agency), and fostering a mutually beneficial approach to job creation. The state/federal vocational rehabilitation (VR) system has long recognized this fact and authorizes the purchase of tools and equipment regularly for job seekers. Under the Workforce Investment Act (WIA) of 1998 (PL 105-220), the community One-Stop Centers, where all job seekers can now begin their career search regardless of disability or other barriers to work they face, can also authorize similar purchases that enhance employability.

Resource ownership is primarily a small business job development approach. Most larger businesses can afford to exploit market opportunities and make investments that might typically be provided under a resource ownership scenario, whereas many smaller enterprises across the country are undercapitalized and cannot always afford to tool-up to attract new customers (Burlingham, 2005; Hamlin & Lyons, 2003).

Suppose it were determined, through the discovery process, that the mobile crew employee above really wanted to be a custodian. A resource ownership approach using a personal budget would reallocate a portion of the $9,100 annual funding in a rather simple scenario. There are janitorial services in every community. Approaching the owners of a particular custodial services company and recommending how they might attract more customers, or be able to provide new services to existing customers, can reveal their needs. If only one custodial service owner responds by suggesting he needs a drapery steam cleaner, and provided that the job seeker wants and can be taught to clean drapes, the job matching and development process has begun.

Employers generally know the type of equipment they need, and have often already investigated the purchase. In this scenario, assume the steamer is $3,500. From the initial $9,100 funding provided, this leaves $5,600 for job coaching and other supports (e.g., transportation, uniforms), and administrative costs, such as clerical support, rent, or phone service. Plus, in most states, extended employment services are billable to Medicaid, VR, and other funding systems based on the ongoing support needs of the individual. Resource ownership saves the taxpayer money by increasing earnings; lessening public benefits and decreasing the reliance on tax-based social programs; increases the individual's personal wealth and status; allows the CRP to concentrate on the next employment candidate; and augments the stability and value of the local business.

Presentation of the job seeker to the business owner, and revealing the job seeker's excitement about drapery cleaning might simply result in a job offer; however, resource ownership can be used to clinch the deal if needed. The individual must always remain the focus of attention in any job development effort; never allow the promise of equipment to become the driving force. There must always be a quality job match, the individual must want the job, and the promise of mutual benefit must be obvious.

The closing negotiation in such a scenario might follow this outline:

| | |
|---|---|
| Employment Specialist: | Well, both Mike and I recognize that you are not hiring at this current time. I wonder if there is a service that you are not now offering, that if you could offer, would generate additional profits. Is there a service your customers ask for that you can't provide right now? |
| Business Owner: | That would be drapery cleaning. The steam cleaner is a bit expensive, but if I had one I could easily charge another $1,000 a month for that service. |
| Mike: | What if I owned a drapery steamer and did the cleaning? |
| Employment Specialist: | In the past our agency has helped create employment by outfitting new employees with the tools that make them more productive, that match the employer's needs, and that create jobs in the community. It's an economic development approach we use to partner with employers. If you were to hire Mike, we might be able to provide him with the steamer so that you can capture these customers. |
| Business Owner: | What happens if Mike decides he doesn't like working for me? |
| Employment Specialist: | We'll draw up a nonbinding letter of agreement. Basically if Mike quits or is fired, he'll either take his equipment with him to get another job, or he will give you first right of refusal to buy the machine. We'll also ask that your insurance cover the equipment in case of theft or damage, and that you repair it once it's out of warranty. If we can buy this first machine, after its usable life, you will be expected to purchase the next machine. We can also ask the company that makes the steamer if they can train Mike on it, and of course, we'll want you to supervise Mike as he learns the job. And we'll be here to assist you, as well. |
| Employer: | The steamer is about $3,500. If you can buy it, I'll call my insurance agent to add this to my inventory list. |
| Employment Specialist: | Great. If you can get the information to me about the steamer, I'll check on the budget. |
| Mike: | When do I start? |

## CAUTIONS AND CONCERNS

All techniques contain the roots of their own destruction, and resource ownership is no exception. Resource ownership should be used cautiously, and always on behalf of the job seeker. Quality job development strategies must be employed regardless of the situation, and a proper job analysis and match should guide the effort. Critically important, too, is that, in most instances, the equipment being purchased, while profiting the employer, functions as assistive technology enabling the new hire to perform the tasks of the job efficiently. For example, a computerized sewing machine allows someone with an interest in making clothes to sew for the first time; a scanner and software creates a job in an office for someone who cannot read or sort alphabetically, electronically storing files; and a pressure-washer creates employment at a powder-coating company for someone with chemical sensitivity who cannot degrease parts using traditional solvent and scrubbing methods.

Over the past 15 years of utilizing resource ownership in dozens of job development situations, the authors have never witnessed an employer hiring someone simply to acquire the tools or equipment promised. This is because the job development strategies presented throughout this book guide the process, and because the negotiation is subtle, never leading with the promise of tools or equipment, but instead using them to improve the employability of the individual. No job developer should ever promise equipment in return for a job. This is a negotiation that first and foremost highlights the contributions of the job seeker; the resources serve only to augment that contribution.

A recent example of proper job development using a resource ownership approach involves Shirley, who hopes to someday become a fashion designer. The prospecting process revealed a children's boutique with a resident designer. This retail manufacturer had no jobs available, but was a perfect match for someone needing a mentor in the business. The owner was approached and, in conversation, the job developer asked about services customers requested but which the employer could not afford to provide. She revealed that many customers wanted the option of adding their child's embroidered initials on clothing items. The job developer wondered aloud if Shirley might want to do something like this, provided she had the proper equipment. The employer could not afford the equipment, but using the annual CRP allocation and money from a U.S. Department of Labor demonstration grant, several thousand dollars was tapped to buy a computerized embroiderer, thus creating a job with an obvious career track.

## RESOURCE OWNERSHIP QUESTIONS

The typical concerns raised about this and other resource ownership scenarios are important. These are the most common questions:

1.  *Isn't resource ownership the same as buying a job?*

    No. Resource ownership is an investment strategy similar to earning a college degree, learning a trade, or buying a business. Owning resources that generate wealth provides the opportunity for using those resources. The exploitation of the resource produces profits that pay wages, creating an employment relationship of mutual need, obligation, and reward. With the unemployment rates of people with disabilities so high, resource ownership uses accepted capitalist processes to open the job market. Using rehabilitation funding to secure jobs is the purpose of these funds in the first place.

2.  *Who owns the equipment?*

    Generally any resource ownership situation is guided by a written letter of agreement stating simply the conditions of the relationship. In most cases, the job seeker retains ownership of the resource, just as an auto mechanic retains ownership of the hand tools she takes to work at her employer's garage. The usable life of the equipment is determined by an accountant or by the company making the equipment and it is recommended that following the usable life of this equipment, the employer be required to purchase the replacement, or make repairs once the item leaves its original warranty.

Should the employee decide to leave the job, or if the employer fires or lays off the employee, the employee may choose to keep the equipment; to offer the employer first right of refusal to purchase it; or, in cases where the equipment's title is still held by a funding agency, to return it to that agency for disposal or use in a new job creation scenario.

3. *Where does the money to buy the equipment, tools, or training come from?*

   There are numerous sources for purchasing equipment or specialized training. Generally, the entire job development funding package, including job analysis, development, coaching, etc., requires multiple financial sources. Typically money derives from day program vocational funding through school transition programs and developmental disabilities, mental health, or specialized Medicaid waivers (e.g., those available for individuals with brain injuries). These funds are amalgamated with other sources, including VR or WIA, or a Plan to Achieve Self-Support (PASS) from the Social Security Administration (SSA), which allows SSA recipients to leverage their benefits to pursue a career goal. A common approach is to use mental health or developmental disability Medicaid funding for job coaching, case management, transportation, and extended employment supports, while tapping VR for job development and equipment purchases, and using WIA One-Stop funding for ongoing skills training. A majority of states now allow for person-centered planning and many are using state general funds and Medicaid templates, such as the Independence Plus option, to customize spending, making resource ownership and amalgamated funding a more common practice (Griffin & Hammis, 2003; O'Brien, Ford, & Malloy, 2005; O'Brien, Revell, & West, 2003).

4. *What about liability?*

   Generally, liability is the employer's responsibility, although every agency should check both with their legal counsel and their insurance company. In the letter of agreement governing any resource ownership situation, it should be stated simply that the employer accepts typical liability, as they would with any piece of equipment operated by any employee. Also included should be a statement that asserts the employer's responsibility to insure the equipment in case of theft, fire, or natural disaster. If for some reason the employer cannot guarantee this coverage, which usually represents no additional cost to their existing policy, the employee should consider insuring the item.

5. *Who does the training?*

   As mentioned earlier, the use of the natural worksite trainers (i.e., co-workers or supervisors) is preferred, but not always possible, especially when new and unique equipment is introduced. The best option available may be arranging for the equipment manufacturer to provide on-site instruction. If this is not available, companies often have instructional videos or other means that an employment specialist, co-workers, and the new employee can review and apply the information.

6. *How is the employee protected against exploitation?*

   Following the recommended discovery, negotiation, job match, and job analysis processes provide substantial safeguards against the misuse of this tactic. Offering equipment in exchange for a job is not the intent of resource ownership. Quality usage requires that:

   a. The individual obviously wishes to perform the job or learn the trade that this technology or training accommodates

b.  The individual operates this resource as a core and essential component of their job

c.  The acquisition of this resource fosters steady employment with growth potential

d.  The resource elevates the status and productivity of the individual

e.  The resource complements and enhances the employee's contribution to workplace profitability

f.  The employee determines if anyone else can use the resource, for instance on a second shift, or while the employee is performing other valued tasks that build their career potential

g.  The employee earns wages commensurate with others performing similar duties

7.  *What happens if the employee quits or gets fired?*

    If the employee leaves the job, the employee can keep the equipment to use in leveraging another job, offer the employer first opportunity to purchase it, or, in cases where the equipment's title is still held by a funding agency, return it to that agency.

8.  *Is this approach handled in writing?*

    Yes, and while a contract is perhaps too formal a document, a mutually signed letter of agreement should be proffered. The authors do not provide this as a legal document; therefore, any such agreement should be reviewed by agency or family legal counsel prior to use. For example, see Draft Letter of Agreement: Resource Ownership (Figure 6.1).

## EXAMPLES OF RESOURCE OWNERSHIP

As with all examples in this book, each was derived from using a discovery process coupled with sound person-centered techniques, and as such are intended to illustrate the topics herein, not to serve as model job ideas. A personal budget format was used in each example, which detailed the funds available through various sources. The power of personal budgets is that they make clear to all stakeholders the revenue generated by the individual within the rehabilitation system, and when used properly reinforce, and indeed exemplify, the powerful framework of freedom, authority, support, and responsibility self-determination advocates. Generally, such funding is available through

•  State developmental disability or mental health services day program

•  Special education funding as authorized per pupil

•  VR supported employment or general job placement funds

•  WIA Intensive Services or Individual Training Account funds for job placement and career-development assistance

•  Grants through a variety of sources including such federal programs as the Office of Special Education and Rehabilitative Services (OSERS) and the Department of Labor

•  Projects through local foundations, city or county Community Development Block Grants, or state developmental disability councils

This letter of agreement details the use of employment resources provided by Mike Nevels and the Tulsa Employment eXchange (TEX) for use in the commercial enterprise of Jorge Gonzales, owner of Super Clean Housekeeping. This is not an employment contract.

Mike Nevels will begin work on July 1 of this year in the position of Home Maintenance Technician with the beginning pay of $8.50 per hour for 35 hours per week, plus benefits as afforded all employees in this job classification. Mike's primary task will be drapery steaming, but he will also have other duties assigned as necessary. Mike has agreed to purchase and provide a Whirlwind Model 355 fabric steamer, serial number B341782A, with drapery attachment, for use in this job. The stated value of this equipment is $3,500.

The following conditions apply:

1.  Mike will be instructed in the use of the steamer, on the job by a Whirlwind technician, by staff at Super Clean Housekeeping, and by TEX employment specialists.

2.  Mike will be the sole operator of this equipment, except in event of work absence due to illness or other event.

3.  The usable life of this equipment, provided in writing by Whirlwind Corp., is 2 years. After this period, Super Clean Housekeeping is responsible for the repair or replacement of the equipment. Mike is not responsible for providing additional equipment or the replacement of the original steamer.

4.  The factory warranty on the steamer is 90 days. Following this period, Super Clean Housekeeping is responsible for maintenance and repairs to this equipment.

5.  Super Clean Housekeeping will maintain fire, theft, and natural disaster insurance coverage on the steamer during its 2-year life span, and, as with any employee situation, assumes all legal liability resulting from the equipment's use.

6.  Should Mike separate from Super Clean Housekeeping within this first 2-year time period, he will offer the employer first right of refusal to purchase the equipment based upon the manufacturer's estimated market value.

All other standard state and federal employment regulations apply. This is a nonbinding agreement not enforceable in a court of law.

| TEX, 7/30/07 | Mike Nevels, 7/30/07 | Jorge Gonzales, 7/30/07 |
|---|---|---|
| TEX, Date | Mike Nevels, Date | Jorge Gonzales, Date |

**Figure 6.1.** Draft letter of agreement: Resource ownership.

- Expansion and innovation funds from state VR agencies, specialized hiring programs through state departments of Labor and Commerce, Welfare to Work, local civic and corporate foundations, and others

- Self-financing through family private pay

- Social Security work incentives (often lucrative and self-directed; most notably, PASS).

Colleagues at the Cobb and Douglas County Georgia Community Services Board (CSB), a developmental disability and mental health service provider, regularly use resource ownership to secure employment of choice and invited the authors to work with them on some of the examples below. These are interspersed with other successful employment scenarios from across the country, including examples illustrating the use of resource ownership to expand job duties, add hours to the work week, and increase pay or profit-sharing. While the CSB used a U.S. Department of Labor CE demonstration project grant to underwrite their efforts, they built a reputation for delivering quality, lasting employment that now allows them to continue leveraging funds without use of the grant. The examples that follow illustrate best practice in job development approaches, resource ownership, and amalgamated funding. Funding amounts are estimated expenditures to date.

## James

James is in his mid-50s and has a developmental disability and a severe hearing impairment. He has a demonstrated interest in maps and roads. A job was developed for him at a local sign shop where he laminates maps and signs using an industrial laminator he purchased and brought to the shop. Prior to this development, the shop was outsourcing over $3,000 in laminating a month. James's personal budget reflects the funding sources (see Figure 6.2).

| Item | Amount | Source | Notes |
|---|---|---|---|
| Planning, job development, and initial coaching | $3,250 | Vocational rehabilitation | |
| Extended employment supports | $400 | Developmental disability Medicaid waiver | |
| Resource | $9,000 | U.S. Department of Labor grant | Laminator and training |
| Total | $12,650 | | |

**Figure 6.2.** James's personal budget.

## Errol

Errol has a developmental disability and he is labeled as occasionally violent. He made it clear that detailing cars was his career of choice. A job was created for Errol in a new car-detailing operation that needed a technician to shampoo carpets. Errol was matched to the job and to his resource, a new carpet steamer. Initial on-site training was provided, for free, by the manufacturer of the carpet cleaner. Errol's personal budget reveals several funding sources (see Figure 6.3).

| Item | Amount | Source | Notes |
|---|---|---|---|
| Planning and job development | $1,500 | Vocational rehabilitation | |
| Job coaching and extended employment supports | $800 | Developmental disability Medicaid waiver | |
| Resource | $1,840 | U.S. Department of Labor grant | |
| Total | $4,140 | | |

**Figure 6.3.** Errol's personal budget.

## John

John is in his mid-20s and is labeled with a significant psychiatric disability. His love of dogs led him to grooming classes and state certification paid for by VR. Currently he is taking advanced certification classes and works at the grooming school, with employment specialist support, using two height-adjustable tables he bought to improve and enhance his productivity (see Figure 6.4).

| Item | Amount | Source | Notes |
|---|---|---|---|
| Planning, grooming classes, job development, and initial coaching | $3,000 | Vocational rehabilitation and One-Stop | |
| Extended employment supports | $600 | Developmental disability Medicaid waiver | |
| Resource | $4,500 | U.S. Department of Labor grant | Two adjustable-height work tables |
| Total | $8,100 | | |

**Figure 6.4.**  John's personal budget.

## Jessie

Jessie, a young woman with psychiatric and developmental disability labels, loves books, conversation, and entertaining. Creating employment matched to her profile involved purchasing a cappuccino maker, purchasing several large comfortable reading chairs for customers, investing in additional book inventory, and placing them within the bookstore that employs her. Her contributions created her job selling coffee drinks, and she also profits proportionately from her inventory investment (see Figure 6.5).

| Item | Amount | Source | Notes |
|---|---|---|---|
| Planning, job development, and coaching | $4,500 | Vocational rehabilitation | |
| Extended employment supports | $500 | Developmental disability Medicaid waiver | |
| Resource | $10,000 | U.S Department of Labor grant | Purchased reading chairs, signage, a cappuccino maker, and inventory, which earns her a return on investment |
| Total | $15,000 | | |

**Figure 6.5.**  Jessie's personal budget.

# Ted

Ted experiences a developmental disability and has a love of automobiles. At a local new car lot, the salespeople complained of having to spruce up the new cars as they arrived from the factory. Their duties also included transcribing long Vehicle Identification Numbers (VINs), which invariably got transposed, causing inventory, insurance, and legal ownership issues. Ted, with a simple mobile tool cart and some supplies, polishes the new cars, cleans the windows, and removes factory paperwork and stickers, freeing up other staff to concentrate on sales. He also uses a barcode scanner and a computer to register each car as it enters the dealership, and this technology has eliminated the confusion over VINs. (See Figure 6.6.)

| Item | Amount | Source | Notes |
|---|---|---|---|
| Planning, job development, and initial coaching | $2,500 | Vocational rehabilitation (VR) | |
| Extended employment supports | $2,000 | Developmental disability Medicaid waiver | |
| Resource | $2,000 | VR and U.S. Department of Labor (DOL) grant | VR purchased the cart; DOL purchased the computer equipment |
| Total | $6,500 | | |

**Figure 6.6.**   Ted's personal budget.

# Georgia

Georgia, a single mom with muscular dystrophy and a psychiatric disability, was referred to a local CRP for job development services. She asked for work in an office setting and shortly began work as a part-time clerical assistant. In order to increase her hours and pay, she used a PASS to purchase a new full-featured copier. This machine provided various collating and copying features that allowed more complexity of tasks assigned, increased speed, and drove down the cost per copy. Bringing her resource into the company boosted her income by over 25%. She has now been employed by the same company for 15 years, earning full benefits and an employer-matched retirement. (See Figure 6.7.)

| Item | Amount | Source | Notes |
|---|---|---|---|
| Planning and job development | $600 | Vocational rehabilitation | |
| Job coaching | no cost | Provided by the employer | |
| Resource | $8,000 | Plan to Achieve Self-Support, Social Security Administration | |
| Total | $8,600 | | |

**Figure 6.7.**   Georgia's personal budget.

## Samuel

Samuel uses a wheelchair following his car accident. His long recovery caused the loss of his job as a mechanic, and finding another position was fruitless. Using a resource ownership strategy, the local VR counselor and CRP were able to create a position for Samuel at a local garage that needed a qualified mechanic and a new diagnostic engine analyzer operator (see Figure 6.8).

| Item | Amount | Source | Notes |
|---|---|---|---|
| Planning and job development | $1,100 | Vocational rehabilitation (VR) | |
| Job coaching | Free | Employer | |
| Resource | $5,000 | VR | Various hand tools and a computerized diagnostic engine analyzer |
| Total | $6,100 | | |

**Figure 6.8.** Samuel's personal budget.

## Roberta

Roberta secured a part-time job as a clerical assistant through her personal connections with People First, a self-advocacy group. Her hours were restricted, though, because the job created for her accommodated her inability to drive, a function of the job that had been carved out and was now assigned to a co-worker. State case management staff believed Roberta's cerebral palsy made it impossible for her to drive, but a local advocate thought otherwise, developing a large PASS, which paid for driving lessons and made monthly payments on a new 4-wheel drive car with hand controls. Once driving, the employer added errands, deliveries, and other tasks to Roberta's job, increasing her wages enough that she now also takes annual vacations and lives on her own. Roberta has been employed with the same company for over 7 years. (See Figure 6.9.)

| Item | Amount | Source | Notes |
|---|---|---|---|
| Job development | Free | Personal network | |
| Job coaching | Free | Employer | |
| Resource | $25,000 | Plan for Achieving Self-Support (PASS), Social Security Administration | Roberta made a personal $3,000 down payment and the PASS made the monthly car and insurance payments |
| Total | $25,000 | | |

**Figure 6.9.** Roberta's personal budget.

## Russell

Russell was referred by VR to the local mental health employment program with a label of schizophrenia. He refused job coaching assistance, and his job at a car dealership doing engine degreasing and repainting fell through when his auditory hallucinations disrupted the workplace. VR had purchased Russell a new steam cleaner that seemed to match his fastidiousness, so with this equipment, and repairs to his aging pick-up truck, a new position was sought. The result was working late nights at a job with a large grocery chain in the city, which accommodated both his medication's side effects and his preference to work alone, steam-cleaning shopping carts. The part-time nature of this job led to a self-employment venture as Russell developed late-night contracts with several local gas stations, steam-cleaning their self-service gas pumps, and also with several restaurants, cleaning their grease traps. (See Figure 6.10.)

| Item | Amount | Source | Notes |
|------|--------|--------|-------|
| Planning and job development | $800 | Vocational rehabilitation (VR) | |
| Business development services | $1,000 | Mental health Medicaid waiver funds | |
| Resource | $3,500 | VR | Portable steam cleaner, new truck engine, brakes, and insurance |
| Total | $5,300 | | |

**Figure 6.10.**   Russell's personal budget.

## Mary

Mary had a strong attraction to chocolate, as most people do, as well as an interest in computers. Although unable to read and write very well, Mary had used a computer set up with macros in her day program classes at the developmental disabilities center to repeat common tasks such as printing mailing labels and entering quality assurance data. Combining her two passions, a job was developed at a small candy company specializing in individually wrapped chocolates. The operation hand wrapped the chocolates and used a manual stamp pad to affix the expiration date to thousands of candies every week. By bringing in a computer with a label printer, a job was created for Mary, who went on to master several other jobs within the company, including prepping and cleaning the candy molds, mixing chocolate, and stocking shelves in the attached retail store. (See Figure 6.11.)

| Item | Amount | Source | Notes |
|------|--------|--------|-------|
| Planning, job development, and extended employment supports | $3,000 | Developmental disability Medicaid waiver | Includes limited transportation |
| Resource | $2,300 | Vocational rehabilitation | Computer workstation, software, computer consultant/programmer, printer |
| Total | $5,300 | | |

**Figure 6.11.**   Mary's personal budget.

## CONCLUSION

Resource ownership follows the tradition of career investment so ingrained in the psyche of our culture that at first glance it appears as a radical departure from accepted job development practice. Using resource ownership tempts the harried job developer to lead with the money, putting the job seeker second. The structured approach and the guiding principles advocated throughout this book provide a shield against such a distortion. The job seeker's satisfaction must remain the focus of attention, blended through careful negotiation in the marketplace to reveal mutual gain between the employee and the employer. Anything less than the consumer-driven approach wastes taxpayer money, makes the job seeker appear incompetent to the community, and is not CE.

## REFERENCES

Braddock, D., Hemp, R., Rizzolo, M., Parish, S., & Pomeranz, A. (2002). *The state of the states in developmental disabilities: 2002 study summary.* Boulder: University of Colorado, Coleman Institute for Cognitive Disabilities and Department of Psychiatry.

Burlingham, B. (2005). *Small giants: Companies that choose to be great instead of big.* New York: Portfolio Publishers.

Griffin, C.C., Brooks-Lane, N., Hammis, D., & Crandell, D. (2006). Self-employment: Owning the American dream. In P. Wehman (Ed.), *Real work for real pay: Inclusive employment for people with disabilities.* Baltimore: Paul H. Brookes Publishing Co.

Griffin, C.C., & Hammis, D. (2003). *Making self-employment work for people with disabilities.* Baltimore: Paul H. Brookes Publishing Co.

Hamlin, R., & Lyons, T. (2003). *Financing small business in America: Debt capital in a global economy.* Westport, CT: Praeger.

Hayward, B. (1998). *A longitudinal study of the vocational rehabilitation service program.* Research Triangle Park, NC: Research Triangle Institute.

Human Services Research Institute. (2001). *The Robert Wood Johnson self-determination initiative: Final impact assessment report, November 2001.* Cambridge, MA: Author.

Metzel, D.S., Boeltzig, H., Butterworth, J., Sulewski, J.S., & Gilmore, D.S. (2007). Achieving community membership through community rehabilitation provider services: Are we there yet? *Mental Retardation, 45,* 149–160.

Nerney, T. (2001). *Filthy lucre: Creating better value in long-term supports.* Ann Arbor, MI: The Center for Self-Determination.

Nerney, T. (2004). *Lost lives: Why we need a new approach to quality.* Ann Arbor, MI: The Center for Self-Determination.

O'Brien, D., Ford, L., & Malloy, J. (2005). Person-centered funding: Using vouchers and personal budgets to support recovery and employment for people with psychiatric disabilities. *Journal of Vocational Rehabilitation, 23*(2), 71–79.

O'Brien, D., Revell, G., & West, M. (2003). The impact of the current employment policy environment on self-determination of individuals with disabilities. *Journal of Vocational Rehabilitation, 19*(2), 105–118.

Workforce Investment Act of 1998, PL 105-220, 29 U.S.C. §§ 2801 *et seq.*

# 7

# Interest-Based Negotiation, Problem Solving, and Conflict Management

*Cary Griffin, David Hammis, and Tammara Geary*

Customized employment (CE) is defined by the negotiation of job duties and arranging a myriad of workplace elements, including training, supervision, and ongoing support. Negotiating a job placement can be quite challenging when creating a work environment that flatters unique personal attributes. Implicit in any job negotiation are the combined elements of problem solving, communication, and conflict management challenges prompted by changes in typical routines. Mastering these fundamental building blocks of negotiation signals an efficacious approach to job development.

The competitive employment model contains useful approaches for the job seeker. Résumés, networking, and interviewing skills are proven essentials for the applicant. Yet individuals with complex barriers to employment do not fare well in the traditional system of hiring, so moving from a *You're Hired/You're Not Hired* to a *Let's Negotiate* approach opens up a world of possibilities for uniquely crafted jobs. This chapter provides problem-solving and conflict management strategies and tools that make employment specialists better negotiators.

## INTEREST-BASED NEGOTIATION

Interest-based negotiation is founded on the belief that parties are more likely to reach a satisfactory understanding if their mutual interests are met, rather than the outcome typified in traditional, or positional, negotiation where one party's needs win out over the other's needs (Fisher & Ury, 1991). Competitive employment is based on a positional approach to hiring. The applicant brings specific gifts and talents to an employer and the employer states the desired skills and conditions of employment in a job description. Both parties state their positions, and the give and take of negotiation is limited by the confines of the essential job functions and the formal personnel policies. If a particular applicant matches the requirements of the employer better than the other candidates, the job is secured.

People with disabilities are selectively culled through this competitive process. On the other hand, a negotiated approach, totally voluntary on the part of the employer, emphasizes the common ground of both job seeker and employer and increases the likelihood of a meaningful audience with the hiring authority. Maneuvering into an opportunity to illuminate shared interests is a first step for staging the job negotiation. Hence, work experience, on-the-job training, going-where-the-career-makes-sense, and other strategies for gaining proximity to employers are recommended to demonstrate the potential contributions of a job seeker.

Interest-based negotiation in employment is a straightforward undertaking. Employers need workers; people with disabilities want to work. The common ground is obvious, but building the bridge to creating that unique job description for each individual necessitates a studied and planned approach. All negotiation requires that we communicate with someone who is different from us. This situation leads both parties to believe that what we each want is different, when in fact employers often state that their most important accomplishments include the creation of jobs (McKinsey, 2001). Starting with the basic common ground of creating employment relieves anxiety and breaks the ice.

Positional negotiation assumes that when two people from different societal sectors (in this case, the private versus the public) negotiate, the one who pulls hardest will eventually tug the other into their way of thinking. Interest-based job negotiation, on the other hand, illustrates to all parties that mutual gain is possible. The strength of Business Leadership Networks (BLNs) and Active Employer Councils (AECs) is their emphasis on similarities rather than differences, mutual education regarding employment possibilities, and the shared experience of building the members' local community.

## COMMUNICATION

Traditional approaches to negotiation emphasize talking more than listening (Fisher & Ury, 1991). To a job developer or job seeker, information gathering is of primary concern. When one is talking, one is neither listening nor learning. The skilled negotiator sets up the job development situation in a manner conducive to a conversation, not a sales pitch. The portfolio, picture book, workplace tours, and other recommended activities, as described in Chapter 4, create a conversational milieu that gently but firmly augments the case for hiring based on the potential for mutual gain, and turns the cold calling of competitive employment into the warm calling of CE.

Communication is the nexus of interest-based negotiation, but excessive talking is low on the priority and efficacy list. Studies show that over 50% of what others understand us to say is a direct result of what we communicate visually through our dress, movements, posture, facial expressions, and eye contact. Almost 40% of the messages we send emanate from the sound of communication, including our rate of speech, tone, timbre, and volume. Less than 10% of our conversation has to do with the actual words we use. Therefore, effective communication means matching the expectations of the other party regarding dress and similar language, making eye contact, and showing true interest in their circumstances while speaking less and observing more. In short, the skilled job developer moves from the traditional sales approach typified by the smooth talker to that of the more refined and interested smooth listener (Aronson, 1995; Griffin, 1999; Grinder & Bandler, 1979; Mehrabian & Ferris, 1967; Shapiro & Jankowski, 1998).

Understanding that communication occurs on numerous levels of consciousness augments the negotiation skill set of both job developer and job seeker. As the conversation unfolds with an employer, the negotiator must pay attention to the employer's choice of words for insight into the best communication methods. For instance, if during a tour of the company the employer uses phrases like, "I'd like to see this work," and "from my point of view," chances are she leans towards a visual communication preference. The picture book and fact sheet may be the best leave-behinds for this situation, coupled with follow-up e-mail messages. If the employer notes that "I hear what you're saying" and "this proposal is music to my ears," then the job seeker may wish to narrate his or her portfolio or the job developer may wish to maintain verbal conversation with this auditory learner, and schedule a follow-up telephone call. And, if the individual notes that "this just doesn't feel right" or "I have a firm grip on this," chances are this is a kinesthetic, or hands-on, learner who will peruse a hard copy résumé and picture books that they can physically grasp (Cialdini, 1993; Gardner, 1983).

Communication often breaks down when the two or more parties involved have differing expectations. Planning and preparation, illustrated by earlier recommendations in Chapters 1 and 3 for work experiences and job analyses, minimize the surprises that often accompany job development activities. Still, communication gaps will occur, so anticipating and structuring conversations beforehand, or even on the spot, provides a safety net as anxiety or unexpected situations arise.

For instance, let's examine a job development call that goes wrong almost from the start. The job developer shows up at the appointed time, but the employer has forgotten, and though distracted by other events, decides to get this brief interruption over with. Chances are this visit will not be productive, but maintaining the relationship, better known by students of negotiation as respecting "the shadow of the future" (Fisher & Ury, 1991) is important. The AEIOU approach is recommended:

- **A**ssume the other person means well.

- **E**xpress your reasons for meeting.

- **I**dentify what you would like to have happen.

- **O**utcomes you expect should be clearly stated.

- **U**nderstanding should be reached on a mutual level.

Such a tactic will not do the hard work of addressing the conflict apparent in this circumstance, but it will help maintain the relationship, anticipate problem areas, and identify where more information or support is needed. The conversation, using the above framework, might progress as follows:

| | |
|---|---|
| Employer: | Sorry, I totally forgot we were meeting this morning. It's been very hectic around here. |
| Job Developer: | I understand. Perhaps we should reschedule for tomorrow? (Assume) |
| Employer: | No, that's all right, I can squeeze you in. |
| Job Developer: | As you'll recall, I wanted to come in for a tour just to see your operations and see if we might work together in the near future. As a career counselor, I am working with several people who have expressed an interest in your company. (Express) |
| Employer: | As you know, good employees are hard to find, so we are always on the lookout for solid candidates. |
| Job Developer: | Our approach is to conduct a thorough job match by performing a job analysis. Perhaps we should just go ahead and schedule a time when I can come back and observe your operations. I am particularly interested in observing the shipping and receiving department. (Identify) |
| Employer: | When would work best for you? |
| Job Developer: | How about Thursday? I'll come in first thing so I can observe the |

| | morning rush. Is there someone I should set this up with back there? (Outcomes) |
|---|---|
| Employer: | That should be ok. You'll need to check in with Randy, the manager. I'm headed back there now. I'll let him know to expect you. |
| Job Developer: | Great! I'll give Randy a call tomorrow to confirm. (Outcomes) |
| Employer: | Thanks for understanding. Again, sorry for the confusion. |
| Job Developer: | No problem. Glad we could work this out! Thanks! (Understanding) |

This scenario, of course, may not tell the whole story. The employer may have staged this event because he did not want to appear unfriendly to people with disabilities and was hoping the job developer might just go away and never return. Giving the benefit of the doubt, however, is a requirement of proper negotiation. Had avoidance been the employer's motivation, it is unlikely the job developer would have secured the next appointment. This tactic, the AEIOU approach, clarifies the reason for the meeting or tour and gives the employer an opportunity to gently back out. Negotiating with someone who sees no purpose in doing so is a dead end, and knowing that there are 20 million other employers in the country means that abandoning one, for now, is no big deal.

Suppose that the job developer returned, performed the job analysis in shipping and receiving, and discovered a potential job carve for a young woman interested in working for the company. The negotiation of the job carver might go something like this:

| Job Developer: | Thanks for seeing Jillian and me this morning. |
|---|---|
| Employer: | My pleasure. Randy, the department manager, tells me you have an employment proposal you'd like to run by me. Of course, I am sure he told you we are not hiring right now. |
| Job Developer: | As you know, Jillian has been doing a work tryout in the back for about a week now. (Assume) |
| Jillian: | I have been scanning bills of lading, tagging pallets, and repackaging the overstocks. |
| Job Developer: | Randy suggested that these were all jobs that require him to pull workers off their own jobs to complete. I think there's a chance that if we combined these tasks into a new job description, it might result in a 30-hour a week job that pays for itself in efficiency savings. (Express) |
| Employer: | Randy told me about this and seems to think it'll improve his operation, though he wasn't sure it'd save him any money. |
| Job Developer: | Jillian and I drew up a sample job description for your review. Perhaps you and Randy can sit down and go through it. (Identify) |
| Jillian: | I have another job I am trying out next week at Cost-Save Warehouse, but I'd like to work here. |
| Employer: | Have you done this type of work before, Jillian? |
| Jillian: | Here's a copy of my résumé. Yes, I worked on my family's farm growing up and we shipped tomatoes on pallets. I had to enter the numbers of each load into the computer, and, of course, I had to lift a lot of boxes. I like doing this kind of work. |
| Job Developer: | I know there's no job open right now, but we've done this sort of job carving for several other companies, such as Cormil Restorations, Public Service Company, and the county administrative offices, and I am sure they'd give you a good reference concerning our work. I can have one of them call you if you'd like. (Outcomes) |
| Employer: | Yes, that might be good. This way I can have some ammunition to take to personnel. Let me talk with Randy this afternoon and I'll get back to you tomorrow. |

Job Developer:   Great. I'll have Roger Harkin from Public Service Company give you a call since we created a similar job in their warehouse. I'll follow up with you on Wednesday. (Understanding)

Employer:   Sounds good.

Jillian:   Thanks. I look forward to working for you.

Here, the job developer and Jillian work as a team to explain the process concisely, set their expectations, and identify a reference, showing their willingness to put more effort into the relationship and also not allowing the employer to stall for time. The job developer and Jillian also made sure they had the support of Randy, the shipping and receiving manager, before scheduling this meeting. Of course, several other scenarios would work just as well. Having Randy sell this idea to the boss would work; having Randy in the meeting would work, too. Think through the process and aim for the best circumstance available.

## NEGOTIATING THE ESSENTIALS

Another key area of negotiation centers on the various components of the job and the support strategies needed for employee stabilization and job retention. Employment specialists and new employees should enter into any negotiation with a win–win mindset. The negotiation process becomes less cumbersome when a thorough job match is completed prior to any placement. This may minimize the actual negotiation time, but still some details of the job are likely left unresolved even as the first day of work looms. Paying close attention to the use of natural supports, including transferring the direct training and supervision to the proper personnel, means that the transition from job coaching may need negotiating, but the fact that the actual responsibility remains with the employer should not come as a surprise to anyone on the worksite (Hagner, 2000).

Commonly negotiated items in a worksite include supports related to

- The sharing of tools and equipment

- Resource ownership details

- Co-worker support and quality checks

- Supervision and quality improvement

- Productivity enhancement

- Templating and jigging the manufacturing process

- Equipment modifications

- Worksite accommodations

- Personal assistant services on the job

- Toileting and eating assistance

- Transportation

Many of these work ingredients are issues faced with every employee and should be handled in as natural a means as possible. Before replacing an existing training or work-related support, attempt to use it, modify it slightly, or adapt it to the new hire (Callahan & Garner, 1997). For example, transportation is often provided by employment specialists or an agency van. Generally, transportation is a personal responsibility. Investigate the existence of car pools at the workplace. A job developer, or new employee, may need to negotiate with co-workers to share transit with the nondriving employee, or work hours may require a negotiated modification to accommodate public transportation schedules. Using this resource increases shared experiences that foster employment longevity and speeds personal emancipation from the disability system.

Machine fixtures and templates are commonly employed throughout the manufacturing industry, but a truly unique adaptation may be required for some workers. This can be negotiated with the employer, or perhaps the plant's engineering staff. The expense of such adaptations may require further negotiation with the employer, the Social Security Administration (SSA) for a Plan to Achieve Self-Support (PASS), or with vocational rehabilitation (VR) for additional tooling support.

Using the most typical means and people in these circumstances stays true to the intent of natural supports theory and engages the employer in the success of the worker. Asking for too much, though, is a concern, and a position that must be so heavily modified that it stigmatizes the new employee is probably a sign that the job match was not done properly. Experience with practical application of job analysis techniques guides the proper match and an appropriate level of job accommodating negotiations.

In traditional supported employment, employment specialists occasionally offered, at no additional cost to the employer, to complete the work of an employee who was not reaching the industry production standard, and also to substitute for the worker in event of absence (Mank, Cioffi, & Yovanoff, 1997). This is highly unusual and not recommended as a negotiable. Instead, the employee should receive the same considerations as other workers regarding illness and absences and should be afforded proper training and job accommodations to boost productivity. Again, if productivity is a key requirement of the job, a proper job match will screen in the correct worker. Still, many potential workers have medical or self-care concerns that, at least until they are accepted into the fabric of the company, may require specialized supports beyond the ability of the employer to provide. In such cases, worksite Personal Assistance Services (PAS) might be available, and their presence on the jobsite launches another negotiation episode (Unger, Kregel, Wehman, & Brooke, 2002). In such a case, the employee and the employment specialist may want to spend time with the personal assistant cluing them into natural supports and allowing for a systematic fade from the worksite, to the greatest degree possible.

## REFRAMING

The entire employment process is linked together by a long chain of negotiations. Maintaining a focus on the win–win aspects of the process at each step assures long-term success and that proper attention is paid to the essential stakeholders and concerns. When barriers are encountered, reframing the negotiation uncovers other options. Reframing is the process of changing the way a thought is presented so that it maintains its fundamental meaning but is more likely to support resolution efforts. For instance, a co-worker complains that the new employee is not mastering the use of the band saw and production is subpar. The employment specialist can offer more powerful training techniques, ask for assistance with diagnosing the problem, suggest a template, or perhaps research the cost of a more automated band saw that improves production. The important point in reframing is accepting the complaint or oppositional position, thereby validating the shared concern, then offering options for resolution. Without reframing, the focus remains squarely on the complaint: in this case, the inability of the person to master the band saw. Reframing diverts the complaint to possible solutions.

Reframing involves circumventing problems. Some problems are simply not easy to solve, but with a little thought can be reconfigured with a simple but elegant solution. One of the authors, for instance, was working with a major computer manufacturer at the time of the passage of the Americans with Disabilities Act (ADA). The regional vice president for operations was interested in hiring people with disabilities, but also mildly complained that replacing all the water fountains in the huge factory to accommodate individuals using wheelchairs was going to cost the company over $10,000. The author suggested he install disposable cup dispensers next to the water fountains, thereby meeting the intent of the law and saving money as well. The company went on to hire several people with significant disabilities throughout its many departments and installed the accessible fountains as well. A debate on the merits of the ADA was not in the interests of the job seekers, and with the gentle suggestion of an answer, the relationship was secured.

Reframing is strongly tied to the philosophy of interest-based negotiation. The parties need to reveal their common ground through discussion and the generation of options. Often, an issue may appear unsolvable, but reframing opens new opportunities. For instance, an employee demands a raise. The boss knows the individual is deserving, but her budget will not allow any increases. A skilled reframer might suggest that the issue is one of reward, not of pay. Knowing this, and assuming that the worker wants a reward and that employers enjoy giving rewards, common ground is revealed. Perhaps nonmonetary benefits, such as a few extra days off per year, use of a company car, or promotional passes to local baseball games, generally reserved for customers, will be satisfactory to both parties.

Another common barrier to job development is transportation to and from the worksite. Historically, national transportation policy put an emphasis on maximizing the use of private automobiles in lieu of mass transit, resulting in significant mobility problems for people who do not drive. Reframing the circumstance, however at least in most major cities is easy. There exists, in most metropolitan areas, an overabundance of transportation, illustrated by daily traffic jams. In such locations, the issue is not the lack of resources; it is perhaps the lack of social ties to those who own the transportation. With reframing, addressing transportation no longer involves the massive and unfathomable task of rewriting federal policy and funding formulas. Instead it brings solutions down to a personal networking arena. Reframing does not minimize the importance of an issue; it simply presents broader options for exploring mutually agreeable solutions.

## ANCILLARY NEGOTIATIONS

The overriding concern for any job seeker, job developer, or employment specialist is securing the position and negotiating the terms of employment. However, there are several ancillary negotiations conjoined with the job that are important for decisive success. Employer negotiations are largely straightforward affairs, whereas ancillary negotiations are fraught with issues of policy, politics, trust, safety, and money. One placement may represent concerns from various parties, such as

- *The family:* Concerns over the health and safety as the individual moves from a day or school program to the community; concern about the possible impact of earnings on SSA benefits

- *Developmental disability/mental health/local educational agencies:* Concerns over the level of funding required for equipment and tools, job coaching, and ongoing supports

- *Day program administrators:* Concern over providing one-to-one community supports when day program coverage is less cumbersome; concern that day program may become irrelevant for families and consumers; concerns over managing a decentralized staff; concern over coordinating decentralized and individualized services such as transportation

- *VR/Workforce Investment Act of 1998 (PL 105-220):* Concern over purchasing services that many believe the community rehabilitation program is already paid to provide; concern over spending more for people with significant disabilities than the accepted average for job placements

- *Social Security and Medicaid:* Concern over approving PASS applications for people historically considered unemployable

- *Case management:* Concern over health and safety of the individual moving from protected settings to community settings; concern over proper use of funding streams

- *Residential service providers:* Concern over individualizing staff coverage for consumers working varied hours; concern over providing work-related supports, including packing a lunch, assuring proper dress, and arranging for transportation

This long list of concerns is typical, especially for adults receiving services through the developmental disability or mental health systems. These circumstances also provide many areas of overlap in responsibility, policy, and funding, catapulting a simple employment situation into a complex bog of competing interests, concerns, rules, and opinions. These situations eventually generate systematic approaches for collaboration among the varied rehabilitation partners, but still manage to foster anger, confusion, and politics with regularity.

The successful management of complex ancillary job development negotiation remains tied to the application of proper methods and accurate communication, as explored in this chapter. Regardless, conflict will arise as the many points of view and competing interests and policies clash. Understanding the causes of conflict is vital to preparation for the negotiation.

## CAUSES OF CONFLICT

There are five major causes of conflict. In diagnosing a job development conflict, understanding these descriptors help to communicate with the stakeholders and to formulate an intervention strategy.

1. *Relationship problems:* These are characterized by strong emotions, misperceptions, and stereotypes; poor communication based on personality conflict; negative or misunderstood behavior; and a history of mistrust.

2. *Values conflicts:* These are defined as conflicting day-to-day or general values; conflicting spiritual values; and conflicting beliefs regarding the superiority of one person over another or one idea, value, or ethic over another.

3. *Systemic or structural disconnects:* These are identified as conflicts or confusion regarding roles and responsibilities between parties, disagreement regarding levels of authority, and issues of time resources in which an individual or team feels overworked or overpressured to perform.

4. *Data problems:* These are characterized by people or agencies lacking data, receiving the wrong data, or getting incorrect data necessary for the successful completion of their work. These circumstances are regularly compounded by poor data collection methods and instruments, and improper data analysis, leading people or teams to take incorrect actions based on the inaccurate work of others.

5. *Interest issues:* These are defined as competing interests and desires (i.e., politics), perceptions that resource acquisition or loss is inequitable, and procedural policies that are deemed to be restrictive or unclear and that contribute to confusion or delay (Bell, 1992; Griffin, 1999).

Each of these root causes easily combines with others to create multifaceted and complex amalgams of conflict. The job seeker, job developer, and employment specialist can diagnose and potentially anticipate conflict by giving some thought to the planning of team membership, communication strategies, and resource availability prior to engaging in the job search. And when forethought fails to achieve a smooth transition to work, acknowledging the existence of a cause for conflict establishes common ground from which to negotiate. Acknowledging conflict is a critical first step in legitimizing conflict and developing a plan for moving onward.

## COMMUNICATION AND CONFLICT MANAGEMENT PLANNING GUIDELINES

Conflict is unavoidable, but is less intense when proper approaches, such as those detailed here for job development, are applied (Heyman, 1994). Accepting the inevitability of conflict and the ongoing necessity for negotiating reinforces the application of efficacious communication and situational management skills. The following guidelines are helpful.

1. *Anticipate reactions.* Talk to others in confidence, recall past experiences, and construct a variety of possible scenarios that address the issues. This creates positive and generative conversation resulting in the promulgation of possible solutions.

2. *Anticipate the greatest point of resistance.* Typically there exists a key issue or a proximate cause for the conflict. Often it is camouflaged by other related items or hidden agendas. Identify the most critical point and address it without becoming distracted by minor points.

3. *Determine the best time and place.* If the individual(s) representing the main point of contention respects power, it may be best to hold the meeting in an environment symbolic of authority, such as the board room, the family home, or agency headquarters. If the threat of authority will flare tempers, choose a more neutral arena. Consider the time of day, week, or month to address the issue. If the conflict is with a family member, it is better not to schedule the meeting during his or her work hours. Be smart and accommodating. The goal is to minimize conflict, not to wield power. Also, make certain to schedule the meeting(s) at a time when stress levels are lowest and when attentions can be focused.

4. *What's in it for them?* Can the other party's needs be satisfied? Are his or her needs (motivations) known? Consider what the target behavior is communicating and what unmet needs have reinforced this conflict. Consider what the bargaining chips are and anticipate that a solution to the current demands may be unattainable. Have a Plan B.

5. *Outline key points and phrases.* Do not stoically recite a rehearsed speech. Problem solving and listening benefit from a certain level of spontaneity. But finding precise words and descriptors to help ferret out information and making key points defines intelligent negotiation. Not everyone thinks quickly or wisely in the heat of conflict; relying on a few key points and phrases can reduce the negotiator's stress and serve to redirect meandering arguments.

Another tactic to utilize in negotiation and in conflict management circumstances is active listening. Applying the following points illustrates a commitment to finding a reasonable resolution to a situation. Negotiators should be fully committed to the process and not simply use these tools to appear empathetic. Insincerity is, by nature, difficult to conceal for long, and when stakeholders recognize efforts as disingenuous, the conflict may reappear even stronger than before.

## Active Listening

Active listening is a technique employed during conversation and negotiation wherein the receiver of information shows that he or she is engaged, concerned, and seeking clarity from the speaker. Active listening creates an atmosphere of caring about both the conversation and the parties involved.

1. *Provide acknowledgment during the conversation.* (Uh-huh; No kidding; Yes, I understand.)

2. *Offer periods of silence.* (Being silent encourages others to expand and explain in greater detail. Silence helps to slow the pace of the conversation, removes the hint of interrogation common to problem-solving sessions, and reduces stress.)

3. *Ask questions.* (Wait for a natural break and ask questions that probe more deeply into the issue. Ask questions that help reveal important issues for the speaker.)

4. *Paraphrase for clarity.* (Restate what you have heard, without interpretation. This augments the clarification process and hones the issues to one or two key concerns [Griffin, 1999; Scholtes, 1988].)

Applying these strategies necessitates an ongoing analysis of the conflict while avoiding reaction or criticism. This is a most difficult task for any engaged negotiator, and the following structure may help.

## Avoiding Destructive Criticism

- Do not act or react while angry.

- Focus on the behavior in the conflict, not on the personalities.

- Use neutral language. Do not generalize with phrases such as, "You always..."

- Indicate a commitment to resolution and give hope for a positive outcome.

- Anticipate as much of the conversation and salient points as possible beforehand.

Being able to answer a few probing questions will help structure the interaction of negotiation and identify the source of the conflicts. The answers often point to personal—that is, negotiator—behaviors that contribute to the conflict. Entering the discussion knowing where to compromise or what to change increases one's bargaining power, and makes for better negotiators.

1. Are each party's roles understood and respected? How can better understanding be pursued?

2. Are all parties clear on time frames and quality standards? How can greater clarity be achieved?

3. Are potential conflicts confronted and dealt with before they become unmanageable? How can communication improve?

4. Does one particular party compromise too often and feel cheated later?

5. Is adequate time allowed for deep conversation? Would an up-front investment in communicating more clearly save time in the long run?

6. Can the parties work with each other? Is there hope for common ground, or should a different structure be considered?

## CONFLICT MANAGEMENT MYTHS AND QUESTIONS

Myths about conflict inhibit us from using its energy opportunistically. The following myths are commonly accepted as fact.

### Myth: Conflict Is Dysfunctional

Conflict can be quite dysfunctional unless those affected take actions to analyze the message of the conflict. Conflict is a symptom announcing that an important component of the negotiation or problem-solving process is being overlooked, slighted, or discounted. Therefore, conflict is generative: It energizes and challenges people to design new solutions to problems.

### Myth: Conflict Represents a Communication Breakdown

This can certainly be true, but is not universal. Conflict is often the result of perceived injustices, of differing values, and of other stressors poisoning a safe environment where conflict itself is actually acceptable. If other concerns are getting in the way of the communication, the negotiator must analyze the circumstances and resolve or minimize the influence of these other factors. Conflict is communication; the message, however, is not always easily discerned.

### Myth: Ignore Conflict and It Goes Away

Behavior does not go away when ignored. If there is a major conflict, there are major reasons for its existence. Analyzing the conflict is the first step to progress. Because behavior is often the result of strained communication (e.g., no opportunity to share concerns), opening up opportunities to discuss changes or circumstances that created the behavior is important.

### Myth: All Conflicts Can Be Resolved

Believing this diverts the negotiator from the work at hand. People have strongly held beliefs, values, and opinions. The negotiator's job is to respect the other parties, give them the time and tools necessary for problem solving, and direct the focus on the desired outcome and away from the conflict. Still, people who cannot work together can seldom be made to work together. Common ground either has to be established or the negotiation has to be reassigned. If a party has no interest in solving a problem, the negotiation is generally futile.

Accepting that conflict is a part of work and life in general is a meaningful first step that relieves people of the responsibility for the actions of others. Still, negotiators do have a responsibility to manage conflict and focus on the tasks of job development. Conflict is a natural state; most people juggle numerous conflicts at once, continuously. And while taking steps for staying out of conflict in the first place is helpful, it is also unrealistic to expect a complete absence of disagreement in one's life.

## COMMUNICATION AND CONFLICT MANAGEMENT METHODS

There are myriad proven methods for managing conflict arising during negotiations. These tools present a framework of intervention useful in decreasing mixed messages and inaction. Good negotiators and problem solvers seek first to control their own behavior in order to model the behavior desired from others. In preparation for a heated negotiation, consider these elements of problem solving and communication (Griffin, 1999).

1. Realize that when conflict exists, communication may be misinterpreted. Give examples, be specific, and choose words carefully.

2. Understand that the larger the audience, the more likely there will be misunderstanding. Try to communicate one-to-one or in small groups first.

3. Do not assume that everyone involved agrees with the facts as presented. Ask for questions and points of clarification as the issue is discussed.

4. Ask people what other sources or types of information stakeholders need that may help shed light on the topic.

5. Do not assume that written communication is clear or complete. Follow up memos or e-mails with discussions at staff meetings.

6. Keep discussions brief and to the point, but allow for relevant discussion.

7. Invite discussion by asking nonthreatening questions to clarify the issues.

8. Assume that there are many sides to every story.

9. Separate fact from opinion and feelings; act on the facts.

Often it is necessary to give constructive feedback to someone who is in, or is causing, conflict. Anxiety about such encounters stalls the quest for resolution, leading to greater frustration on this person's part because he or she feels ignored or attacked, while others involved also become enraged or dysfunctional due to the dispute-caused delay. Conflict can arise from mistakes made by people in the process of job development, funding designs, logistical support, and policy interpretations, and these must be corrected, sometimes publicly. The following structural framework recognizes arising conflicts and offers avenues for moving onward during difficult negotiations (Heyman, 1994; Scholtes, 1988).

1. *Acknowledge the need for feedback.* Make this a substantive part of all complex negotiations by asking along the way if folks are satisfied with the process, if their concerns are being heard, and if they remain committed to an agreeable solution. Make it clear that mistakes do happen within the cumbersome rehabilitation system, but that the benefit of the doubt should be given to all parties; seldom do people make mistakes on purpose.

2. *Make a practice of giving positive and negative feedback.* Too often, good work and deeds go unrewarded. Recognize publicly and privately the accomplishments of the stakeholders. Building a culture of support allows criticism to seem less negative and corrective, and more supportive and generative. Do point out precisely the issues that need correction, but do not overstate mistakes at the expense of someone's ego and reputation. Everyone makes mistakes, and most people operating in a positive environment will self-correct if given the opportunity to learn from errors.

3. *Time the feedback appropriately.* Make certain that the timing is right for the person(s) to hear the feedback. Do not embarrass others or make examples of people. Be careful not to accidentally slight someone by giving credit to someone else when none is due. Studying personalities and circumstances is critical. Make certain that team efforts are rewarded in team settings. Do not publicly criticize, do not offer correction when tempers are flaring, and do not speak before knowing the facts (Scholtes, 1988).

4. *Follow the rules of giving feedback:*

a.  Describe the issue concretely. Use the following opening sequence structure:

When you…

I feel…

Because I…

(Pause and discuss briefly)

I would like you to…

Because…

What do you think?

Using this structure, the following discussion might take place between one stakeholder and the negotiator in a private space:

> *When you* come unprepared with the funding information for Joe's job development team meetings *I feel* disappointed *because I* need you to share this vital information on his funding status. (Pause for brief discussion). *I would like you to* bring the correct Medicaid, VR, and Workforce Center funding information to next week's meeting *because* I value your knowledge of these systems and your recommendations for Joe's career. *What do you think?*

b.  *Do not use labels.* Simply, do not characterize individuals or their behavior as immature or unprofessional or egotistical. Describe the behavior but do not malign the person. Instead of saying, "Failing to bring the funding policies to the meeting shows how irresponsible you are," say, "You did not bring the data needed for the meeting."

c.  *Do not exaggerate.* In anger and haste, issues are sometimes overstated. Such actions only increase emotion. Instead of saying, "You *always* forget the proper materials for these meetings," simply state the concern: "This is the second meeting without the required information."

d.  *Do not judge the person.* Bad bosses sometime ridicule personnel, asking rhetorical questions such as, "Why were you late? Out at the bars again last night?" A good problem solver lowers anxiety a bit by restating the concern in a more somber tone. "Your work quality is typically quite good. I am concerned, though, by the lack of funding information for the meeting."

e.  *Speak for yourself.* Avoid the temptation to make the discussion someone else's issue. Do not say, "Well, *the team* is really concerned by your inattention to the funding details." This outnumbers the person and heightens emotion. Instead, take responsibility for your duties as the negotiator: "*I* am quite concerned about not having the facts and figures."

f.  *Speak first about yourself.* Maintain focus on the behavior and its impact on the negotiator. At first blush this seems egocentric, but it demonstrates the vital role the person plays as a member of the job development team. If *you* statements are used, the other person becomes defensive. By starting with the *I* statement by saying, "I am disappointed when you do not bring the necessary information for the meeting," the negotiator is offering honest concerns and not speculation. If a problem solver uses a *you* statement and says "You rarely bring the proper information to meetings," the other person is put on the defensive because the statement is confrontational.

g.  *Use statements, not questions.* "How many more times do you plan to forget the vital information for this meeting?" is quite different from, "I am disappointed when you don't bring the information requested." This statement puts responsibility for a specific instance of behavior on the errant stakeholder. Asking someone how many more times they might misbehave is an invitation to an argument full of excuses, blaming, and rationalization.

h. *Focus on the facts.* Do not present opinions regarding the consequences or causes of the behavior. Discuss only what is known to be true (i.e., the funding data were not delivered to the team).

i. *Help people hear the positives.* Unfortunately, many individuals are so unaccustomed to hearing compliments that they often shrug them off with an "Oh, it was nothing, really" statement. Be persistent and drive home the fact that the team really does pay attention and does value the accomplishments of everyone. Ask individuals and job development team members frequently about why they think the process worked and how they might want to change it next time. Ask for ideas for upcoming job development situations. Help people see the value in this difficult work.

Negotiators also need to know how to take feedback if they are going to be giving it in an adaptive teamwork culture. Few of us are reinforced for our listening skills. Many students take speech class in school and participate in show-and-tell. Few ever take a listening class and fewer still participate in show-and-listen. However, one of the most frequently cited skills for success is listening. On the job, the average manager is expected to talk 35% of the time, write 9% of the time, read 16% of the time, and listen a full 40% of the time (Scholtes, 1988; Senge, Ross, Smith, Roberts, & Kleiner, 1994). Practice listening following these basic steps:

a. *Breathe deeply.* This is a traditional technique used to slow down and relax.

b. *Listen carefully.* Instead of anticipating the gap to be filled with a response, listen until the speaker finishes. Do not pretend to be listening while constructing a studied response.

c. *Seek clarity.* Ask for specific examples of the behavior or issue that concerns the other person.

d. *Recognize the information.* Restate the information to illustrate to the speaker that the meaning is understood. This launches the finding-common-ground portion of the exercise; it creates common language about the issue.

e. *Accept valid points.* Agree with what is known to be true or possible. Accept others' interpretation of the issue. Accepting this interpretation furthers the development of common ground, but it does not signal agreement with their interpretation. Do not challenge the interpretation at this stage; listen and slow down the communication process. This is not the time to react or to negate the interpretation. Communication and understanding is not a contest; do not compromise the livelihoods and needs of others by trying to prevail at an event that has no winners.

f. *Agree on next steps.* Finding closure is what many people desire after receiving feedback. Perhaps there is need for behavior change; perhaps there is a need for an assignment that brings better data to the decision-making process; or perhaps the criticism is unfounded or based on a unique occurrence. Take some time to consider the comments. Assume that confidences will be kept. Seek a solution for all stakeholders (Scholtes, 1988).

Once these feedback skills are learned, several negotiation and problem-solving methods can be effectively implemented.

## Conflict Management Method 1: Competition (Win–Lose)

Linear problem-solving approaches teach the win–lose orientation. The process is socially reinforced by the belief in One Authority, One Boss, One Right Way, and One Correct Answer. This is the essence of the traditional educational system that encourages competition, assigns grades, draws little distinction between collaboration and cheating, and enforces an either-or orientation to the world (Kohn, 1993). However, there are times when the win–lose scenario makes sense and should be used. For example,

- When quick action is required, such as when a deadline is very short and salvaging any shred of success means taking action or when someone may be harmed by delay. For example, a part-time job may be accepted with a desired employer to get one's foot in the door at the start of a career, rather than accepting a full-time undesirable job.

- When unpopular changes must occur, such as when new billing regulations are required of agencies. They may not agree, but if the paperwork is not submitted, no matter how legitimate the argument, the doors will close.

## Conflict Management Method 2: Accommodation (Lose–Win)

Savvy negotiators know that giving in on some issues will grant political power useful in more important debates later. This strategy is used

- When preserving relationships matter, such as when two collaborators approach the same employer. If the job developer and the local VR counselor are in conflict over the same customer, one party may decide that the relationship is too important to jeopardize and back off the situation. This represents an example of invoking the Shadow of the Future (Fisher & Ury, 1991).

- When seeking Growth from Others, by demonstrating cooperation and graceful losing to a team that is becoming increasing insular or competitive.

- When setting the Stage for Reason, such as when the work culture becomes so concerned with winning that ethics and values take a back seat to common courtesy. Giving up power is a strong signal that there is sometimes a greater good.

## Conflict Management Method 3: Avoidance (Lose–Lose)

While it is best not to ignore difficult negotiations or behavioral conflicts, there are times when avoiding a situation pays off. For instance, a situation arose in which a young woman wanted a job in a local company. The family feared for their daughter's safety and refused to allow her to work. The state reacted by advocating for the daughter's rights as an adult and by reminding the family that the purpose of funding was to emancipate people with disabilities. An impasse was reached, and after 6 months of cooling off and subtle education, the family came to support their daughter's wishes. Avoidance, or the lose–lose approach, may be triggered

- When both parties see the issue as minor. If the circumstance is minor, do not feel pressured to resolve it. Attention sometimes increases tension. Many problems do work themselves out over time by becoming irrelevant. Also, people are smart; most can solve their own problems if the environment allows risk taking and honesty.

- When no one will gain from resolution. There are times when people simply agree to disagree and move on. Disagreement does not mean one party is right and the other is wrong. Just as easily, both could be wrong or both could be right.

- When cooling-off time is needed. The situation may simply have to play itself out and opportunities for moving forward may be lost. If the circumstance is not critical, it may be better to pull away from the conflict and let the calming influence of time take control.

## Conflict Management Method 4: Compromise (Win–Lose, Win–Lose)

Compromise is not always the best method for problem solving; for example, when it weakens the morale of teams and renders an organization useless in pursuit of its mission. However, the consequences of compromise are not usually so dire. For example, a young woman sought to get her driver's license in order to get to and from work, and around town, independently. The state case manager argued that this person's driving posed a safety risk to herself and the community. A compromise was reached by creating an adaptive driving curriculum with the assistance of a local, certified instructor. After passing the class and the state driving test, the individual was free to purchase her first car. Compromise is commonly used

- When there is a need for agreement and both parties have equal power. In this case a tug of war can dominate, but such circumstances are not productive. If two people of equal standing are deadlocked, progress stops. Compromise is needed to jump-start the work effort once again.

- When common ground is needed to meet mutual goals. Employers need employees and people with disabilities need jobs. Skilled negotiation makes common sense visible and understandable. In CE the employer is asked to voluntarily reconfigure hiring and production methods, and job seekers and job developers are asked to create job accommodations and training methods that mesh with the company's culture, quality, and production expectations.

## Conflict Management Method 5: Collaboration (Win–Win)

This strategy is a cliché of sorts, but for those negotiators who practice it, the future is open to countless opportunities. Collaboration is the essence of the modern organization. It is the underpinning of healthy companies and communities. It is the ongoing result of interdependence. Recently, for example, the authors flew overseas to work. Starting on a commuter flight to a hub airport, they boarded a partner airline to the coast, and then boarded another flight to the destination. Only one ticket was purchased by each passenger. Three competing airlines collaborated by linking their routes. Instead of two airlines losing and one winning the fare, they shared the fare and thereby all generated income. Collaboration, or the win–win approach, is used to

- Preserve important relationships. The challenge of collaboration is slowing down in order to speed up. Collaboration takes time and practice, but working together makes for strong and successful alliances. Many community rehabilitation programs and local VR offices have strong working relationships even though they could as easily compete with one another for job placements. Both succeed by sharing resources and talent.

- Do more with less. There is strength in numbers, and there is profit in sharing resources. By working together, less work falls on each individual, and costs are spread across various entities. People are taught as children to compete; collaborative strategy, however, deemphasizes individual success while glorifying the team. Reducing competition reduces conflict (Kohn, 1993).

- Do more with more. Collaboration means sharing resources. Common property reduces political intrigue, backstabbing, and petty arguments. It also weeds out those who do not contribute to the development of the outcome. By working together in a job development situation, for instance, each contributor saves money and time because the effort is spread across several partners, such as SSA, the state developmental disability or mental health systems, VR, or the local workforce center. Working together multiplies the level of intellect applied to the situation as well, and sharing success generates excitement and security that promotes further collaborations.

## MANAGING THE IMPACT OF CHANGE

As the saying goes, people love change, but they hate being changed. Asking employers to hire people with disabilities is regularly greeted with reluctance because it is perceived as an imposed change. Interest-based negotiation minimizes the anxiety spawned by change by welcoming the creation of new circumstances through the promise of mutual benefit. Unfortunately, the change process is not always well managed by the job seeker or the job developer, so the promised benefits are never realized. Managing change and conflict is vital to CE negotiation.

By understanding the change process, the job developer and job seeker shape communication to support all stakeholders by using language that deflects aggression and by timing each negotiation point for safe transition through the process. The fallout from change is somewhat predictable and has been studied exhaustively (Floyd & Wooldridge, 1996; Friedman, 2005; Gilbert, 1978; Mintzberg, 1989; Wycoff, 1995). Reactions to change compare to the grieving process and the skilled negotiator knows to support the loss of status quo conditions and the assimilation of new circumstances. A model representing the stages of the change process (see Figure 7.1) is helpful in managing the changes that the employment of people with significant disabilities represents to the many stakeholders.

The employment negotiation process involves a host of stakeholders, each affected by the process. Managing both the individuals' reactions to change and the group's combined behaviors is important. The negotiation process in Figure 7.1 begins with a stakeholder in a state of relative contentment: the world is pretty much as it was the day before. A new idea or situation enters the picture pushing the person, or team, into a denial state. Depending upon the severity of the change, anger may or may not occur. Anger takes a great deal of energy to sustain, so movement towards a depressive stage results. Depression is taxing and disorienting as well, however, so over time, the individual, or team, moves on to confusion. This stage is marked by acceptance that things will not remain as they have in the past and the realization that the individual or team is not equipped with the tools or strategies needed to adapt. At the point of confusion comes acceptance and willingness to learn new approaches. Eventually, the newness wears off and becomes status quo. From this point contentment either returns, or the individual or team becomes so energized by the new circumstance that they proselytize its acceptance to others (Kübler-Ross, 1997; Weisbord & Janoff, 1995).

Employers who have not been exposed to hiring people with disabilities experience this change pattern predictably. A first meeting between a job seeker, a job developer, and an employer might yield the following transcript. (In the transcript, the change stages of the employer appear in parentheses.)

| | |
|---|---|
| Job Seeker: | Thank you for meeting with us. |
| Employer: | My pleasure. What can I do for you two? (Contentment) |
| Job Seeker: | As I mentioned at the Kiwanis meeting, I am looking for a job in aviation, and I brought along my career counselor to explain her role in the process. |

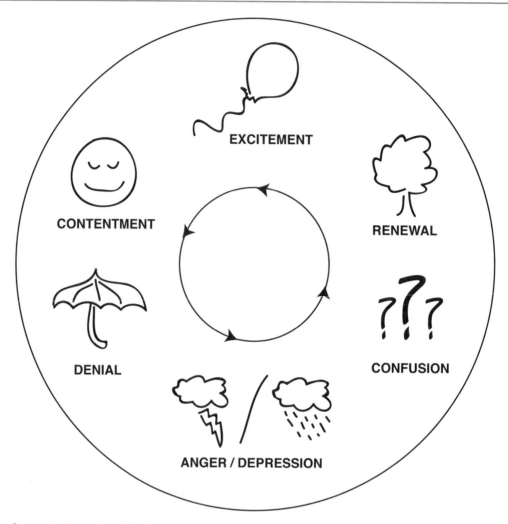

**Figure 7.1.** Communication and conflict. *Sources:* Kübler-Ross (1997); Weisbord & Janoff (1995).

| | |
|---|---|
| Job Developer: | Briefly, my job is to match qualified workers with employers. Since John is interested in aviation and weather prediction, we naturally thought the municipal airport would be a great place to begin our analysis of employment possibilities. |
| Employer: | I see. I can tell you that our organization believes strongly in diversity. We have a varied and productive workforce here. (Contentment) |
| Job Developer: | Terrific. As John mentioned to you, he is interested in working with the meteorologists and air traffic controllers here at the airport. Perhaps we could start there with a brief tour and see if we can get some ideas. Of course, we're not sure this is the right match for either you or John; it's just a starting point to research the field of aviation. |
| Employer: | Well, right now we don't have any jobs open for people with disabilities. If we did, we would have been seeking out applicants from one of the local agencies. Of course, this is a very hectic operation; if a crisis occurs, it could mean life and death, so we have very high standards for all employees. (Denial) |
| Job Seeker: | I was thinking that I could print out updated weather maps and take them to the controllers; maybe take readings off the instruments for the meteorologists. I plan to enroll in the meteorology class over in |

Helena if there is a job available; it's a course that requires work-applied study.

Employer:        Well, like I said, I am afraid the liability of hiring someone with a disability prevents us from considering it right now. (Denial)

Job Developer:   A lot of the employers we work with feel this way at first, but they find that there is rarely a liability issue, and we can assist in streamlining work processes and actually improve operations. We've worked with over 50 local employers, creating new positions that are benefiting their companies.

Employer:        As I said, we have a diverse workforce. We are in full compliance with all laws, including the ADA. Our airport is completely accessible. Since you use a wheelchair, John, I'll bet you found it easy to get around throughout our building. Still, we just don't have any jobs open right now. (Anger)

Job Developer:   I certainly understand that. And we're not asking for a job. I should have been clearer. We'd just like a tour to get some career planning ideas.

Employer:        I understand. You have to understand also that being overseen by a board of directors, I am not at liberty to just create jobs and hire people simply because it might feel good to do so. (Depression)

Job Seeker:      I wouldn't want you to hire me unless there is real work to be done.

Employer:        Well, tell me how the process works. (Confusion)

Job Developer:   Basically, we do an analysis of the tasks people are performing that hold an interest for John. We look for bottlenecks, missed opportunities that might enhance customer service, and we look for opportunities to introduce new tasks or equipment that improve profitability or internal operations. I have some examples here on this fact sheet I'll leave with you.

Employer:        Well, I am pretty busy today. (Renewal)

Job Seeker:      Perhaps we can schedule time for a tour next week?

Employer:        Certainly. (Renewal)

Avoiding disputes at several junctures by gently pulling the employer through the stages allowed the job developer and job seeker to move the negotiation along. Following this template not only allows the negotiator to offer support to the stakeholder(s) as needed, but also provides a check on his or her own behavior and serves as a reminder not to react negatively to the natural stages of denial and anger that derail complex conversations.

This negotiation process can be used with all stakeholders, including funders, policy makers, case management staff, residential providers, family members, school principals, transportation vendors, co-workers, and others. The power of the process is in its linearity, which offers predictable milestones along negotiation's rutted path. Of course, as with any tool or device, practice and adaptation are essential to guide the unpredictable nature of some human interactions. The negotiation process reduces stress, provides logical direction, and restores some predictability to even the most heated debate.

## CONCLUSION

The voluntary negotiation employers engage in with job seekers and employment specialists is a manageable process. There is no fail-safe approach for negotiation, but good self-management skills, strong values, open communication, a focus on accomplishment and outcomes, and a reputation for honesty contribute to functional problem solving. Developing these critical professional characteristics contribute to high performance and inventive, mutually beneficial job development.

## REFERENCES

Americans with Disabilities Act of 1990, PL 101-336, 42 U.S.C. §§ 12101 *et seq.*

Aronson, E. (1995). *The social animal.* New York: W.H. Freeman Company.

Bell, G.M. (1992). *Getting things done when you are not in charge.* San Francisco: Berrett-Koehler Publishers.

Callahan, M., & Garner, B. (1997). *Keys to the workplace: Skills and supports for people with disabilities.* Baltimore: Paul H. Brookes Publishing Co.

Cialdini, R. (1993). *Influence: The psychology of persuasion.* New York: William Morrow & Company.

Fisher, R., & Ury, W. (1991). *Getting to yes: Negotiating agreement without giving in.* New York: Penguin Publishers.

Floyd, S., & Wooldridge, B. (1996). *The strategic middle manager: How to create and sustain competitive advantage.* San Francisco: Jossey-Bass.

Friedman, T.L. (2005). *The world is flat: A brief history of the twenty-first century.* New York: Farrar, Straus & Giroux.

Gardner, H. (1983). *Frames of mind: The theory of multiple intelligences.* New York: Basic Books.

Gilbert, T.F. (1978). *Human competence: Engineering worthy performance.* New York: McGraw-Hill.

Griffin, C.C. (1999). *Working better, working smarter: Building responsive rehabilitation programs.* St. Augustine, FL: TRN Press.

Grinder, J., & Bandler, R. (1979). *Frogs into princes.* Salt Lake City, UT: Real People Press.

Hagner, D. (2000). *Coffee breaks and birthday cakes: Evaluating workplace cultures to develop natural supports for employees with disabilities.* St. Augustine: TRN Press.

Heyman, R. (1994). *Why didn't you say that in the first place?* San Francisco: Jossey-Bass.

Kohn, A. (1993). *Punished by rewards.* New York: Houghton Mifflin.

Kübler-Ross, E. (1997). *On death and dying.* New York: Touchstone.

Mank, D.M., Cioffi, A., & Yovanoff, P. (1997). Patterns of support for employees with severe disabilities. *Mental Retardation, 35,* 433–447.

McKinsey & Company. (2001). *Knowledge unplugged: The McKinsey & Company global survey on knowledge management.* Bath, England: Author.

Mehrabian, A., & Ferris, S.R. (1967). Inference of attitudes from nonverbal communication in two channels. *Journal of Consulting Psychology, 31,* 248–252.

Mintzberg, H. (1989). *Mintzberg on management.* New York: Free Press.

Scholtes, P. (1988). *The team handbook: How to use teams to improve quality.* Madison, WI: Joiner Associates.

Senge, P., Ross, R., Smith, B., Roberts, C., & Kleiner, A. (1994). *The fifth discipline fieldbook: Strategies and tools for building a learning organization.* New York: Doubleday.

Shapiro, R., & Jankowski, M. (1998). *The power of nice.* New York: John Wiley & Sons.

Unger, D., Kregel, J., Wehman, P., & Brooke, V. (2002). *Employer's view of workplace supports: Virginia Commonwealth University's Charter Business Roundtable's national study of employer's experiences with workers with disabilities.* Richmond: Virginia Commonwealth University, Rehabilitation Research and Training Center on Workplace Supports.

Weisbord, M., & Janoff, S. (1995). *Future search: An action guide to finding common ground in organizations and communities.* San Francisco: Berrett-Koehler Publishers.

Workforce Investment Act of 1998, PL 105-220, 29 U.S.C. §§ 794 *et seq.*

Wycoff, J. (1995). *Transformation thinking.* New York: Berkely Books.

# 8 Job Carving

## Creating Jobs that Fit an Individual's Ideal Conditions of Employment and Benefit the Workplace

*Tammara Geary, Cary Griffin, and David Hammis*

Susanna is a 28-year-old woman with severe mental retardation and a full-scale IQ of 38. She is referred for vocational evaluation, with the referral noting concerns about her ability to work in the community. She recently lost a supported employment (SE) job after 2 years. Records indicate ongoing performance issues at the job and ongoing support visits required every other day. The SE staff at Carter Vocational Options have been trying to determine if there are any good jobs or industries for her. Her history demonstrates a significant lack of success in both school and work. She left school without completing her special education certificate. Records indicate she was challenging in the classroom, often refusing to participate. There were several serious behavioral outbursts in school. Behavioral management plans were only mildly successful. She attended the Carter Vocational Training Center (CVTC) for 6 years, working on various contracts. Records indicate that she was often unwilling to work. Her production rate was 15%. She was frequently off task and would not remain in her work area.

She presents well, has good hygiene, and is neatly dressed. She is pleasant and talkative but has been unable to adequately describe past work experiences. She admits that she did not like school, the CVTC, or her job. Susanna says she wants a job but cannot identify a job she wants. She indicates that she likes to go outside. She appears confused by many questions, is unable to sequence events, and frequently responds in ways that seemed irrelevant to the question. Her mother and sister have been providing support. Evaluation and testing revealed good matching skills, simple counting skills, basic letter recognition, minimal word recognition, and absent reading. She is frequently off task but is generally cooperative. She frequently asks to go outside or just gets up to go. She is unable to follow even simple directions and her attention span does not allow completion of all tests. In general, Susanna appears to need constant redirection. In this evaluator's opinion, she has a limited potential for success in the community workforce without regular supervision. This evaluator would recommend some sort of arrangement where there is constant supervision and direction. Perhaps one of CVTC's lawn crews would be appropriate, given her demonstrated desire to go outside.

Susanna's report and history are not all that unusual. In working with over 200 employment sites across the country, and through years of direct experience serving people with disabilities, we have encountered numerous job seekers who, though unique individuals, have had experiences with similar issues and recommendations. Needless to say, community employment providers are not lining up to serve people with such limited recommendations and perceived ability and whose work skills and potential are not readily apparent. It is likely that readers are at least somewhat familiar with this concept.

We have often been asked to help providers figure out how to serve many individuals who present real or perceived work challenges. In the words of one site director, "We just can't figure out how to serve him, and we haven't done a good job of it." For many people, the solution lies in job carving, with its foundation in the discovery, planning, and job development processes.

Job carving is not new; the concept has been around for many years. It is probably safe to say, however, that it is underutilized as a strategy for creating well-fitting jobs for people with disabilities while providing benefit to the workplace.

Job carving is a process of analyzing the duties performed in a given job, or the duties of several different jobs, to identify discrete tasks that could be combined to create a job that meets the specific aspirations and support needs of an individual (Griffin & Sherron, 2006) while meeting the needs of the business. Job carving seeks to maximize an individual's gifts, skills, interests, and contributions to a workplace and is therefore distinctly different from traditional approaches to developing jobs for individuals, in which the focus is on the labor market (Griffin & Hammis, 2003a). Here the approach has been to look at the local job market, determine what businesses and jobs exist, and provide training and other strategies with the goal of making the individual fit the job. Based on the continuing high unemployment rates of people with disabilities, it is clear this approach has not been successful. Furthermore, years of using a labor market–driven approach to job development has not produced much variety in the types of jobs secured by people with disabilities, particularly those with developmental disabilities. There is a high incidence of placement in stereotypical jobs, such as janitorial, food service, retail, stocking, greeting, grocery bagging, laundry, and hotel housekeeping. These jobs are in industries with which providers are familiar and are not necessarily ones that represent the best fit for an individual.

Carving jobs expands opportunity through true customization, selecting essential tasks performed in a workplace to create a job that contributes critical functions to the workplace and at the same time is highly focused on the individual's abilities, interests, skills, preferences, and general support needs. With skillful carving, the jobs that are created also create profit for the business.

## THE UTILITY OF JOB CARVING

Job carving is useful in a variety of situations. Its ultimate utility, however, is in creating the right employment situation for people with disabilities. Some people receiving Temporary Assistance for Needy Families, and others considered hard to serve, will likely find it very difficult to find a form-fitting job in the community. Carving allows a person who wants to work, but who is unlikely to find an existing job and description of duties that he or she can successfully perform, to create a job in which he or she can be successful.

While it is perfectly appropriate to carve a full-time job, carving can be an ideal strategy for people who may be seeking part-time employment. Although the provider should always strive to meet the individual's goals for hours of work per week, there are many reasons a person may need to limit hours to part time. Physical disability, psychiatric illness, intellectual capacity, medical fragility, available supports, and choice represent some of those reasons (Griffin & Winter, 1988).

Further, job carving allows an individual to maximize contribution, something that should be at the heart of any job search or creation effort, as well as integral to small business development. Contribution refers to any individual's specific sets of skills (existing and potential), personality traits, and potential assets that are *exploitable resources* for an employer (Callahan & Garner, 1997; Griffin & Hammis, 2003b). In this case, the term *exploitable* refers to usable or profitable resources and should not be mistaken to refer to the more negative connotations of the word, that is, gullible or easy to take advantage of. The more exploitable resources a person has, the more marketable they are. Commonly, existing or off-the-shelf jobs do not include a set of tasks that take advantage of an individual's contributions. They just don't fit an individual very well. Job carving allows a person to work in jobs that fit; ones that maximize use of his or her unique resources and contributions, offering clear advantages for both the job seeker and the employer. It is important to note that exploitable resources are not only limited to skills, but also include personality, relationships, tools, or other qualities that create profit or enhance the workplace.

## Considering Susanna

Susanna spent several years in a sheltered workshop doing whatever was assigned to her, based on whatever contract work was in house. Until recently, she spent 2 years in SE working in a laundry room at a local hotel, requiring high levels of ongoing support for the duration. She was never really good at the job. She made lots of mistakes, such as mixing up sheets and towels and folding improperly. She was frequently late coming back from breaks, and often said she got lost in the back hallways of the hotel. Nonetheless, she liked having a job and getting a paycheck. Co-workers and supervisors liked her, saying she was pleasant and fit in well, but they were increasingly irritated by her slow pace, mistakes, and inconsistency. She was getting more frustrated, too, but continued to go to work. She finally admitted that she did not really like the job at about the same time her supervisor let her go.

Susanna; her mother and sister; a few friends; various support staff, including her case manager, employment consultant, and a few additional staff from the employment provider organization formed a team to learn more about Susanna with hopes of creating or carving a job that fit her. Through the discovery and planning process, several of Susanna's attributes were identified and developed. It turns out Susanna had been taking care of people's pets in the neighborhood for a few years. Her mother or sister help her go in and out of houses, but Susanna has learned to walk the dogs, feed them, clean up accidents, bathe and brush them out, and she frequently performs those tasks on her own for her neighbors shortly before they return from trips. She also takes care of cats and changes litter boxes. Before the owner's return, she vacuums and cleans up with help from her sister or mother. Her mom and sister both agreed that Susanna could probably do this herself, but they just wanted to make sure everything gets done and the house gets locked.

She walks the dogs in the park next to her neighborhood. As a result, she is fairly well known in her small community, and she often stops to chat with other dog walkers and moms watching their kids at the playground. People seem to enjoy her. Despite the obvious fact that she is essentially running a small business already, and that she would like to keep taking care of her neighbors' animals, she doesn't want that to become a regular obligation. She'd rather work part time for somebody else and continue to enjoy her neighbors' animals on her own time. As part of her job-planning process, she starts to volunteer for a dog rescue and adoption group a few evenings and most Saturdays. She has an easy way with the animals and is able to work with even the most distressed and neglected among them. She is well liked and pretty good at drawing people in to take a look at the animals on Adoption Saturdays. After a while, Susanna believes that she would like to work for a veterinarian who offers some additional services, such as boarding, daycare, and grooming.

Take a few minutes and consider this: What are Susanna's exploitable resources? Remember to consider not only her existing, but also her potential, exploitable resources.

## Some of Susanna's Exploitable Resources

- Dog and cat care skills (e.g., walking, feeding, bathing, drying, brushing, playing with, and cleaning up after dogs and cats) (existing)

- Other skills may include additional grooming (e.g., hair trims, nails, ears, teeth) and other care-related tasks (potential)

- Caring for other types of animals (potential)

- Ease with dogs and cats, including injured and distressed ones (existing)

- Provides thorough and extra services (e.g., clean-up and bathing when she cares for animals) (existing)

- Is friendly, chatty (but not too much so), and well liked (existing)

- Can draw people in and attract customers (existing)

- May be able to purchase some tools for her job (potential)

- Network of people with pets (e.g., her neighbors, the dog rescue shelter) (existing)

This is just a start to a list of existing and potential exploitable resources. There are probably more. It is also important to note that many of these attributes, both existing and potential, may require on-the-job training and further development to solidify particular contributions. It is, therefore, critical to consider training and support strategies in the process of creating jobs based on exploitable resources. The identification of contributions and exploitable resources is the foundation of solid job carving.

Recall that solid carving creates profit for the employer. Now take a moment to consider how Susanna's contributions would benefit a veterinary business.

## Veterinary Business Benefits from Employing Susanna

Here are just a few ways that a veterinary business might profit from employing Susanna.

- Susanna loves to work with dogs and cats and is motivated by the work

- She is motivated to do little extras that enhance customer service

- She has quite a few existing skills and the potential to develop several others

- She likes to do a variety of tasks

- She could assume responsibility for specific billable services (e.g., bathing, caring for boarded animals, playing with and walking boarded animals), allowing the business to maximize volume and profit

- She could take care of many different support tasks (e.g., preparing exam rooms; retrieving and returning animals to and from crates and delivering them to the groomers and trainers; preparing monthly reminder post card for mailing), which are essential tasks that directly produce revenue

- Susanna is able to draw people in to look at dogs on Adoption Saturdays, so she likely has some natural sales skill that may be put to good use

- Susanna may be a good up-seller, that is, she may be good at getting people to buy little extras (e.g., an extra plaything, a blanket or bed for boarders, a special treat, some gourmet biscuits, collars, toys), which increases business revenue

- She knows many people who trust her with their animals

Susanna will surely bring in many new customers. People she knows will be glad to have their pets go to a place where the pets are familiar and comfortable with staff. New customers are a clear profit to businesses. Susanna's contacts could be particularly valuable to a new veterinary clinic or to one that is expanding or adding services.

## JOB CARVING

As mentioned earlier, job carving is a process of analyzing the duties performed in a given job, or the duties of several different jobs, to identify discrete tasks that could be combined to create a job that meets the specific aspirations and support needs of an individual (Griffin & Sherron, 2006). While the carving is focused on creating a collection of tasks that suits the individual, the selected tasks and negotiation with the employer ensure that the business benefits as well.

Many use the terms *job carving* and *job creation* interchangeably, while others draw distinctions between the two (Geary, Griffin, & Hammis, 2005). For the purposes of this book, the terms are used interchangeably to refer to the host of carving, creation, negotiation, and self-employment development strategies that result in a customized employment outcome.

## What Is Job Carving?

Job carving is the process of sectioning out a portion of an existing job and creating a new one that allows the worker to contribute his or her strengths to the workplace and perform a job he or she likes and desires (Callahan, McLoughlin, & Garner, 1987; Geary, Griffin, & Hammis, 2005). While a carved job has to meet the needs of the employer, the carving should be centered on the person and the goals set forth in the individual's employment plan.

There are many examples of job carving, and each situation is different. It is critical to be observant, sensitive, thoughtful, and strategic when figuring out, planning, and negotiating a job carve. The following is an example that highlights essential cultural considerations and a few strategies used to carve the position.

## Marjorie's Experience

Marjorie, a young transition-age woman, wanted to work at a huge distribution center. She lived in an area where the majority of residents worked either at the center or at a very large factory down the road. Essentially all the work in this center involved various shipping tasks. The majority of the workforce did essentially the same task but on products of various sizes. Working from a list provided by supervisors, employees

- Requisitioned items from the various warehouses

- Confirmed the inventory upon arrival

- Packaged and labeled items

- Prepared items for shipping

- Confirmed shipping on all items on the list

In addition, there were substantial work culture routines, including

- Ride sharing

- Taking breaks at the same time

- Taking turns bringing coffee and doughnuts for the crew

- Playing poker and Crazy 8s during down time and breaks

From everything known about Marjorie, it was clear that her limited math and reading skills and the complexity of the requisition forms would make it very difficult for her to master the tasks involving paperwork, including requisitioning items, confirming inventory, and confirming shipments. She would, however, have no problem with the packaging and labeling, and she could master the shipping preparation with a slight modification involving physically stacking boxes a certain way so they matched the order on the mail labeling sheets.

Ultimately, the employment specialist proposed that the packaging, labeling, and shipping tasks be pulled from the overall job description to carve a job to fit Marjorie, and a co-worker who really enjoyed the paperwork part would take on that responsibility. In return, Marjorie would assume responsibility for a portion of her co-worker's packaging tasks.

This was handled delicately to not upset the balance of the strong workplace culture. Restructuring a co-worker's job in order to accommodate somebody can backfire in terms of the individual's acceptance by the team, so it was essential that the employment specialist be thoughtful and observant while negotiating the job carve.

By conducting a thorough job analysis, the employment specialist was able to get a strong sense of all the tasks involved, including the flow of the work and the relationships between team members. By blending in well, she was able to observe the workplace culture. She was able to identify a person, who was clearly valued by the team and supervisor, who saw taking on the paperwork associated with Marjorie's workload as an advantage. The employment specialist did not want to approach the supervisors with a proposal without checking it out with the targeted co-worker, but at the same time, she did not want to ask the co-worker about the plan specifically, out of concern that the co-worker might really jump on the idea, only to have the proposal refused by the supervisors. This could unintentionally create disharmony for her and perhaps the entire unit.

The employment specialist decided it was critical to check this out with the co-worker before approaching the supervisor with a proposal. Realizing it must be done subtly, she asked the co-worker to show her a few steps and help her understand a few details related to the requisition process. As they worked, she started a conversation about the different tasks by commenting on the complexity of the requisition process. The co-worker indicated that she liked that complexity. Within a 5-minute conversation that started with the employment specialist commenting on the relative simplicity of the packaging and labeling, the co-worker revealed a preference for paperwork and a desire to be free of some of the packaging tasks. In general, the employment specialist followed the conversational lead of the co-worker, seizing on nuggets of pertinent information to learn more.

Having a fair level of certainty that the co-worker would be happy with the arrangement, the employment specialist presented a brief proposal to the supervisor suggesting the shifting of job responsibilities as outlined. She noted that she had reason to believe the co-worker would like the change in responsibilities, but she did not want to pursue it if it was not desirable to the co-worker. In addition, the employment specialist highlighted a few potential benefits of the arrangement, including potential increase in efficiency, with Marjorie and the co-worker focused on specific tasks while essentially collaborating to complete two requisition lists. With less shifting of focus and tasks, it seemed likely that each could be more efficient, not just in terms of speed, but also in terms of quality. Also, the co-worker was very good at the requisitioning and shipping confirmation. Her low error rate, self-direction, and attention to detail were valued by everyone in the unit. The supervisor identified another benefit. He had heard rumors that this person was "burnt out" and was seriously considering quitting. He did not want to lose her and saw this as a valuable way to keep her.

Marjorie was hired in the carved job that met her needs, the co-worker benefited with a carved job that met her needs, and the distribution center benefited with two dedicated, long-term employees, increased efficiency, and quality. The team concept was subsequently used with other pairs of employees as a strategy to maintain interest, focus, and quality. Marjorie never became a decent poker player, so her co-workers pair up with her for games and give her a pair of dark glasses to help her "master the bluff."

## JOB CREATION

Whereas job creation or negotiation is slightly different from job carving, both techniques are based in the same concept, that is, creating a job that is consistent with the individual's desires and that allows the individual to contribute his talents and strengths to benefit the workplace.

The subtle difference: job creation or negotiation pulls a variety of tasks together from several existing jobs to create a position tailored to the individual. (Callahan, McLoughlin, & Garner, 1987; Geary, Griffin, & Hammis, 2005) Contrary to popular belief, the job is not assembled from cast-off, unwanted jobs from other workers. Rather, the created job is a collection of tasks that meet the job seeker's objectives (Griffin & Hammis, 2003a).

These tasks can be found throughout a workplace simply by looking for tasks that never get done. Often those tasks remain undone simply because nobody has that task as one of their primary responsibilities, or because those tasks have been added on to an already overloaded job description. Even as a customer, employment specialists or job developers should take note of demand that overwhelms a business's staffing, customer needs that cannot be met, and unnecessary or excessive waits or delays in service (Bissonnette, 1994). It also helps to look at tasks that do not directly produce revenue and take direct revenue producing employees from their roles. For example, a salesperson copying and preparing his or her own information packets takes that person away from making sales calls; a paralegal who does his or her own filing takes that person away from billable client service hours. This example presents an opportunity to carve a separate job handling tire changes.

### Lola's Experience

Lola had not worked for several years after an injury that left her with minimal use of her left arm and hand and a significant tremor in the right. She has since recovered some use of her left arm and hand, and she is making steady progress in her physical therapy. Her right hand tremors occur only with very fine motor work and when fatigued. She has some ongoing mental health issues as well, although she has been doing very well for a few years. In trying to figure out what she wanted to do, she revealed a desire to work in a dental office. She sustained significant injury to her teeth and jaw in her injury, and she identifies the restoration of her teeth as a significant turning point in her recovery. She refers to it as "when I got my smile back." She really liked the idea of working in a dental office.

She wanted to be a dental assistant but physically could not handle the precision required. The discovery and planning process revealed that her first passion was working with the patients, followed by a sincere interest in the tools and instruments used. Observation and job analysis at a local orthodontics office uncovered several tasks consistent with her interests that could be pulled from several people's responsibilities to create a new position.

Initially, the new position combined several tasks from several sources:

- Cleaning the treatment area between patients, sterilizing equipment, and stocking each chairside unit (tasks of the eight orthodontic assistants)

- Greeting and seating patients (tasks of the receptionist)

- Placing the monthly giveaways, such as pens, pencils, and toothbrushes bearing the practice's contact information, in the waiting room and reception desk and calling patients to confirm appointments (tasks of the office desk staff)

The created job allowed her to work in the treatment area, handle the instruments, and have personal contact with each and every patient. Once again, this strategy resulted in mutual gain. Lola got a job customized around her needs and interests. Further, the job holds great significance for her due to her personal experience. The practice benefited because other staff could focus on income-generating activities. The assistants were able to see more patients in a day, the receptionist could focus on booking appointments and answering phones, and the office staff could attend to processing insurance claims, billing, and collections.

After a few months on the job, more tasks were added. Desiring more patient contact, Lola was taught to use the photography equipment and learned what shots the orthodontist wanted to have taken of each patient. Lola now takes the "before" and "after" photographs of each patient. She maintains a wall of photographs of all the "after" shots, and she makes a card for every patient when they get their braces removed. The card has the "before" and "after" shots with a simple note reading, "Congratulations on your new smile!"

Again, job carving and job creation are shades of the same concept, selecting a set of tasks that results in mutual benefit for the employee and the employer. Regardless of where the tasks come from, preparing a brief written proposal outlining the proposed job description and related details, along with the benefit of profit to the business, is a useful exercise (Bissonnette, 1994) that can aid negotiation. Networking, informational interviewing, Internet searches, and other techniques outlined in previous chapters are key to building a good plan.

## CONSIDERATIONS FOR JOB CARVING

For the remainder of this chapter, the terms *job carving* or *job creation* refer to any of the strategies outlined above that result in customized employment. Job carving requires effort, observation, and careful analysis. It is not simply walking into a business with a predetermined set of tasks and starting a negotiation. Successfully carving a job for an individual requires several critical elements.

### Ideal Conditions of Employment

Solid knowledge of the ideal conditions of employment for the individual, including contributions and exploitable resources, environment, work skills, and preferences are outlined earlier in this chapter and in Chapter 2. There are several examples and individual stories that demonstrate how an individual's ideal conditions serve as the foundation for further job customization.

Readers may recall the example of Melinda in Chapter 3. Melinda's story illustrates how the discovery and planning process blend learning from past experiences with new exploration and experience that, along with thoughtful reflection, reveals her ideal conditions of employment. It also shows how these ideal conditions guide conceptualization and investigation of possibilities to create a well-fitting job.

Melinda's vocational profile, following discovery, revealed that she

- Is of transition age

- Is friendly

- Has a strong work ethic

- Resists supervision vigorously

- Orients well and rides the city bus independently after training

- Uses some sign language and minimal verbal language

- Reads and writes a little

- Is very street smart

- Enjoys gardening

- Likes office work

Her ideal conditions of employment are

- Work alone

- Work with others

- Inside work

- Outside work

- Planting/gardening work

- Clerical work

- Wants a workplace bowling team

- Wants to be around wealthy people

- Needs autonomy

- Wants to move around

If traditional testing and evaluation had been used, Melinda would present a contradictory picture. The power of discovery is again illustrated by accepting what the process reveals. In this case, Melinda is as inconsistent as most people are; she enjoys variety, likes being in control, and has a complex personality. She prefers working both outside and inside; working alone and with others. Most of us have complex preferences, but traditional approaches to assessment seem to hold these truths as mutually exclusive. Proper job development and carving demands respect for the complexity of lives.

Melinda's past was critical to further job development. As a special education student, she had several paid and nonpaid work experiences and part-time jobs. She showed an interest in wealth and accepted a job doing clerical tasks, along with some light janitorial work, at a local branch bank. Melinda's resistance to supervision turned out to be more an issue of predictability and personal autonomy. As long as she knew her work schedule and no one singled her out to perform a last-minute task, everything was fine. At the bank, an officer gave her a previously unassigned duty, and Melinda refused, costing her that job. At an insurance agency, she was doing well with filing and copying a few hours a day but lost her job when she loudly protested being asked to make a pot of coffee.

Her ideal conditions of employment slowly became apparent. Melinda relished working but not taking orders because she felt singled out. Perhaps working in a team where everyone does the same jobs or in a setting where work orders are regularly used might modify her behavior. Working in a team-based setting also increases the interesting tasks, thereby lessening the role of a job coach, who again could be considered just another boss giving orders, thus prompting behavioral issues. People with disabilities are often labeled as being frustrated by change, which is a trait characteristic of humans in general. Melinda did not mind change per se; she resisted change that she felt singled her out and showed disrespect for her previously assigned duties. Melinda actually enjoyed, as do most people, a variety of work tasks and challenges.

Prospecting and networking led to the development of a carved position at a city botanical park. Working with a program director there, the employment specialist and Melinda developed a job that involved her working alone weeding plant beds indoors and out, building displays and cutting plant stakes with a team of people in a woodshop, and handling watering and plant relocation with other teams. Other carved duties included assisting the mailroom with bulk-mailing jobs, which advertised educational and theatrical events hosted at the gardens; delivering mail, by herself, across the campus, thereby utilizing her great sense of direction and autonomy; and working in the gift shop, alongside the wealthy patron volunteers who supported the gardens financially and who take great civic pride in this establishment. Later, another task was carved and added to her job: helping a team to set up and break down conference rooms and garden areas where classes, weddings, and special events regularly occurred. Table 8.1 illustrates how Melinda's ideal conditions are satisfied through the carved job.

Over time a co-worker learned that Melinda's interest in wealthy people had an interesting logic about it. She reasoned, silently for a long time, that wealthy people travel and that if she had wealthy friends, perhaps they would invite her along some time. Again, the power of discovery is in accepting the information and not speculating about motivations; if the information is important, its importance will be revealed. Further, although the gardens did not have a bowling team, the money she earned allowed Melinda the opportunity to bowl on a regular basis.

## Job Analysis

Job analysis is the other fundamental piece of finding the right job. It is a detailed study of the job and the workplace. Its purpose is to ensure the best possible job match, through full understanding of the intricacies of the job as they relate to the essential needs and interests of the individual, and as documented in the vocational profile. Poor job analysis and job matching are closely related to job termination (Brooke, Inge, Armstrong, & Wehman, 1997). In order to be useful, the job analysis must be written.

Successful carving requires understanding of the intricacies of a business and its operation. A thorough job analysis examines multiple factors, which are outlined in Chapter 3. Tasks to be carved are found by looking at, among other things, multiple roles, jobs, projects, jobs within jobs, along with efficiencies/inefficiencies, and unmet needs of a business. The details of the job analysis yield the discrete tasks that can be used to carve a job. Committing time to the job analysis provides the access needed to identify and observe what goes on. Carving cannot be successful without this knowledge.

## Social and Natural Supports

Good carving must factor in social and natural supports. Considering natural supports involves not only the social structures of the workplace, but also the various training strategies and elements that already exist in the workplace, which may be used to assist

**Table 8.1.**   Ideal conditions and related elements of carved jobs for Melinda

| Ideal conditions | Related elements of carved job |
| --- | --- |
| Work alone | Weeding<br>Delivering mail |
| Work with others (teams) | Building displays and cutting stakes<br>Watering and relocating plants<br>Bulk mail<br>Gift shop<br>Meeting set-up |
| Inside work | Weeding plants<br>Building displays<br>Cutting stakes<br>Watering plants<br>Preparing bulk mail<br>Delivering mail<br>Working in gift shop<br>Setting up meetings |
| Outside work | Weeding plants<br>Watering plants<br>Relocating plants<br>Delivering mail |
| Planting/gardening work | Weeding plants<br>Watering plants<br>Relocating plants |
| Clerical work | Preparing bulk mail<br>Delivering mail |
| Wants a workplace bowling team | There is no bowling team, but Melinda spends part of her earnings to bowl regularly |
| Wealthy people should be in the area | Wealthy people are present in the gift shop and are involved with some of the meetings |

Note that even the tasks that involve working with others involve some tasks that are semiautonomous (i.e., she works on her own segment of work within the team unit). For example, the person is responsible for specific bulk mailing zip codes while others take care of other zip codes. Other tasks, such as relocating large plants, require direct cooperation among team members. However, the teams include only staff of an equal level, so nobody directs or instructs her. The job was also modified slightly to deal with this issue; she checks her mailbox when she arrives and picks up a simple list of daily responsibilities using words she recognizes, which may include some additional tasks. She looks forward to getting her morning mail and has no problem asking someone to help her read something if she can't figure it out. In this way, the carved job itself accommodates and alleviates her "behavioral issues" related to resisting supervision and needing personal autonomy.

the individual to master the various tasks and self-manage or self-direct (see the Training and Support Strategies section in this chapter).

Sociological studies of integration and neighborhood belonging illustrate that sharing physical space over time is one of the strongest predictors of social integration; therefore, it follows that proximity at work is also an important consideration in job carving (Oldenburg, 1989). Fostering co-worker interrelation is especially critical for individuals with high support needs. Having friendships or respected roles at work helps increase job retention and improves acceptance (Griffin & Sherron, 2006; Hagner & DiLeo, 1993; Nisbet & Hagner, 1988).

Clearly, an essential consideration in carving is the identification and facilitation of natural supports to speed the safe emancipation of the consumer to the workforce, cultivate sustaining workplace relationships, and set the stage for fading reliance on paid support staff.

One useful approach to maximizing the impact of natural supports is identifying existing or potentially shared or overlapping work tasks during the job analysis, and preserving these circumstances, or carving them in, during the job development and training negotiations (Griffin & Sherron, 2006). These intersecting tasks set the stage for interaction and developing valuable workplace relationships.

The following example, modified here for confidentiality reasons, but true to the actual job design, illustrates what Patricia Rogan at Indiana University noted, as early as 1990, as the crucial role of shared, or intersecting, tasks in lessening the impact and stigma of job coaching by relying instead on natural workplace assistance in performing routine operations (Rogan, 1990). It is a good example of how intersecting tasks and natural supports merge to meet a worker's support requirements.

## David

David is a young man with a label of Down syndrome. He was intent on becoming a welder, but even with instruction, this vocation seemed out of reach in his rural surroundings. Complicating matters, the program serving David was over 70 miles away and could not afford to provide lengthy job coaching in the very small town where he lived with his mother. After some investigation, David agreed that just working in a welding shop would meet his career goals. An appointment at the local welding shop was secured and his employment specialist Lisa proceeded with a job analysis. She spent a total of 7 hours over 2 days listing the major duties of the 3 welders at the shop and made lists of tasks she thought the welders could relinquish to David, while improving their own performance. Lisa was careful not to give David the less desirable work but instead analyzed the tasks and pulled duties into a new job description that involved joint or intersecting tasks with the welders. David might be cleaning a work area for a welder, but he was there during regular work hours, doing work important to the business, alongside his co-workers.

As Lisa observed, she noted that the welders often stopped their projects and cleaned their surrounding area. This was because the waste they created was heavy and cumbersome steel that, if left unattended, was bothersome, impeded their work, and created a tripping hazard. She also noted that the big recycling cans were carried out back to the Dumpster on a regular basis by two welders. She also noted that supply deliveries, changing acetylene tanks, project set-ups and tear-downs, and other tasks, often required two people working together, largely because most items in a welding shop are heavy.

Obviously, having well-paid welders handling lifting and cleaning tasks is a wasteful practice. The carving around David's talents to create a welder assistant position allowed the welders to concentrate on their projects, and David became a vital member of the team, assisting with joint tasks throughout the day. The job was developed to solve the production problems at the shop, create a job that David enjoyed, and eliminate the need for job coaching since co-worker support was already the norm throughout the day (Griffin & Sherron, 2006).

## WORK CULTURE

Any job analysis must consider the impacts of corporate culture on acceptance and accommodation of a new worker. In the rush to succeed at job carving, sometimes culture is not analyzed nearly enough. As a preventative illustration, Jack's story is presented here. Again, all these examples are disguised and modified to protect confidentiality.

## Jack

Jack's vocational profile reveals a young man in his mid-30s who experiences schizophrenia. He attends regular counseling and takes psychotropic medications that control many of his symptoms. He does, sometimes, still have auditory hallucinations and, as a personal management strategy, tends to seek solitude rather than display these occasional conversations. Because of this, Jack can sometimes seem antisocial or aloof, according to his support staff. Regardless, Jack loves to drive (often a solitary task); is not mechanically inclined, though he likes cars; and would like to perhaps detail or wash them. Jack has had several custodial jobs, but he does not enjoy that type of work. He is personally fastidious and does not like being dirty. Jack also has computer skills and enjoys surfing the Internet and writing e-mails. Jack and his employment specialist are exploring the possibility of his working at a local car dealership, since it is near his home and offers several jobs that might be to his liking.

The employment specialist visits the dealership and discovers they have a "lot-boy" position open. Jack, however, is not interested in washing cars outside all day, though it is a solitary task; Jack insists this is too much like janitorial work. He reemphasizes that he wants to drive or learn higher-level skills.

The employment specialist returns and observes the dealership for several hours over a week's time. He discovers through watching and talking with the service manager, mechanics, and parts department manager that

The specialized shop tools owned by the dealership are in disarray and not inventoried. He believes Jack could set up an efficient tool check-in system on the computer.

The parts manager is often assisting others when the mechanics need a tune-up or routine part. Rather than having the mechanics wait at the parts counter, they can pull the part and enter the part number on the computerized work order. Unfortunately, the mechanics regularly forget to enter these data. When the bill is settled, the part number is assigned a price, but without the part number, the customer's bill is not charged. The parts manager makes a point that he needs help to stop this loss of revenue and the irritation he feels at the forgetful mechanics.

Throughout the week, the service manager pulls mechanics off the line to run errands to a parts warehouse, to the local paint company to pick up auto body supplies, and so forth. While the mechanics see this as a reward, the employment specialist believes that well-paid mechanics performing errands cost the dealership money in down time and delays completion of their work, which affects customer satisfaction.

After discussing his observations with Jack, the employment specialist proposes a job carve to the dealership manager. The carved tasks include

- Detailing cars

- Managing the tool inventory

- Assisting the parts manager with entering part numbers on the computer

- Working in the body shop, assisting with bodywork (learning a trade)

- Taking over all the driving, to retrieve parts, and running other errands

The pressure on the employment specialist to close Jack's case contributed to the job's ultimate failure. First, Jack is fastidious and working in the body shop does not suit him particularly well. Although it would teach him a valuable trade, his hallucinations and shyness make him seem aloof to the mechanics. To complicate matters, the mechanics resent that Jack now seems to be in a position of management because they must request parts and specialty tools from him. Even more significant to them, by taking over the driving duties, Jack has stripped the mechanics of their unofficial break-time, an informal reward doled out by the boss, which relieves each of them from leaning over hot engines at least once or twice weekly.

So what happens? All these factors add up to Jack's not being accepted in the culture, and, sensing the resentment, he feels unwelcome and quickly departs. A little more rigorous analysis and job matching could have saved Jack this embarrassment and failure. The culture, of a workplace should be studied and honored; too much disruption to a work culture can have devastating impacts on job seekers (Deal & Kennedy, 1982).

## Existing and Potential Attributes and Competencies

The reader may recall the example of Susanna earlier in the chapter. Part of that chapter focused on identifying Susanna's existing and potential exploitable resources. Discovery involves searching for not only what is present today but also for what might be possible. Through observation, learning, and trying new things, much is learned about the individual, including motivators, learning style, and learning and teaching strategies that help the person expand their present competencies and acquire new ones.

Carving requires the same mindset. When conducting a job analysis and carving the job (i.e., selecting the specific discrete tasks or projects that will combine into a new job), attention should be given to discrete tasks that match existing competencies and attributes and those that a person is likely to be able to learn. This allows the creation of jobs that are appropriately challenging, maintain interest, and allow the person room for personal and career development.

Susanna's story provides a few simple examples. It is clear that Susanna is already able to handle certain tasks involved in pet care: walking, feeding, bathing, drying, brushing, playing with, and cleaning up after dogs and cats. A job could be carved where Susanna deals only with those specific tasks. However, what is now known about her, gathered from the process of discovery and planning, indicates that she may well be able to learn other tasks involved in pet care, such as grooming, trimming nails, and cleaning ears and teeth. If based only on her existing skills with dogs and cats, a job could be carved where she works exclusively with dogs and cats. However, she has the potential to learn how to provide care for other animals—maybe guinea pigs, rabbits, ferrets, birds, and reptiles—the many different types of animals seen in veterinary offices.

When the focus is only on existing attributes and competencies, the person's value to the workplace may be inadvertently limited; there are fewer exploitable resources and therefore tasks that can be carved. The employment consultant may, unfortunately, dismiss as beyond the individual's ability, or even fail to identify, certain tasks that may be well within the individual's potential. With a dual focus on existing and potential attributes and competencies, the opportunities are expanded; the individual has more exploitable resources and therefore more tasks may be carved. Focus on potential opens great options and opportunity.

## TRAINING AND SUPPORT STRATEGIES

Evaluating and selecting tasks to be included within the carved job requires thoughtful analysis of the teaching and learning, modification, self-management, and other training and support strategies that may be used by the individual to do the task, particularly if it is a new task for the person. Whereas the carving process designs the new job as defined by its collection of duties, the process must include a training plan that incorporates various tools and strategies, with emphasis on those natural to the workplace.

Natural supports in the context of the training and support plan involve not only the people and social structures of the workplace discussed previously, but also those strategies and elements that already exist in the workplace such as clocks, timers, movement of staff, arrivals and departures of people, changes in lighting or sound, and so on. An individual can employ these elements as cues, timekeepers, motivators, and signals to learn and perform tasks. If the natural training elements are not sufficient to nurture mastery of specific tasks, supplemental training strategies and potential modifications can be employed, such as in the example of having Melinda get her list of daily duties from her mailbox rather than getting it from a boss.

The importance of the application of training knowledge and skill to the carving process should not be underestimated. It is key to stretching the individual and the employer, and, maybe even more critically, it is key to changing perceptions of the professional community, allowing vision beyond the existing to the creation of fulfilling jobs where people can contribute the best of themselves.

## Returning to Susanna

Initially, Susanna did not appear to have a lot of employment prospects in her future. Staff saw her as very limited and did not see options for her because they were focusing predominantly on past experiences, records, evaluations, mixed with a certain amount of misinformation and outright misperception that sometimes perpetuates itself through the oral history of an organization. Susanna initially appeared to have no skills or interests. She had been labeled "noncompliant" and "stubborn" because she would strenuously refuse work at the workshop (as she did in school), and "lazy" and "unmotivated" because she appeared to find ways to avoid work at the hotel laundry by getting "lost," returning late from breaks, and so on. Susanna appeared to be somebody whose behavior presents more barriers to employment than skills for employment.

Through the discovery and planning process, the team learns of her pet-sitting enterprise. In going to her house and observing her going through some of her routines, including her pet-sitting tasks, they begin to see a completely different person. Susanna is engaged and largely self-directed. She is friendly and seems to know many people in the area. She is skillful with many animal care tasks.

The discovery process reveals many of Susanna's attributes and contributions. In order to expand some of those and learn more about her potential, she begins to volunteer for an animal rescue shelter. One of her new friends, Daniel, who also volunteers, joins Susanna's support team and agrees to mentor Susanna through a few informational interviews and job-shadowing experiences at two veterinary offices in the area. Those opportunities grew out of Susanna's connections from shared work at the rescue shelter. It is important to note that having Daniel serve as her mentor through those experiences is a great advantage as he is knowledgeable and naturally valid in those settings; that is, he shares the passion and experience in working with animals. For Susanna, having a mentor like Daniel is clearly better than having as a mentor an employment specialist who has never owned a pet.

During the job shadowing, Daniel tapes some videos of the activities, and the employment specialist joins Susanna for brief periods to observe her, particularly noting how she learns, where she tends to need cues, and what she responds to or not, and even tries out a few different strategies and self-management tools to see how Susanna responds. This is the beginning of the training plan.

Susanna tries out some of the activities that were identified as potential skills. She works with a groomer to give Phoebe, a miniature poodle, a fresh haircut complete with bows and a nail trim. She also has the opportunity to help with several other animals, including a bird, a snake, a ferret, a turtle, and a gerbil. Through that experience several things are learned. Among them, Susanna does pretty well with both experiences, which suggests that she is likely to be able to expand into some of the potential roles identified earlier. She also has a clear preference for furry creatures, as she didn't much care for the turtle or the bird, and was particularly unmotivated to deal with the snake.

Considering the discovery experience, and her now clear list of exploitable resources, her vocational profile is developed. It includes the following ideal conditions of employment:

- Work inside

- Work outside

- Prefers to work with furry and hairy animals

- Prefers not to work with reptiles, birds, hairless cats, and other nonfurry/hairless animals

- Likes to know what needs to be done but does not do well with rigid schedules, time-frames, and sequencing of tasks

- Loves to talk to people who share her enthusiasm for animals

- Will do tasks related to animal care (e.g., cleaning cages, floors), but her main interest is actual involvement with the animals

- Prefers morning work (she has a significant decline in her ability to focus after about 3:00 p.m.)

- Wants to work in her immediate community

The support team develops a plan to find a situation that will work for Susanna. Among the first steps is talking informally with people in her animal network about her interest in working for a veterinarian. During one Adoption Saturday event, when she had assumed the role of luring soft-hearted and unsuspecting people to the animals, transforming them from mere shoppers, walkers, and joggers to new pet owners, Suzanne encounters a woman, Pat, whose best friend is a veterinarian. Susanna tells her about her plans to work at a veterinary office. It turns out that this veterinarian, Dianne, has recently bought a fairly large building with hopes of expanding her practice and offering boarding, dog training, and grooming. Pat gives Susanna the contact information, and Daniel helps Suzanne record it and communicate this possible "eureka!" moment to her support team.

Pat calls Dianne to tell her about Susanna. Because Susanna and Daniel are the ones who met Pat, they decide it is best that they make the initial contact with Dianne. Samantha, the employment specialist, coaches Daniel about asking for the opportunity to come in to learn about the operation, and when Susanna and Daniel call Dianne, she remains nearby to support them. They are successful in setting up a meeting with Dianne, and Daniel lets her know that Samantha will come with them. He makes no mention of her employment specialist role, as there is no need to do so. Pat has introduced Dianne to the fact that Susanna has an obvious disability and discussing the role of the employment specialist at this juncture would only serve to emphasize Susanna's disability. When Pat meets Susanna, she sees enthusiasm, competence, and contribution.

During the initial meeting and job analysis, Dianne tells them the specifics of her plans to expand to other services. She currently provides only veterinary services, but plans to offer a doggie daycare, dog training, boarding, and grooming, though she says it will be a while before she can afford all of it. She has, however, already finished the spaces she plans to use for each service, but she is without supplies and equipment needed to set it up. There are great opportunities here for Susanna, for carving a job and for resource ownership.

Because these jobs are not yet in existence, Susanna decides to return to the other full-service veterinary office for a more thorough analysis of the tasks involved. Susanna and her team get together and review the vocational profile and the job analysis to begin to carve a job. They select the tasks that are consistent with Susanna's ideal conditions, consider the benefit to the business, and identify the training or modification strategies that may be required.

In Susanna's carved job, she is responsible for

- Maintaining the lobby

- Stocking the sales area

- Receiving inpatient pets from their owners in the early morning

- Settling inpatient pets in their crates

- Providing food or water as appropriate for each animal

- Walking and playing with waiting animals

Susanna has direct contact with pets. The receiving task is modified slightly so that she is not responsible for discussing the procedures to be done; the front desk person handles that while Susanna focuses on the animal. To ensure that Susanna provides the appropriate food or water, or withholds it during postsurgical recovery, they devise a system using color-coded labels to represent the type of food the animal should get (the print color on the labels matches the bag color) and labels with a photo of water on them as well as the time the food or water should be removed or started. They are printed out by the reception desk staff the night before the animal's arrival along with other paperwork. When the animal checks in, Susanna gets the labels and places them on the door of its crate so she knows what to give each animal. She checks it off after she completes the task. If changes are made postsurgery, the veterinary assistant changes the label or writes an adjusted time on it per the doctor's orders. Note that this set of tasks also meets her need for morning work.

The business benefits in many ways. Animals get special attention when they arrive, which customers really appreciate.

The doggie daycare tasks involve taking a proposal to Dianne that includes resource ownership. Susanna will purchase several pieces of equipment for the operation of the doggie daycare, through a combination of vocational rehabilitation and Plan to Achieve Self-Support (PASS) funds, including

- Several large indoor play yards that can be connected and reconnected to make smaller or bigger play spaces as needed. These will be used to divide the room into play areas for different sizes of dogs.

- A few crates of various sizes for dogs that may need to be temporarily separated from the others

- Water and food bowls

- Food and doggie treats

- A pager so the reception staff can let her know when a dog arrives regardless of where she is

- A variety of toys for inside and out

- A few small stain-resistant inexpensive area rugs

- An 8-foot folding table and a few chairs Susanna is bringing from her parents' garage, along with a few tablecloths. Daniel is giving them a sofa he was about to take to the local thrift store.

They propose to open a Monday–Friday doggie daycare in one section of the building that has easy access to the outdoor fenced-in area. Using Dianne's vision as their guide, they plan to create a warm and somewhat homey play area within that space. The area rugs will not be used within the play areas but will be placed between them and near furniture to warm up the room. Area rugs have the advantage of being movable, which will accommodate rearrangement and resizing the play areas. A small sitting area will be built around the sofa, including a rug and clothed table. In addition they propose setting up a small display of various toys, treats, food, collars, and leashes they use in the daycare. Based on informational interviews and job analyses at other veterinary offices that offer doggie daycare or other services, they know that most of their sales of those items occur as people pick up their dogs from daycare. Further, they propose that the reception desk handle check in and check out of the daycare dogs and that, in addition to Susanna, a few other staff be hired or that staff wanting more hours be committed to the daycare so that the center can operate from 7:00 a.m.–7:00 p.m. with at least two staff working in the daycare initially, and increasing as the number of participating dogs increases. They develop a few recommendations in terms of the prices they would have to charge for daycare to cover staff and the other minimal operational costs. They also propose that Susanna work 30 hours per week at $8.00 per hour to start, increasing to $11.00 after they have regular enrollment averaging 20 dogs per day.

They present this proposal to Dianne and she is quite excited by it. She thinks it will work but is somewhat concerned with having to hire additional staff, particularly in the early stages of the business, and struggles with the numbers. She decides to increase the hours of a few employees but indicates she would prefer to try to get a minimum enrollment of 10 dogs per day before they open.

Susanna and her team focus on envisioning the space, and Dianne says she will buy some paint, fake plants, and donate some window curtains to the decorating crew. They will set up the space themselves and begin marketing efforts by hosting an open house every Saturday for a month before they open. They will offer early enrollment discounts at those events. They create an inexpensive flier advertising the open house and daycare and distribute it through local pet supply stores, grooming outlets, and veterinary offices that don't have a doggie daycare. The animal rescue shelter also distributes flier to passersby on Adoption Saturdays, and they make sure every pet's new adoptive family gets the information. And, of course, they will use their substantial networks of friends with pets to publicize the new service.

Ultimately, Susanna benefits from a job that is highly tailored to her interests, skills, preferences, and support needs, and she is able to earn a good wage. She is able to connect with a host of people who share her enthusiasm for dogs in particular. The business benefits not only in the ways mentioned above but also by adding a new source of revenue, expanding sales of accessories, and having another way to attract people to the place of business, who in turn become new customers of the veterinary practice. Many of Susanna's friends begin to use Dianne as their vet, as do the animal rescue people. Further, Dianne gains from her investment in the building. What was previously dead space is now generating revenue. Incidentally, through Dianne's ongoing relationship with the rescue via Susanna and Daniel, she decides to donate a section of her building for use by the rescue, which allows her some tax advantage rather than dead space.

These examples represent both the complexities and the ease with which jobs can be carved. While job carving relies on thoughtful implementation of discovery, job analysis, and carving strategies outlined in this book, along with training considerations, networking, and negotiation, it is typically not particularly difficult. Considering the value created for the individual and the business, efforts are well worth it.

## REFERENCES

Bissonnette, D. (1994). *Beyond traditional job development: The art of creating opportunity.* Chatsworth, CA: Milt Wright & Associates, Inc.

Brooke, V., Inge, K., Armstrong, A., & Wehman, P. (Eds.). (1997). *Supported employment handbook: A customer-driven approach for persons with significant disabilities.* Richmond: Virginia Commonwealth University/Rehabilitation Research and Training Center.

Callahan, M., & Garner, B. (1997). *Keys to the workplace: Skills and supports for people with disabilities.* Baltimore: Paul H. Brookes Publishing Co.

Callahan, M., McLoughlin, C., & Garner, J.B. (1987). *Getting employed, staying employed: Job development and training for persons with severe handicaps.* Baltimore: Paul H. Brookes Publishing Co.

Deal, T.E., & Kennedy, A.A. (1982). *Corporate cultures: The rites and rituals of corporate life.* Reading, MA: Addison-Wesley Publishing.

Geary, T., Griffin, C.C., & Hammis, D. (2005). *Customizing employment and workplace supports.* Atlanta: Georgia's Project Access.

Griffin, C.C., & Hammis, D. (2003a). *The training connection series for employment specialists: A collection of articles on supported employment and self-employment. Job Training and Placement Report.* Wisconsin: Impact Publications.

Griffin, C.C., & Hammis, D. (2003b). *Making self-employment work for people with disabilities.* Baltimore: Paul H. Brookes Publishing Co.

Griffin, C.C., & Sherron, P. (2006). Job carving and customized employment. In P. Wehman (Ed.), *Life beyond the classroom* (4th ed.). Baltimore: Paul H. Brookes Publishing Co.

Griffin, C.C., & Winter, L. (1988). *Employment partnership: Job development strategies in integrated employment.* Paper presented at the Winter Group Marketing, Rocky Mountain Resource & Training Institute and Colorado Developmental Disabilities Planning Council, Denver, CO.

Hagner, D., & DiLeo, D. (1993). *Working together: Workplace culture, supported employment, and persons with disabilities.* Cambridge, MA: Brookline Books.

Hagner, D., Rogan, P., & Murphy, S. (1992). Facilitating natural supports in the workplace: Strategies for support consultants. *Journal of Vocational Rehabilitation, 1.*

Nisbet, J., & Hagner, D. (1988). Natural supports in the workplace: A reexamination of supported employment. *Journal of the Association for Persons with Severe Handicaps, 13,* 260–267.

Oldenburg, R. (1989). *The great good place: Cafes, coffee shops, bookstores, hair salons, bars, and other neighborhood hangouts at the heart of a community.* New York: Marlowe & Company.

Rogan, P. (1990). *Strategies for facilitating natural supports in the workplace.* Paper presented at the Virginia Commonwealth University National Symposium on Supported Employment.

# 9

# Using Social Security Work Incentives

*David Hammis, Cary Griffin, and Tammara Geary*

This chapter is designed to provide immediate and practical tactics for job developers to effectively support the use of Social Security work incentives by prospective employees. An overview of current work incentives used by job developers, concerns, issues, opportunities, as well as examples and a completed Social Security Administration (SSA) form sets the stage for two clear approaches for job developers and employment specialists to put work incentives in effect. This chapter does not attempt to describe and cover all human services programs, such as SSA, Medicaid, Housing and Urban Development (HUD), and food stamps, or all laws and policies related to work incentives, but focuses rather on a very narrow and less complex set of specific job development Social Security work incentives and tactics that can be implemented efficiently, quickly, and effectively during job development activities.

The first tactic enables job developers to take clear and decisive action by recognizing and facilitating the direct implementation of an easy-to-calculate Plan to Achieve Self-Support (PASS). This SSA work incentive is low-risk and high-yield and is immediately accessible for approximately 30% of the prospective customized employment employees with complex disabilities.

The second tactic is based on job developers building relationships with, and requesting assistance from, SSA-contracted (non–SSA employees) benefits planners, available in all states, to indirectly facilitate more complex work incentives analyses, advisement, and implementation by third-party benefits planners. These tactics work well separately or together. Both can be implemented today and do not require significant work incentives education beyond the information in this chapter.

## THE CURRENT STATE OF JOB DEVELOPERS' USE OF SOCIAL SECURITY WORK INCENTIVES

Very few job developers and employment specialists discuss with prospective employees, promote, or use Social Security work incentives prior to, during, or after job development activities as a source of job development funding or enhanced community employment support funding. There is no clear study that targets the job developer's and the employment specialist's discussions, knowledge base, and use of work incentives, yet SSA's Annual Statistical Reports reveal that work incentives such as PASS, which are directly applicable to job development, show a use rate so low it's almost not measurable compared with the number of jobs developed each day around the country.

The current processes, policies, and sources of funding, from vocational rehabilitation (VR), Medicaid, and the U.S. Department of Education school-to-work funding for job development are generally understood by job developers and employed wherever job developers work, yet do not include processes and policies to access and use Social Security work incentives as a source of job development or community employment support funding. Securing adequate agency funding and paying a job developer's salary seems like it should not be a job developer's task but rather like it should be one of the multiple tasks of the directors and managers of local community rehabilitation programs (CRPs), high schools, mental health centers, centers for independent living, and so forth. And yet, job developers are often directly tasked with developing their own salary funding and, as a result, tend to mold and strategize each of their daily activities based on exact external and internal policies that are directly related to securing job development funding. Job developers are often under significant funding pressures to develop jobs quickly with strict funding oversight of their discrete daily job development activities, through fee-for-service agreements or flat-fee outcome payments, based on specific payment points related to outcomes.

One current concern, as noted in earlier chapters, is that many job developers do not amalgamate funding from various potential sources, but are locked into only one or two funding sources, and are therefore at the mercy of their funding needs. As a rule, job developers working for CRPs do not focus on Social Security work incentives (such as direct funds from PASS) as a source of funding, and instead focus on Medicaid day program funds and VR funds as their primary source of revenue. Even though it appears that job developers do not proactively address Social Security work incentives, such as PASS, they do seem to act daily on perceived SSA information, concerns, and often misinformation, in very serious and limiting ways.

As an example, a job developer may be requested to develop a part-time job for a prospective employee receiving Medicaid health care benefits and a Supplemental Security Income (SSI) check of $603 per month. SSI monthly checks, by law, are gradually reduced $1 for every $2 gross wages earned after the first $85 of gross wage earnings each month, assuming no work incentives such as PASS are used and there is no other monthly income. Due to mistaken fears of loss of benefits held by the SSI recipient's family or employment agency, the job developer might have been instructed to limit the job being developed to a part-time job that produces gross wages less than $85 per month to protect and preserve the prospective employee's SSI and Medicaid, when, in fact, the prospective employee could potentially earn thousands of dollars each month in gross wages and still be eligible for SSI and Medicaid.

From the author's experiences, it seems to be commonplace, either by choice, agency policy, or directions from others, for job developers to intentionally limit their prospective employee and employer wage negotiations, outcomes, and efforts, based on perceived barriers related to possible Social Security income thresholds. A real-life example is an employment agency where job developers are instructed by policy to develop only part-time jobs for most (if not all) prospective employees served by that employment agency—jobs that are designed to yield reduced monthly incomes targeted to be safely below various perceived Social Security eligibility income limits and other perceived interrelated systems income limits, such as Medicaid waiver eligibility thresholds.

Job developers' use of Social Security work incentives during job development seems to be almost an afterthought on the heels of the customized employment (CE) process. Even in leading state community employment projects that are clearly embracing most of the foundations and principles of community and customized employment—which specify the planned amalgamation of funding from multiple sources (including Social Security work incentives as outlined in CE principles), the use of Social Security work incentives in job development activities is so minimal that it is still for the most part nonexistent. For example, an exemplary employment project in a progressive state recently sent the authors confirmed, yet unpublished, data on 30 employment situations for which a local CRP provides employment services, all of which were developed over the past few years through the employment project. Of 30 employment outcomes listed, not one community employment situation supported by the CRP job developers accessed SSA's PASS work incentive.

Statistically, as an average, 30% of the new community employees, according to SSA's annual reports statistics, were eligible at the onset of their employment for very low-risk and high-yield PASS funding, estimating on average $9,000 per person, due to the probability that 30% of the employees concurrently receive both SSI and Social Security Disability Insurance (SSDI) monthly cash benefits in the age and disability type and severity brackets related to the employees in the data provided. Another 30% of the employees, eligible for just SSI monthly cash benefits (no SSDI), became eligible for extremely low-risk and moderate-yield PASS funding as soon as their employment started, conservatively averaging a bit less at roughly $3,000 per PASS per employee.

The employment support funding not accessed through failure to use SSA's PASS work incentive in this example affected 20 of the 30 employees and represents approximately $120,000 over a timeframe of 18–36 months, typically. This funding was probably not considered or presented as a choice to the new employees. The objection could be posed that perhaps the 20 employees did not need $120,000 in employment support funding, yet the data provided on the 20 employees indicate employment support funds needed and acquired by the employees as totaling $517,855 (see Table 9.1). Clearly, the potential $120,000 in low-risk, high-yield PASS funds could have been a part of the required $517,855 employment support funds. Not even one small $3,000 PASS was accessed.

This project's example of not using PASS is for the most part the current norm. Any use of Social Security work incentives before, during, and after job development is the exception. National PASS use has a statistically minute approximate rate of use of .04% nationally, from SSA's Annual Statistical Reports, which equates to one person with a disability per every 2,500 who could access and use SSA's PASS work incentive. Of the .04% who do access and use a PASS, most access PASS on their own and are not supported in accessing a PASS by local job developers. In comparison, 30%, or one person with a disability per every three receiving SSI and/or SSDI served by job developers at local CRPs, could use and benefit from a low-risk, high-yield PASS. There certainly are untapped potentials for one out of three potential PASS users versus one out of 2,500 current PASS users.

**Table 9.1.**   Employment funding example of 30 actual customized employment outcomes

| Source | Total employment funding for 30 jobs | Average funds per person |
|---|---|---|
| Personal funds | $22,945.00 | $764.83 |
| State vocational rehabilitation funds | $125,500.00 | $4,183.33 |
| Loans | $22,500.00 | $750.00 |
| Customized employment grant funds | $346,910.00 | $11,563.67 |
| Total | $517,855.00 | $17,261.83 |
| Potential Plan to Achieve Self-Support (PASS) funds not accessed | –$120,000.00 | –$4,000.00 |
| Reduced total cost to employees and other systems funding if PASS had been used | $397,855.00 | $13,261.83 |

## THE JOB DEVELOPMENT SYSTEM AND SOCIAL SECURITY WORK INCENTIVES

As noted in Chapter 1:

> The high unemployment rate for people with disabilities is not the result of a flaw in the system; it is the system. In order to change the realities of poverty and isolation endured by people with significant disabilities, changes in our approach to employment services must take top priority.

From a job development perspective, the initial question becomes: How do we make effecting changes in our almost nonexistent approach to the use of Social Security work incentives a reasonable and viable priority for job developers? If we assume that the high unemployment rate for people with disabilities is the system, then the system is the problem. If the current job development system continues to lead to high unemployment rates and almost no use of work incentives by job developers, what systemic changes need to occur to support job developers to access and use work incentives?

## PRACTICAL TACTICS FOR INCREASING THE JOB DEVELOPER'S USE OF WORK INCENTIVES: TODAY—SIMPLE TACTICS FOR IMMEDIATELY USING SSA WORK INCENTIVES; AND, TOMORROW—LONG RANGE LEADERSHIP CHANGES AND PLANNING

### Today: Quick-Start General Assumptions and Practical Tactics for Job Developers to Use Work Incentives Immediately

This chapter is not intended to be a course attempting to duplicate exacting Social Security work incentives training manuals and policies. There is no need to wait, attend classroom trainings, and be completely trained in the precise details of work incentives to begin to support the use of them. Understanding the few key concepts and basic general presuppositions outlined here will work well to get started today. At the end of the chapter, technical resources are listed, including free and low-cost publications and web sites.

The first task is to find out what type and amount of SSA disability monthly cash benefits each person seeking community employment receives. It's important to know that there are only two major types of Social Security disability-related monthly cash benefits. One is Title XVI (Title 16), Supplemental Security Income (SSI); the other is Title II (Title 2), Social Security Disability Insurance (SSDI). Finding out what cash benefit types and monthly check amounts each person receives can be daunting, since many SSI and SSDI recipients or beneficiaries who use electronic funds transfers from SSA do not see actual paper checks and are not sure of some of the technical terms in SSA postal letters. The simplest way is to ask the person or family directly. The next simplest way is to ask the person or family to show you some recent letters they have received from SSA, copies of recent SSA checks, or copies of bank deposit statements listing electronic deposits by SSA into individual bank accounts monthly. Asking the person or family to call the local SSA office or the national SSA toll-free number to verify the type of checks and amounts can be done while the person or family is with you. SSA will need to talk to the person directly, yet you can certainly be present to provide a cell phone and phone number to support the phone call. Once you have confirmed the type of SSA disability benefits received (either SSI or SSDI or both) you can use the three generalizations in Table 9.2 (which fit most situations) to be very effective immediately.

The first work incentives scenario, with lowest risk and highest yield, occurs when a prospective employee, who is not working, receives both SSI and SSDI checks each month. Roughly 30% of the potential employees who are both served by employment agencies and receive monthly cash benefits from SSA receive both SSI and SSDI checks each month (unless the employment agency provides employment services for only youth under age 22 or only older potential employees over age 50). The majority of youth tend to receive only SSI (yet some do receive SSI and SSDI), and the majority of

Table 9.2.    Three scenarios of low risk

| Scenario | Risk | Difficulty | % of potential use |
|---|---|---|---|
| 1. Prospective employee receives Supplemental Security Income (SSI) and Social Security Disability Insurance (SSDI) | Very low risk | Very easy to develop Plan to Achieve Self-Support (PASS) applicable both retroactively in time and forward in time and also easy to use all other work incentives | 20%–30% |
| 2. Prospective employee only receives SSI | Very low risk | Very easy to develop PASS, yet PASS applies only when a job or business that produces earned income is started | 10%–20% |
| 3. Prospective employee only receives SSDI | Moderate to high risk | Difficult to develop PASS, cannot go back in time, requires more skills and support to develop | 10%–20% |

older adults tend to receive only SSDI, with some exceptions. Most CRPs do not limit their services only to youth or to older potential employees and instead provide employment services to a wide range of potential employees of varying ages.

Simply focusing efforts on supporting the use of Social Security work incentives using this first common concurrent SSI and SSDI PASS scenario could change the use of work incentives in job development efforts from the average of less than .04% use to 10%–30% use almost overnight. This simple scenario for supporting individuals receiving both SSI and SSDI will produce a dramatic increase in your local SSA work incentives use efforts, well beyond the national use rate of less than .04%. Even if you increase your work incentives use rate to only 5%, your agency will still be outpacing the dismal national .04% rate.

Each job seeker receiving both SSI and SSDI can be immediately supported to develop a fairly quick and simple PASS with the lowest risk possible and highest yield associated with such a low risk and will receive thousands to tens of thousands of dollars of employment support funding for her or his work goal from SSA, in the form of SSI offset employment funds that can pay for almost any employment-related expense, such as paying for college degrees years before searching for or acquiring employment, technical school expenses and certification, discovery and job development, on-the-job-training support, co-worker paid supports, equipment, supplies, vehicles, transportation, gas and repairs, clothing, operating capital, and equipment and services to start a business—almost any employment-related expenses that do not need to be directly justified and related to the person's disability but do need to be related to the person's employment goal.

James (Jim) Dodge, whose situation is used as an example of this initial concurrent SSI and SSDI scenario, illustrates core job development tactics in Chapters 1, 2, 3, and 4, with details of Jim's situation listed in filled-in version of a PASS plan Customized Employment (CE) Management Plan (see Figure 1.1) and a Job Analysis Record (JAR) (see Figure 3.1), which covers the specifics of Jim's employment development. In the CE Management Plan, Jim is listed as receiving both $303 SSI and $320 SSDI each month prior to his employment. Quite a few employment funding sources, supports, enhancements, and needs are listed, including the need for a car with hand controls, equipment, and training for Jim's employment. The JAR shows that Jim's employment at Engine Rebuilders, Inc., began with a starting rate of pay of $1,200 per month, noting a PASS approval for modified adjustable-height work benches, engine stands, new parts washers, and various hand tools, as examples of resource ownership (see Chapter 6), with an additional approval for a modified personal car with hand controls needed by James to get to and from work each day.

The potential exists for a retroactive PASS going back in time 24 months due to Jim's part-time job in the past, his goal during and after that job to become an assistant machinist, and his current open VR case. The math is very simple for the retroactive PASS, and for any PASS for someone receiving both SSI and SSDI. It's simply the SSDI check amount minus $20 per month times the number of months of retroactivity. In Jim's case, it would be $323 SSDI – $20 × 24 months in the past = $7,272 lump sum from SSI as soon as the PASS is approved. Then after that, the easiest math to go forward in time is to continue to use the $323 SSDI – $20 and then roughly one-half of his gross wages he will be earning in his new job: $323 – $20 + $1,200/2 = $303 + $600 = $903 PASS funds each month forward in time. If his PASS extends forward about 12 months due to the time to learn and stabilize on his new job and pays for the car and equipment, his forward in time PASS budget will be $903 × 12 months = $10,836. A conservative estimated budget for PASS funding going back in time 24 months and forward in time 12 months = $7,272 from a 24-month retroactive lump sum set of PASS funds + $10,452 PASS funds forward in time at $903 per month for 12 months = $17,724, in this case for a new or slightly used vehicle with hand controls, GPS system, insurance, gas, maintenance, and repairs. It's possible more PASS funds are available, yet it appears that budget will be sufficient and reasonable to support Jim's work goal. Jim's PASS is very easy to develop both retroactively and forward in time due to his concurrent receipt of both SSI and SSDI, and also in this case, the work already accomplished and recorded in the JAR and CE Management Plan. Jim's PASS example is included at the end of this chapter in the chapter appendix.

In this example, the year is 2006 and Jim lives in Montana, where SSI allows individuals to earn up to a threshold of $25,977 (without losing their SSI eligibility or their Medicaid eligibility), and possibly even higher if Jim uses Medicaid at high levels. Income thresholds related to SSI change slightly each year and are posted on SSA's web site around November or December each year for the upcoming year. Jim's SSI and SSDI combination is very low risk, as noted before, due to his earning of $1,200 per month, or $14,400 per year, well below the Montana threshold of $25,977, which means Jim will retain his SSI eligibility and his Medicaid eligibility.

Jim plans to eliminate his SSDI cash benefit on purpose, by earning over the 2006 amount when SSDI will go away in June of 2007, based on Substantial Gainful Activity of $860 per month in 2006 and approximately $900 per month in 2007 (he will be earning $1,200 per month), since he has the fallback position of SSI and Medicaid eligibility. It's not necessary to know these additional threshold and Medicaid details initially to begin to assist Jim. SSA will explain these to him at the PASS approval level.

A second work incentives scenario occurs when someone receives only SSI (no SSDI or other income). Then a very low risk PASS, only going forward in time, can be developed and implemented as soon as the person starts earning a wage, or starts a business producing net income from self-employment. If, for instance, Jim received only SSI of $603 in 2006, then the calculation is quite simple when he starts work: monthly gross wages – $85/2 = PASS amount. Using Jim's predicted wages of $1,200 per month, his PASS math would be: $1,200 gross wages – $85/2 = $1,115/2 = $557.50 PASS funds per month available forward in time. Such a PASS would not be as high yield as the PASS was in the previous example where Jim received both SSI and SSDI, yet it is still a significant amount of funds for his employment goals and needs: $557.50 × 12 months = $6,690.00 per year forward in time for his PASS and employment-related expenses.

A third scenario occurs when someone receives only SSDI (no SSI). Then a PASS is typically larger and more complicated  and in some cases is very difficult to solve for mathematically. Such a PASS—SSDI only before the PASS is developed—and the math associated with it requires more training and support than this chapter can provide, yet it could be a very useful PASS, generating quite a bit more funds, than either of the first two PASS scenarios above. For support with individuals who receive only SSDI, it's suggested that the job developer locate a benefits planner for assistance. Local SSA offices can provide the local contact information for benefits planners titled Community Work Incentives Coordinators (CWICs). SSA's web site (http://www.socialsecurity.

gov/work) has links with all current contact information for community agencies funded through Work Incentives Planning and Assistance (WIPA) cooperative agreements and the associated CWICs at each WIPA project agency.

Of the three scenarios explained above, the first two can be developed and implemented today by using the simple math noted in each scenario. They do not require more knowledge than was covered here. The third scenario requires more expertise. Individuals receiving SSDI checks only prior to using a PASS represent one of the most frequent uses of the three scenarios listed previously in this section, since a PASS is the only tool in any system that can get someone receiving SSDI-only to also receive SSI as a result of the PASS. No work incentive can do that except a PASS.

From the percentages noted in Table 9.2, combining scenarios 1 and 2, 30%–50% of individuals who receive SSI and/or SSDI monthly cash benefits can use a PASS easily under these very low-risk plans. For individuals who receive only SSDI in scenario 3, PASS plans are more difficult to develop and pose a higher risk, applying approximately 10%–20% of the time, yet are often the most common type of PASS for which SSA receives requests and funds. Of the 50% low-risk PASS plans, 30% can be written immediately (today) with little or no skills. Following the few paragraphs here and reviewing the attached example PASS for James Dodge, a job developer can write a PASS to generate employment funding both back and forward in time.

## Other Social Security Work Incentives and Resources

There are quite a few Social Security work incentives beyond PASS, most of which are designed to occur on their own. Incentives that occur on their own do not need job developers' support or time. For instance, someone who receives SSDI is entitled to 9 Trial Work Period (TWP) months and 36 Extended Period of Eligibility (EPE) months. The TWP and EPE are called work incentives, yet there is no form to fill out to request those incentives; they simply occur in the background on their own. It's considered useful to be aware of the rules and policies covering those months, yet even awareness will not promote or stop the months from occurring, and no additional job development or employment support funding is derived in any way from such TWP and EPE months. A job developer will probably be asked about such work incentives at times and can reference the many web sites and printed resources available for free online.

## On-Line Work Incentives Resources

**http://www.ssa.gov/work**
General work incentives information site from SSA, some materials available in hard copy; also at local SSA offices

**http://www.ssa.gov/work/ResourcesToolkit/pubsnforms.html**
*Social Security Working While Disabled: A Guide to Plans for Achieving Self-Support*; hard copy may be available at local SSA offices

**http://www.socialsecurity.gov/disabilityresearch/redbook.htm**
*Social Security Redbook*, a summary guide to employment support for individuals with disabilities under the SSDI and SSI programs; hard copy may be available at local SSA offices

**http://ruralinstitute.umt.edu/training/publications.asp**
*Don't Look for Logic, It Doesn't Take a Rocket Scientist*, and fact sheets covering SSI and SSDI benefits; hard copy can be requested from the Rural Institute, The University of Montana, 52 Corbin Hall, Missoula, MT 59812

**http://www.rcep7.org/~ssawork/**
Online PASS and other work incentives calculator, SSA fact sheets, PASS forms

**http://www.workworld.org**
WorkWORLD™ decision support software for personal computers related to complex benefits systems, work incentives, and income interactions and planning

**http://www.passplan.org**
Examples of PASS forms

## Long-Term Use, Assistance, and Support

Helping prospective employees with disabilities, and/or prospective business owners, to understand, choose, and use work incentives is the beginning of a longer period of supporting the long-term implementation of work incentives. Long-term support for work incentives is very similar to long-term support for customized and supported employment, with more intensive support initially fading to less intensive support over time, yet available indefinitely, even for very short periods, say, one hour per month. In James Dodge's example, his PASS development and implementation will continue from the time his PASS was conceived as a possibility (due to his concurrent receipt of both SSI and SSDI in May 2006) to his PASS approval in June 2006, through its completion in June of 2007. Jim's PASS is interconnected with his employment and is tied to his progress toward achieving his work goal. Whereas an employment specialist can facilitate connections for Jim, such as to a skilled benefits planner who can answer benefits questions, it is the employment specialist who possesses the in-depth knowledge of Jim's daily, weekly, and monthly work supports, challenges, and tasks at the workplace.

Job developers or employment specialists providing ongoing follow-up support for individuals with long-term employment support needs are potentially ideal facilitators of long-term benefits support. As with supported employment, the amount and level of support for long-term use of work incentives will vary for each employee or business owner. In James's situation, he may need very little support, or he may need a fair amount of support with his PASS between May of 2006 and June of 2007. Assume that Jerry, the employment specialist working with James, after the initial intense on-the-job training period, checks in on James one day a week, or at least one day per month, to support his ongoing employment. During these visits, James and Jerry could review his PASS recordkeeping, making sure that James is reporting his wages to his local SSA office and depositing the correct amount into his PASS checking account each month (which SSA authorized in his PASS approval letter). They could make sure he is following his PASS steps (milestones) and keeping receipts for all approved PASS purchases.

Aligning a long-term benefits support process with existing ongoing employment specialist support meetings, calls, and e-mails is an ideal method to stay on top of any benefits questions, changes, or issues that may develop over time with a PASS work incentive. Employment specialists are the front line with employees and employers and have the most accurate understanding of the employment situation of anyone at any support agency. An employment specialist may or may not know the nuances of benefits and work incentives or be able to answer detailed questions for every possible situation, yet he or she is in an optimal position to provide significant, yet simple and easy, benefits support. For complex benefits questions and issues, the employment specialist can contact a trained benefits planner by phone or e-mail or set up a meeting in person.

Over time, as employment support agencies begin to understand the value of the use, implementation, and long-term support of work incentives such as PASS, they will set up systems and policies to provide long-term support. In Seattle, Washington, around 1998, King County Developmental Disability Services requested that the authors assist with planning to develop a long-term internal PASS and benefits support system for all individuals with developmental disabilities served in King County, who might choose to use PASS if informed about PASS as a choice. The system was approved by the county and has been in place now for six years. In 2006, roughly $500,000 per year in PASS funding was developed, supported, and tracked weekly by a trained benefits planner and an accountant trained in benefits planning. Weekly payroll from community employers is reported by each person with a disability or his or her support contact such as family or agency contacts, and PASS deposits and expenditures are reported monthly. Ongoing long-term PASS and related work incentives benefits support for anyone with a developmental disability in King County is in place for both the employees with disabilities and their related employment specialists and job developers. Their successful PASS employment funding system, in place now for years, relies on accurate and continual communications among the benefits specialist, PASS accountant, employees, job developers, and employment specialists.

## Tomorrow: Leadership

National, state, and local leaders must make it their goal to support and promote the use of Social Security work incentives by clearly directing job developers to use work incentives. Job developers are the key community employment personnel leading to successful customized community employment development and acquisition for individuals with disabilities. If job developers do not support or promote the use of work incentives, the use of work incentives is diminished to almost zero. In the absence of leaders who will mandate a clear directive and assign responsibility to use work incentives, their use will not improve. However, even lacking national and state level leadership, local community employment supervisors can still lead on their own by making a choice to train and direct job developers to promote and support the use of work incentives.

## SUMMARY AND JOB DEVELOPERS' USE OF WORK INCENTIVES LESSONS TO DATE

Currently job developers and employment specialists are not using job development–related Social Security work incentives, such as PASS, in any significant manner, except perhaps in King County, Washington. Whereas there is no clear study that targets job developers' and employment specialists' use of work incentives, SSA statistical reports show that work incentives such as PASS, which would be directly applicable to job development, are used at a negligible rate compared to the number of jobs developed each day around the country. There is one current clear exception in King County, Washington, which appears to be a solid, replicable model for increasing the use of SSA's PASS work incentive throughout job development and long-term support timeframes for job developers and employment specialists. Replicating such an approach could take time and certainly would require some level of employment support services leadership, yet there are simpler ways to get started right now that could lead to changes as significant as King County's PASS and benefits support program.

The simplest method to get started with very little benefits knowledge or expertise is to first offer PASS as a clear low-risk and high-yield choice to any prospective employee who receives both SSI and SSDI concurrently. Such types of PASS are fairly simple to develop just by answering the questions in the PASS form. (For an example of a filled-in version of this form, see the appendix at end of this chapter; a blank version of this form appears in the appendix at the end of this book.) The math is also quite simple and is provided in this chapter. It's very important to reiterate that individuals receiving both SSI and SSDI are most likely excellent PASS candidates. Assuming the customized discovery and job development processes of this book are implemented and a clear work opportunity exists, then someone receiving both SSI and SSDI has the opportunity to develop a very low-risk and high-yield PASS, if informed of her or his choice. Job developers can at least inform prospective employees concurrently receiving SSI and SSDI that PASS is a choice to support their work goals.

Next, it's important to understand that anyone receiving only SSI before working and then begins working and whose income is reducing his or her SSI check due to SSI's $1 reduction for every $2 earned policy, could potentially develop a PASS of lower financial yield, yet also of low risk. This situation (someone receiving SSI only before working) is common and is a use-it-or-lose-it option that can be chosen by the recipient only if he or she knows it is a choice. If the new employee does not use a PASS, his or her SSI will be reduced through SSI's $1 reduction for every $2 in gross wages earned, yet if the person uses a PASS, his or her SSI will not be reduced by the equivalent of that reduction, if used in a PASS to pay for work or education-related expenses. For individuals who receive only SSDI due to an SSDI check that is larger than the SSI Federal Benefit Rate plus $20 (in 2006, that would be larger than $603 + $20), a PASS is a higher-risk option and more complicated to develop than this chapter can address, yet such types of PASS are often developed and desired when the person is informed of the potential PASS and makes an informed choice to develop a PASS. This option can be very beneficial in many ways, specifically in states with restrictive Medicaid policies. In such states, SSDI-only PASS plans are a premier choice for a prospective employee and create powerful new opportunities for individuals who, prior to PASS, perceived no solutions to issues with Medicaid, long-term support, community living, and working. Although such PASS plans are more complicated, it is recommended that a benefits planner be contacted to assist in developing this type of more complex, yet very high-yield PASS option.

Once prospective employees are informed and choose to use a PASS option and its related work incentives, then some level of long-term benefits and PASS support is needed and highly advised. Long-term PASS and work incentives support is very similar to supported employment long-term supports that are more intensive initially and then fade, and are less intensive, yet still ongoing, should any changes, questions, issues, or new opportunities develop. King County Developmental Disabilities Community Employment Services is the best active long-term PASS and employment support model that could be replicated at an agency or system level, yet similar individualized support can be provided and/or facilitated by job developers and/or employment specialists without developing a large system-level program. Employment specialists, who are already checking with the employee and employer on a regular follow-up basis, are well positioned to coordinate and provide such support. Job developers also are qualified to provide or facilitate long-term PASS and work incentives support due to the fact that PASS and work incentives are tied to employment. No position or staff person knows the employment situation details better than does the job developer or employment specialist.

This chapter addresses the job developer's use of Social Security work incentives and is not intended to be a Social Security work incentives manual nor a duplication of many books and manuals on work incentives. Rather, the chapter reviews issues regarding lack of work incentives and the opportunities to use those work incentives that are missed each day in the field. Solutions that are presented here, step by step, cover the most relevant of work incentives and PASS plans, and can be implemented immediately without years of benefits training and study.

Immediate recognition of potential low-risk and high-yield PASS applications is accomplished by spending a little time to find out if the prospective employee receives both SSI and SSDI concurrently and then informing the prospective employee of his or her easy-to-calculate PASS potential, which could generate thousands of dollars at a minimum, and up to tens of thousands of dollars, of employment support funding. Other possible simple and complex PASS scenarios are also briefly addressed. To keep it simple and easy to start somewhere, the best approach mathematically is to determine if a prospective employee receives both SSI and SSDI. Such individuals account for 25%–30% of the number of people receiving disability benefits on an average job developer's or employment specialist's case load. At 25%, one out of four prospective employees whom job developers around the country are working with at this moment could benefit from significant employment support funding for almost any employment, transportation, education, or self-employment–related expense.

## RECOMMENDED READING

Balkus, R., & Wilschke, S. (2004). Annual wage trends for supplemental security income recipients. *Social Security Bulletin, 65.*

Callahan, M., & Garner, B. (1997). *Keys to the workplace: Skills and supports for people with disabilities.* Baltimore: Paul H. Brookes Publishing Co.

Griffin, C.C. (1999). *Working better, working smarter: Building responsive rehabilitation programs.* St. Augustine, FL: TRN Press.

Griffin, C.C., Brooks-Lane, N., Hammis, D., & Crandell, D. (2006). Self-employment: Owning the American dream. In P. Wehman et al. (Eds.), *Real work for real pay: Inclusive employment for people with disabilities.* Baltimore: Paul H. Brookes Publishing Co.

Griffin, C.C., & Hammis, D. (2003). *Making self-employment work for people with disabilities.* Baltimore: Paul H. Brookes Publishing Co.

Hammis, D., & Griffin, C.C. (2002). *Social security considerations for entrepreneurs with significant disabilities.* Florence, MT: Griffin-Hammis Associates, LLC.

Jensen, A., & Silverstein, R. (2005). *A framework for preparing cost estimates for SSDI $1 for $2 gradual reduction demonstration proposals.* Washington, DC: George Washington University Publication.

Jensen, A., & Silverstein, R. (2005). *Gradual reduction choice option and related proposals.* Washington, DC: George Washington University Publication.

National Council on Disability. (2005). *The Social Security Administration's efforts to promote employment for people with disabilities: New solutions for old problems.* Washington, DC: Author.

Office of Policy and Research, Social Security Administration. (2005). *SSI recipients by state and county.* Baltimore: Social Security Administration.

Ticket to Work and Work Incentives Advisory Panel. (2006). *Strategic plan 2006–2007* (SSA Publication No. 63-021). Baltimore: Social Security Administration.

U.S. Government Accountability Office. (2002). *Social Security Administration disability-SGA levels appear to affect the work behavior of relatively few beneficiaries, but more data needed.* Washington, DC: Author.

U.S. Social Security Advisory Board. (2006). *Disability decision making: Data and materials.* Washington, DC: Author.

# Sample Plan to Achieve Self-Support

Social Security Administration

Form Approved
OMB No. 0960-0559

# PLAN TO ACHIEVE SELF-SUPPORT

Date Received

*In order to minimize recontacts or processing delays, please complete all questions and provide thorough explanations where requested. If you need additional space to answer any questions, use the Remarks section or a separate sheet of paper.*

Name _James Dodge_                    SSN _888-88-8888_

## PART I - YOUR WORK GOAL

A. What is your work goal? (*Show the job you expect to have at the end of the plan. Be as specific as possible. If you cannot be specific, provide as much information as possible on the type of work you plan to do. If you do not yet have a specific goal and will be working with a vocational professional to find a suitable job match, show "VR Evaluation" and be sure to complete Part II, question F on page 4.*)

_Assistant Machinist_

If your plan involves paying for job coaching, show the number of hours of job coaching you will receive when you begin working. _30 hours_ per ☑ week ☐ month (*check one*).

Show the number of hours of job coaching you expect to receive after the plan is completed. _1 hour_ per ☑ week ☐ month (*check one*).

B. Describe the duties and tasks you expect to perform in this job. Be as specific as possible.

_See attached Job Analysis Record (JAR) for details. The duties and tasks I expect to perform include grinding engine valves, deburring and degreasing engine parts, washing parts, painting engines and component parts, and other various machine shop maintenance tasks._

C. How did you decide on this work goal and what makes this type of work attractive to you?

_My ideal conditions of employment are (from discovery): Working in an accessible space within a reasonable driving distance of home; driving my own hand-controlled adapted pickup truck; working during the day rather than at night; learning new things with some assistance available._

D. Is a license required to perform this work goal?    ☑ YES    ☐ NO
(*If yes, include the steps you will follow to get a license in Part III.*)

E. How much do you expect to earn each week/month (gross) after your plan is completed?
$ _1,720_ per ☐ week ☑ month (check one)

In *The Job Developer's Handbook* by Cary Griffin, David Hammis,
& Tammara Geary. (Paul H. Brookes Publishing Co., Inc.)

F. If your work goal involves self-employment, explain why working for yourself will make you more self-supporting than working for someone else. _N/A_

IMPORTANT: If you plan to start your own business, attach a detailed business plan.
The business plan must include:
- the type of business;
- products or services to be offered by your business;
- the advertising plan;
- a description of the market for the business;
- technical assistance needed;
- tools, supplies, and equipment needed;
- a profit-and-loss projection for the duration of the PASS and at least one year beyond its completion.

Also include a description of how you intend to make this business succeed.
For assistance in preparing a business plan, contact the Small Business Administration, Chamber of Commerce, local banks, or other business owners.

G. Have you ever submitted a Plan to Achieve Self-Support (PASS) to Social Security?  ☐ YES  ☑ NO  If "no," skip to H.

Was a PASS ever approved for you?  ☐ YES  ☐ NO  If "no," skip to H.

When was your most recent plan approved (month/year)? _____

What was your work goal in that plan? _____

Did you complete that PASS?  ☐ YES  ☐ NO

If no, why weren't you able to complete it? _____

If yes, why weren't you able to become self-supporting? _____

Why do you believe that this new plan you are requesting will help you go to work? _____

H. Have you assigned your "Ticket to Work"?  ☑ YES  ☐ NO  If "no," skip to Part II.

Show name, address and telephone number of the person or organization it was assigned to.

_Montana Vocational Rehabilitation_

_4444 Ridge Drive_

_Hamilton, MT 77777_

_555-555-5555_

In *The Job Developer's Handbook* by Cary Griffin, David Hammis,
& Tammara Geary. (Paul H. Brookes Publishing Co., Inc.)

# PART II - MEDICAL/VOCATIONAL/EDUCATIONAL BACKGROUND

A.  List all your disabling illnesses, injuries, or condition(s). _Developmental and physical disabilities, wheelchair required for mobility, and somewhat limited reading, writing, and communication skills_

B.  Describe any limitations you have because of your disability (e.g., limited amount of standing or lifting, stooping, bending, or walking; difficulty concentrating; unable to work with other people, difficulty handling stress, etc.) Be specific.
_I require environments accessible to wheelchairs and learn best by clear hands-on instructions._

In light of the limitations you described, how will you carry out the duties of your work goal?
_I will carry out the duties of my work goal with adapted workspace support accommodations approved by VR (two adjustable-height work benches, semi-automated parts washer, hand tools and portable engine stands, and on-the-job training supports)._

C.  List the jobs you have had **most often** in the past few years. Also list any jobs, including volunteer work, which are similar to your work goal or which provided you with skills that may help you perform the work goal. List the dates you worked in these jobs. Identify periods of self-employment. If you were in the Army, list your Military Occupational Specialty (MOS) Code; for the Air Force, list your Air Force Speciality code (AFSC); and for the Navy, Marine Corps, and Coast Guard, list your rank.

| Job Title | Type of Business | Dates Worked | |
|---|---|---|---|
| | | From | To |
| Part-time janitor, shelf stocker | Bitterroot Feed & Supply Store | 4/03 | 3/06 |
| One-week paid work experience | Hamilton Auto Body | 4/06 | 5/06 |
| | | | |
| | | | |
| | | | |
| | | | |
| | | | |
| | | | |
| | | | |

In *The Job Developer's Handbook* by Cary Griffin, David Hammis, & Tammara Geary. (Paul H. Brookes Publishing Co., Inc.)

D. **Select the highest grade of school completed.**

☐ 0  ☐ 1  ☐ 2  ☐ 3  ☐ 4  ☐ 5  ☐ 6  ☐ 7  ☐ 8  ☐ 9  ☐ 10  ☐ 11  ☐ 12

☐ GED or ☑ High School Equivalency    College: ☐ 1  ☐ 2  ☐ 3  ☐ 4 or ☐ more

Were you awarded a college or postgraduate degree?    ☐ YES  ☑ NO
If "no," skip to E.

When did you graduate? _____

What type of degree did you receive? (AA, BA, BS, MBA, etc.)? _____

In what field of study? _____

E. Have you completed any type of special job training, trade or vocational school?    ☐ YES  ☑ NO
If "no," skip to F.

Type of training _____

Date completed _____

Did you receive a certificate or license?    ☐ YES  ☐ NO  If "no," skip to F.

What kind of certificate or license did you receive? _____

F. Have you ever had or expect to have a vocational evaluation or an Individualized Written Rehabilitation Plan (IWRP) or an Individualized Plan for Employment (IPE)?    ☑ YES  ☐ NO
If "no," skip to G.

If "YES," attach a copy of the evaluation. If you cannot attach a copy, when were you evaluated (or when do you expect to be evaluated) and when was the IWRP or IPE done ( or when do you expect it to be done)?
My WIA and VR IPEs are attached.

Show the name, address, and phone number of the person or organization who evaluated you (or will evaluate you) or who prepared the IWRP or IPE (or will prepare the IWRP or IPE.)
Jerry Smith

Montana Vocational Rehabilitation Services

4444 Ridge Drive, Hamilton, MT 77777

555-555-5555

G. If you have a college degree or specialized training, and your plan includes additional education or training, explain why the education/training you already received is not sufficient to allow you to be self-supporting.
N/A

_____

_____

_____

Form **SSA-545-BK** (11-2005) ef (11-2005)          Page 4

In *The Job Developer's Handbook* by Cary Griffin, David Hammis, & Tammara Geary. (Paul H. Brookes Publishing Co., Inc.)

155

# PART III - YOUR PLAN

I want my Plan to begin _____ June 1, 2004 _____ (month/year)
(*This should be the date you started or will start working towards your goal.*)

and my Plan to end _____ May 31, 2007 _____ (month/year)
(*This should be the date you expect to start working in your job goal.*)

List the sequential steps that you have taken or will take to reach your work goal starting with your begin date above and concluding with your expected end date above. Be as specific as possible. If you are or will be attending school, show the number of courses you will take each quarter/semester and attach a copy of the degree program or plan that shows the courses you will study. Include the final steps to find a job once you have obtained the tools, education, services, etc., that you need.

| Step | Beginning Date | Completion Date |
|---|---|---|
| **Part I: Retroactive Events and Steps (2 years Retro PASS)** | June 2004 | June 2006 |
| 1. Part-time school-to-work transition employment to learn work skills and explore my interests (note part-time, $200/month job at Bitterroot Feed & Supply actually started in 2003, yet this PASS is going back in time only 24 months to June 2004). Part-time job ended in May of 2006. Active VR case opened after age 22 (2005) to move from underemployment in part-time job to full-time employment. | June 2004 | May 2006 |
| 2. VR and Hamilton Community Rehab Program (HCRP) worked with me through discovery processes to develop a vocational profile. | April 2006 | May 2006 |
| 3. Jeremy Adams, employment specialist from HCRP, developed a 1-week on-the-job situational assessment, supported by the local workforce center, at Hamilton Autobody, Inc., to evaluate my chosen career field skills by actually working on a similar job. | May 2006 | May 2006 |
| 4. Through discovery, my vocational profile recommendations, and working with Jeremy Adams, an opportunity to work at Engine Rebuilders, Inc., evolved within a month and a series of tasks were analyzed and carved. I started working there on June 1, 2006, for 35 hours a week at $7.50 per hour with the goal of increasing my hours to 40 hours a week at $10 per hour in 1–2 years. | May 2006 | June 2006 |
| **Part II: Future PASS Steps and Activities (June 1, 2006–June 1, 2007)** | June 2006 | June 2007 |
| 1. Work at Engine Rebuilders, Inc., starting June 1, 2006, at 35 hours a week, increasing my skills, hours, and pay every 3 months to 40 hours a week by June 1, 2007. | June 2006 | June 2007 |
| 2. Receive interim transportation to and from work from my family at no charge due to short duration of support needed. | June 2006 | July 2006 |
| 3. VR purchases two adapted-height work benches, an adapted parts washer, adapted engine stands, and hand tools. | June 2006 | June 2006 |
| 4. Engine Rebuilders installs hand bars in bathrooms. | June 2006 | June 2006 |
| 5. WIA (local workforce One-Stop) pays for me to take adapted hand-control driver's lessons on weekends and evenings and I pass the driver's test by the end of June. | June 2006 | June 2006 |
| 6. Using most of the retroactive PASS funds of approximately $6,500 of the $7,200 available, I make a down payment on a loan and purchase a slightly used pickup truck and pay for hand controls and GPS unit to be installed. | July 2006 | July 2006 |
| 7. Using some of the remaining retroactive PASS funds, I pay for insurance and tags for my adapted pickup truck. | July 2006 | July 2006 |
| 8. At my new job I begin to learn the tasks described with the support of Jeremy Adams, my employment specialist (job coaching), who supported me initially at 30 hours a week, fading his support within a month to less than 1 hour a week paid for by HCRP. | June 2006 | July 2006 |
| 9. Increase my skills performance of initial carved tasks, and add additional tasks at Engine Rebuilders. | June 2006 | June 2007 |
| 10. Make large monthly installment payments on my pickup truck to pay off my loan by June 2007. | July 2006 | June 2007 |
| 11. Pay quarterly vehicle insurance payments. | Sept. 2006 | June 2007 |
| 12. Intentionally earn over SGA throughout 2006 and 2007 and eliminate my SSDI check as of June 2007 due to using up my (9) trial work period months and my (3) grace months and yet retain my SSI and Medicaid eligibility through the SSI 1619(b) Medicaid work incentive. Even though I will not be receiving an SSI check, I will remain eligible. | June 2007 | June 2007 |
| 13. PASS completed—work goal achieved, SSDI and SSI monthly cash payments ceased (yet SSI and Medicaid eligibility retained), and all debts paid. | June 2007 | June 2007 |

Form **SSA-545-BK** (11-2005) ef (11-2005)          Page 5

In *The Job Developer's Handbook* by Cary Griffin, David Hammis, & Tammara Geary. (Paul H. Brookes Publishing Co., Inc.)

# PART IV - EXPENSES

A. Do you propose to purchase or lease a vehicle?     ☑ YES   ☐ NO

If yes, list the purchase or lease of the vehicle as one of the steps in Part III and complete the following:     *If "no," skip to B on Page 7*

1. Explain why less expensive forms of transportation (e.g., public transportation, cabs) will not allow you to reach your work goal. ___I live in a rural area of Montana over 20 miles___

___each way from my new employment. There are no public transportation options.___

_____

_____

2. Do you currently have a valid driver's license?     ☐ YES   ☑ NO

*If "yes," skip to 3*

If no, does Part III include the steps you will follow to get a driver's license?     ☑ YES   ☐ NO

*If "yes," skip to 3*

If no, who will drive the vehicle? ___N/A___

How will it be used to help you with your work goal?

___I will use the vehicle as transportation to and from work and I also plan to use it at___

___work as requested by my employer to pick up and deliver products and supplies.___

_____

3. Do you already own a vehicle?     ☐ YES   ☑ NO

If yes, explain why you need another vehicle to reach your work goal.     *If "no," skip to 4*

___N/A___

_____

_____

4. Describe the type of vehicle you propose to purchase or lease:

Make: ___Toyota___

Model: ___Tacoma S-Runner Low Cab Pickup Truck___

Year: ___2001 with 30,000 miles___

Purchase price: ___$13,500 ($14,500 with $6500 down and 8% loan interest for 11 month loan)___

OR Lease price: _____

5. If the vehicle is new, explain why a used vehicle is not sufficient to meet your work goal.

___N/A___

_____

_____

In *The Job Developer's Handbook* by Cary Griffin, David Hammis,
& Tammara Geary. (Paul H. Brookes Publishing Co., Inc.)

B.  If you propose to purchase a computer or other major equipment, describe the computer or equipment you will purchase, including the cost for each item.

N/A

C.  Do you already own a computer?     ☐ YES     ☑ NO
    If yes, explain why you need another computer to reach your work goal.

N/A

D.  Please explain why you need the capabilites of the particular computer and/or equipment you identified.   N/A

E.  Other than the items identified in A through D above, list the items or services you are buying or renting or will need to buy or rent in order to reach your work goal. Be as specific as possible. If schooling is an item, list tuition, fees, books, etc. as separate items. List the cost for the entire length of time you will be in school. Where applicable, include brand and model number of the item. **(Do not include expenses you were paying prior to the beginning of your plan; only expenses incurred since the beginning of your plan can be approved.)**

NOTE: Be sure that Part III shows when you will purchase these items or services or training.

1.  Item/service/training: Toyota S-Runner pickup truck and license plates

    Total Cost: $ 13,500 plus financing interest for 1 year totaling $14,500 and tags

    Vendor/provider: Hamilton Toyota

    How will you pay for this item *(one-time payment, installment or monthly payments)?*
    $6,500 down from retro PASS and 11 monthly installments of $727.27.

    How will this help you reach your work goal? I live in a rural area and need an adapted (hand controls) vehicle to get me to and from work each day. I am working at an engine rebuilding company and a pickup truck will allow me to deliver and pick up supplies and products for my employer during work hours.

In *The Job Developer's Handbook* by Cary Griffin, David Hammis, & Tammara Geary. (Paul H. Brookes Publishing Co., Inc.)

2. Item/service/training: _Magellan 3000T GPS unit_

   Total Cost: $ _900 including installation_

   Vendor/provider: _Magellan, Inc._

   How will you pay for this item *(one-time payment, installment or monthly payments)?*

   _One-time payment when I purchase the pickup truck_

   How will this help you reach your work goal? _I experience some difficulty with directions and the Magellan can be set up to provide voice and map directions telling me what streets to travel and when to turn._

3. Item/service/training: _Full coverage insurance for adapted pickup truck_

   Total Cost: $ _1800_

   Vendor/provider: _State Farm Insurance_

   How will you pay for this item *(one-time payment, installment or monthly payments)?*

   _Quarterly payments of $450_

   How will this help you reach your work goal? _Full coverage is required by my local bank for the loan to purchase the pickup truck._

4. Item/service/training: _Gas, maintenance, and repairs_

   Total Cost: $ _1100_

   Vendor/provider: _Local gas stations and Toyota dealer_

   How will you pay for this item *(one-time payment, installment or monthly payments)?*

   _Weekly or as needed for maintenance at $100 per month for 12 months_

   How will this help you reach your work goal? _Using PASS funds to pay for my gas, maintenance, and repairs will provide the financial support needed to successfully meet my goal._

5. Item/service/training: _N/A_

   Total Cost: $ _____

   Vendor/provider: _____

   How will you pay for this item *(one-time payment, installment or monthly payments)?*

   How will this help you reach your work goal?

6. Item/service/training: <u>N/A</u>

Total Cost: $ _____

Vendor/provider: _____

How will you pay for this item *(one-time payment, installment or monthly payments)?*

_____

How will this help you reach your work goal? _____

_____

F. Will any of the items, services or training costs be reimbursed to you or paid by any other source, person or organization? ☐ YES ☑ NO

If yes, be sure to complete Part V, question F on page 11.

## CURRENT LIVING EXPENSES

G. What are your current living expenses each month? $ <u>623</u> /month

Include all living expenses:
- Rent, Mortgage, Property Taxes,
- Property/Personal Insurance,
- Utilities, Phone, Cable, Internet,
- Food, Groceries,
- Automobile Gas, Repair and Maintenance, Public Transportation,
- Clothes, Personal Items, Laundry/Dry Cleaning,
- Medical, Dental, Prescription,
- Entertainment, Charity Contributions, etc.

H. If the amount of income you will have available for living expenses after making payments or saving money for your plan is **less than** your current living expenses, explain how you will pay for your living expenses.

<u>N/A</u>

_____

_____

_____

_____

_____

_____

_____

_____

_____

In *The Job Developer's Handbook* by Cary Griffin, David Hammis, & Tammara Geary. (Paul H. Brookes Publishing Co., Inc.)

# PART V - FUNDING FOR WORK GOAL

A.  Do you plan to use any items you already own (e.g., equipment or property) to reach your work goal?　☐ YES　☑ NO

If "no," skip to B.  If yes, show the items you will use that you already own:

Item  N/A _____

How will this help you reach your work goal? _____

_____

Item  N/A _____

How will this help you reach your work goal? _____

_____

Item  N/A _____

How will this help you reach your work goal? _____

_____

B.  Have you saved any money to pay for the expenses listed on pages 6-9 in Part IV? *(Include cash on hand or money in a bank account.)*　☑ YES　☐ NO

If "yes," how much have you saved?　$600 _____

C.  List the income you **receive or expect to receive** below. *(Include Social Security benefits, wages, self-employment, assistance, royalties, pensions, dividends, prizes, insurance, support payments, etc.)*

| Type of Income | Amount | Frequency (Weekly, Monthly, Yearly) |
|---|---|---|
| Gross wages at Engine Rebuilders | $1,200 | Monthly |
| SSDI | $326 | Monthly |

D.  How much of this income will you set aside to pay for the vehicle, computer, major equipment and other items, services and training listed in Part IV?

Each month retroactively from June 2004 to June 2006, I will set aside $303 of my SSDI since SSI does not count $20 of my SSDI check for a total of 24 months retroactive totaling $7,272

From June 2006 to June 2007 for 12 months I will set aside the same $303 from my SSDI for 12 months totaling $3,636 from my SSDI and also one-half of my gross wages after the first $65 I earn each month ($1,200–$65)/2 = ($1,135/2) = $567.50 per month for 12 months totaling $6,810. Adding the total from my SSDI and from my wages equals ($3,636 + $6,810) $10,446 between June 2006 and June 2007.

The total including my retroactive PASS funds of $7,272 and my PASS funds of $10,446 between June 2006 and June 2007 equals $17,718.

My expenses listed in my PASS are:

$14,500 pickup truck, (includes loan interest and tags)
$900 Magellan GPS
$1,800 vehicle insurance
$1,100 gas, maintenance and repairs
$18,300

My PASS will provide $17,718. I have saved $600 to start my PASS, for a total amount of $18,318 to pay for the $18,300 PASS expenses.

In *The Job Developer's Handbook* by Cary Griffin, David Hammis, & Tammara Geary. (Paul H. Brookes Publishing Co., Inc.)

## Part V - FUNDING FOR WORK GOAL (Continued)

E.  Do you plan to save any or all of this income for a future purchase which is necessary to complete your goal?

☑ YES　　☐ NO  If "no," skip to F.

If "yes," you will need to keep this money separate from other money you have. How will you keep the money separate. *(If you will keep the savings in a separate bank account, give the name and address of the bank and the account number.)* Hamilton Bank, checking

account number 458999-00767

F.  Will any other person or organization (e.g., grants, assistance, or Vocational Rehabilitation agency) pay for or reimburse you for any part of the expenses listed in Part IV or provide any other items or services you will need?

☑ YES　　☐ NO  If "no," skip to Part VI.

If "yes," provide details as follows:

| Who Will Pay | Item/Service | Amount | When will the item/ service be purchased? |
|---|---|---|---|
| Montana VR | hand tools | $1000 | June 2006 |
| Montana VR | 2 adapted work benches | $800 | June 2006 |
| Montana VR | adapted parts washer | $400 | June 2006 |
| Montana VR | engine stands | $75 | June 2006 |
| VR, WIA, and CRP Adult Service program funding | job trial, development and coaching | $7,500 | May 2006-June 2007 |

## Part VI - OTHER CONTACTS

Did someone help you prepare this plan?　　☑ YES　　☐ NO

If yes, give the name, address and telephone number of that person or organization:

Name　Jerry Adams

Address　444 Mountain Lane

City, State and Zip Code　Hamilton, MT 77777

Telephone　555-555-5555

E-mail address　Jadams@HCRP. Com

Are they charging you a fee for this service?　　☐ YES　　☑ NO

If yes, how much are they charging?

In *The Job Developer's Handbook* by Cary Griffin, David Hammis, & Tammara Geary. (Paul H. Brookes Publishing Co., Inc.)

## Part VI - OTHER CONTACTS (Continued)

May we contact them if we need additional information about your plan?   ☑ YES   ☐ NO

Do you want us to send them a copy of our decision on your plan?   ☑ YES   ☐ NO
If yes, please submit a Consent for Release of Information, form SSA-3288.

*(If you also wish to authorize this person or organization to act on your behalf in matters pertaining to this plan, please submit an Appointment of Representative, form SSA1696.)*

## PART VII - REMARKS

Use this section or a separate sheet of paper if you need additional space to answer any questions:

_____

_____

_____

_____

_____

_____

_____

_____

_____

_____

_____

_____

_____

_____

_____

_____

_____

In *The Job Developer's Handbook* by Cary Griffin, David Hammis,
& Tammara Geary. (Paul H. Brookes Publishing Co., Inc.)

# PART VIII - AGREEMENT

**If my plan is approved, I agree to:**

☑ Comply with all of the terms and conditions of the plan as approved by the Social Security Administration (SSA).

☑ Report any changes in my plan **to SSA** immediately.

☑ Keep records and receipts of all expenditures I make under the plan until asked to provide them to SSA.

☑ Use the income or resources set aside under the plan **only** to buy the items or services shown in the plan as approved by SSA.

☑ Report any changes that may affect the amount of my SSI payment immediately.  (For example: income, resources, living arrangement, marital status.)

I realize that if I do not comply with the terms of the plan or if I use the income or resources set aside under my plan for any other purpose, SSA will count the income or resources that were excluded and I may have to repay the additional SSI I received.

I also realize that SSA may not approve any expenditure for which I do not submit receipts or other proof of payment.

**I declare under penalty of perjury that I have examined all the information on this form, and on any accompanying statements or forms, and it is true and correct to the best of my knowledge.**

Signature _James Dodge_                             Date _June 1, 2006_

Address _114 Fairview Road_

City, State and Zip code  _Hamilton, MT 77777_

Telephone:  Home _777-777-7777_

Work _555-555-5555_

Other _____

E-mail address _jdodge@enginerebuilders.com_

If you have a representative payee, the representative payee must sign below:

Representative Payee Signature _____ Date _____

Form **SSA-545-BK** (11-2005) ef (11-2005)                Page 13

In *The Job Developer's Handbook* by Cary Griffin, David Hammis, & Tammara Geary. (Paul H. Brookes Publishing Co., Inc.)

# PRIVACY ACT STATEMENT

The Social Security Administration is allowed to collect the information on this form under section 1631(e) of the Social Security Act. We need this information to determine if we can approve your plan for achieving self-support. Giving us this information is voluntary. However, without it, we may not be able to approve your plan. Social Security will not use the information for any other purpose.

We would give out the facts on this form without your consent only in certain situations. For example, we give out this information if a Federal law requires us to or if your congressional Representative or Senator needs the information to answer questions you ask them.

**Paperwork Reduction Act Statement** - This information collection meets the requirements of 44 U.S.C. § 3507, as amended by Section 2 of the Paperwork Reduction Act of 1995. You do not need to answer these questions unless we display a valid Office of Management and Budget control number. We estimate that it will take about 120 minutes to read the instructions, gather the facts, and answer the questions. **SEND THE COMPLETED FORM TO YOUR LOCAL SOCIAL SECURITY OFFICE. The office is listed under U. S. Government agencies in your telephone directory or you may call Social Security at 1-800-772-1213.** You may send comments on our time estimate above to: SSA, 1338 Annex Building, Baltimore, MD 21235-6401. *Send only comments relating to our time estimate to this address, not the completed form.*

In *The Job Developer's Handbook* by Cary Griffin, David Hammis, & Tammara Geary. (Paul H. Brookes Publishing Co., Inc.)

# OUR RESPONSIBILITIES TO YOU

We received your plan for achieving self-support (PASS) on _____.
Your plan will be processed by Social Security employees who are trained to work with PASS.

The PASS expert handling your case will work directly with you. He or she will look over the plan as soon as possible to see if there is a good chance that you can meet your work goal. The PASS expert will also make sure that the things you want to pay for are needed to achieve your work goal and are reasonably priced. If changes are needed, the PASS expert will discuss them with you.

You may contact the PASS expert toll-free at 1- ( _____ ) - _____

# YOUR REPORTING AND RECORDKEEPING RESPONSIBILITIES

**If we approve your plan, you must tell Social Security about any changes to your plan and any changes that may affect the amount of your SSI payment. You must tell us if:**

- ☐ Your medical condition improves.
- ☐ You are unable to follow your plan.
- ☐ You decide not to pursue your goal or decide to pursue a different goal.
- ☐ You decide that you do not need to pay for any of the expenses you listed in your plan.
- ☐ Someone else pays for any of your plan expenses.
- ☐ You use the income or resources we exclude for a purpose other than the expenses specified in your plan.
- ☐ There are any other changes to your plan.
- ☐ There are any changes in your income, help you get from others, or things of value that you own.
- ☐ There are any changes in where you live, how you live, or your marital status.

You must tell us about any of these things within 10 days following the month in which it happens. If you do not report any of these things, we may stop your plan.

You should also tell us if you decide that you need to pay for other expenses not listed in your plan in order to reach your goal. We may be able to change your plan or the amount of income we exclude so you can pay for the additional expenses.

**YOU MUST KEEP RECEIPTS OR CANCELLED CHECKS TO SHOW WHAT EXPENSES YOU PAID FOR AS PART OF THE PLAN.** You need to keep these receipts or cancelled checks until we contact you to find out if you are still following your plan. When we contact you, we will ask to see the receipts or cancelled checks. If you are not following the plan, you may have to pay back some or all of the SSI you received.

Form **SSA-545-BK** (11-2005) ef (11-2005)                    Page 15

In *The Job Developer's Handbook* by Cary Griffin, David Hammis, & Tammara Geary. (Paul H. Brookes Publishing Co., Inc.)

# 10 Active Families

## Support, Partnership, and Roles

*Tammara Geary, Cary Griffin, and David Hammis*

Any job developer or employment specialist who has spent any time at all in the field has heard sentiments similar to these:

"The parents are too overprotective."
"We'd love to get her a job, but Mom won't let her."
"Mom is very difficult."
"They don't think she can do anything except go to day hab."
"Frankly, our [the provider's] relationship with the family is strained."
"The sister is too controlling."
"If only the family would just get out of the way."

Sound familiar? For whatever reason, job developers and families frequently end up in combative relationships. This is extremely problematic, as families have a wealth of information about an individual and can exert considerable influence on the job seeker. Families can be amazing allies who provide valuable support to the individual as well as to the provider organization. Establishing trusting, respectful, and active partnerships with families is critical to the employment process. This chapter will look at the family perspective and will give strategies and tips for building partnerships, active family roles, and healthy communication.

## UNDERSTANDING THE FAMILY EXPERIENCE

While certainly every family and every situation is different, there are some commonalities to the experience of having a son, daughter, or family member with a disability. Understanding some of those experiences can help providers establish strong relationships with families, which ultimately can only benefit the individual.

### The System's Focus on Disability and the Family Experience

Entry into the system—whether it is school, adult services, vocational rehabilitation, or Social Security disability programs—requires focus on disability. Time and time again,

This chapter is based on the author's conversations and work with many family members and individuals with disabilities and providers throughout the United States that we have encountered in various venues, along with personal experiences. Thanks to the many individuals and families who have shared their experiences with us.

the individual and the family must focus on the individual's deficits and problems in order to prove total and permanent disability. Families are put in a position where they must focus, at least temporarily, on all the ways a person is not or will never be normal. This can be a significantly disempowering and depressing experience, accompanied by eroding confidence and hope for the future.

Beyond that, involvement in school and adult programs comes with many meetings and ongoing evaluations. Typical vocational evaluations are highly limiting in the information they provide, particularly for those with significant cognitive and/or developmental disabilities.

All too commonly, the meetings continue to highlight deficits, and annual meetings set goals that have to do with remediating identified problems. Most parents who have children with disabilities will note that at some time during their son's or daughter's educational and adult service history, they have participated in a meeting that was an extremely negative, and maybe even a humiliating, experience. This stems from over-focusing on the problems, little recognition of ability, and perhaps even an oppositional or blaming tone to the meeting. In many cases, the family members see the services or supports offered as inadequate. Further, when supports are not working out, the individual receiving support services is often blamed; identified as more incompetent than originally assumed; or, even worse, identified as "noncompliant," "stubborn," "manipulative," or "attention seeking." It is, unfortunately, not the norm for the providers of support to look at the supports provided as the problem.

Families are quite aware of the difficulties and challenges faced by their family member. They look to professionals to help move beyond that and to help build a future. Meetings, evaluations, and situations such as those described here can have many different effects on the family. There can be intense frustration that the professionals providing supports see little value or ability in the job seeker. Even worse, when a parent reacts to the negative labels, evaluations, or inadequate supports by advocating for a better environment or supports, a parent or family member can be labeled as "difficult" or as "trouble." Providers typically respond to this by avoiding the parent or tuning out much of what the parent has to say. If parents perceive that they are considered to be difficult, they may respond by getting louder and more challenging. Here we have the birth of the combative relationship.

On the flip side, many providers indicate that parents are overprotective, that they don't see their son's or daughter's potential, that they are overly concerned with safety, that they won't allow the person to become more independent, and that they won't allow the person to try more things. There are several factors that may contribute to this issue.

Through the many negative experiences throughout life, the system teaches people with disabilities that they can't contribute, perform, work, live independently, and so on. For many people, services have focused on caretaking and protection. Many goals set are never reached, and many supports provided are inadequate. There is a tremendous erosion of confidence here, both in the individual with a disability, in the family's ability to advocate, and in the provider system itself. Families may begin to see the staff and systems that are there to support their child and family as largely incompetent and lacking. Further, families and individuals are frequently trapped, as there are no other options for support, leaving them feeling very powerless.

Families have been taught that their family member has limited value and competence. Furthermore, families have felt that the staff and supports are incompetent. But then a provider agency, which perhaps has fed these notions in the past, announces its intention to help somebody live and work in the community. All along the system has advised a caretaking, segregated, protective approach to services, and now suddenly the provider is seeing the person with a disability as competent enough to contribute something of value (work) and to live independently in the community. If the family has been underwhelmed by the basic custodial and maintenance supports or services provided (something they do at home every day), how can they be expected to have confidence now in the ability of the agency to provide adequate supports for a much more challenging situation—moving into the community? Given their history and experiences, how can we possibly expect families to embrace this shift?

Not only would a serious shift in thinking be required, but also a sincerely trusting relationship with the provider organization as well as demonstration of a high level of competence by support staff would be essential. Those working for any organization that has changed from providing segregated services to providing integrated community services knows that shifting staff attitudes, in terms of seeing people as capable of working in the community, and moving from caretaking to supporting individually-directed services, is a substantial challenge that takes time. Yet providers rarely afford the same adjustment time to families. Thinking can change, but it takes time to reframe working relationships and to trust in the competence of staff.

Even for families who have always believed in the potential of their son or daughter to live in the community, to contribute to the workplace, and to lead as normal a life as possible, this move is fraught with concerns, particularly when there is limited confidence in the staff and organization. Their journey has been one of constant advocacy and self-education and networking. They know what types of services and supports are needed, and the system has been too slow or unwilling or unsuccessful in providing adequate supports. This family is highly hopeful but frequently wary. The highs of new potential were followed by the lows of underperformance of supports too often. Even in families that have persistently advocated for and received services they really wanted, the outcomes are frequently not what they expected. In some cases, the provider builds up hope for outcomes that are never realized. In some cases, the family hopes for more than is possible given the provider's limited skills in creating productive, well-fitting jobs within their community. Regardless of the root cause or situation, individuals with disabilities and their families live with fairly consistent disappointment. For some, daring to hope again is just too much. So it becomes the provider's responsibility to figure out how to demonstrate the responsiveness that will gain the confidence of the family and shift this dynamic.

## Relationships with Providers

For these reasons, the relationship with the individual and family, and the perception of staff and organizational competence, are critical. It is hard to underestimate the impact of this relationship. The best outcomes require respect, willing collaboration, communication, and confidence between the provider and the family. And it is important to remember that this relationship is not about the family member or the provider. This is about the best outcomes for the individual, a goal that despite perceived evidence to the contrary, is typically a goal that both parties share.

Whereas the potential and outcomes of community living and employment related to quality of life, social connections and value, contribution, and normalcy are well worth the effort, community employment presents some unique challenges for families that may not be present in segregated programs. There are more uncontrollable variables, perceived and real, in community employment. Hours may vary, leaving the individual without supports for the nonwork part of his or her daily routine. Transportation is often a challenge, requiring families to plan their days around driving or relying on transportation systems that may not be entirely reliable. There are frequently safety concerns: the what ifs? What if he gets lost when he's riding the bus to work? What if somebody takes advantage of him? What if somebody hurts her or is mean to her? What if she loses her Supplemental Security Income (SSI)? These variables are easier to control in segregated environments. The person is picked up every day, works a predictable number of hours, and is perceived to be protected from harm within the four walls of segregation.

Interestingly enough, these types of concerns are shared to some degree even by those families of people without disabilities who have always worked toward a normal life for their family member, those who hope and plan only for integration and contribution. And these concerns are valid and typical of the concerns parents have for any child when he or she begin venturing out on his or her own. However, in the world of community supports, providers are well in tune with the dignity of risk and may inadvertently dismiss these concerns as worth the risk or as just an outright sign of overprotection or a difficult parent. In order to move forward, a solid relationship must be built where the issues of the family can be heard and addressed to everyone's satisfaction. Strategies for relationship building are addressed later in this chapter.

## A Lifetime Commitment

It is absolutely essential that providers acknowledge and understand that the family is in the individual's life for the long haul. Yes, there are exceptions, and it is easy to point to some example of a family that has basically discharged its role to providers or institutions. It is not for us to judge why those decisions are made, as there are so many variables involved. And for those who don't have family support, we need to apply the same thinking and relationship building to those who are the most significant parties in their lives.

For the most part, people with disabilities have some level of family involvement, and many have significant family support and involvement, particularly those making the transition from school to adult services, a period of rather significant anxiety and hope. These families have been involved, in some cases consumed, with supporting, advocating, and searching for good supports for their son or daughter. They have been there from day one. They have been through countless professionals, sometimes so many it is impossible to remember them all. They are there through every change, through every achieved goal, through every missed milestone, through every success, through every disappointment. What's more important, they will still be there when the individual staff are gone, when the provider is gone, whether the service being offered succeeds or fails. And if it fails, the support frequently falls back on the family. When there is crisis, the family takes responsibility. It is a lifelong commitment. So sometimes, when things are stable and the key supports to the individual are relieved of regular responsibility, it is hard to intentionally rock the boat, even for a life improvement. This is far more complicated for families than it looks from the provider's perspective.

## A Case Study Example

### Maria ▬ ▪ ▬ ▪ ▬ ▪ ▬ ▪ ▬ ▪ ▬ ▪ ▬ ▪ ▬ ▪ ▬ ▪ ▬

Maria is a 34-year-old woman who is being considered for a possible job in the community. She has been supported by an employment agency for 8 years, 3 in the workshop, and 5 on an office cleaning crew. Nothing about the work really matches Maria's interests, and she's clearly losing interest, as it has become necessary to constantly prompt her and provide reinforcement to get her to complete tasks she knows how to do. At the time Maria started with the agency, they only operated a workshop and were just beginning to support people in community jobs. However, right at the time Maria started with the agency, its funding was cut, and they decided to do work crews only. Recently, a new executive director came in, and she is looking to significantly improve the agency's outcomes, focusing on individually driven customized community work supports.

Currently, the provider's relationship with Maria's mother is pretty combative. Maria's mother is perceived as never happy with services and very demanding. The oral history or mythology of the organization has Maria's mother characterized as unrealistic about what her daughter can do, yet critical and demanding. Staff say she treats them all like idiots. They haven't heard from her in quite a while, and they are operating on the no-news-is-good-news principle.

If you ask Maria's mother, she'll tell you that she "treats them like idiots because they are idiots." She feels they've never really taken the time to know and understand her daughter; that they see her as another label rather than as an individual. She feels they've never really tried to do what's best for Maria. Maria's mother hated the fact that they put her in a workshop, but this agency was the only deal in town, and thus represented Maria's only hope for something—and her mother's only respite. She believes that staff is disrespectful to Maria, talking down to her; that they don't know how to teach her; that they spend more effort threatening her with and delivering punishment or negative consequences for her behavior than they do in supporting her; that they could accomplish so much more with her if they were competent.

In the past, Maria's mother advocated. Now she's just tired. She hasn't contacted the agency because Maria's situation is stable; there's nothing right about it, but nothing is going terribly wrong. Maria's mother is disappointed. It's not what she hoped for, and planned for, but it is something. At least, Maria's not depressed and lying around the house. Her mother can work and do some things for herself and others in the family. She's just worn down.

How did it get this way? Looking back, it started during Maria's school years when she had lots of food service training. Maria was never really interested in that kind of employment and made it clear that she did not like it. By the time she finished school, she was "over it." Despite that, and Maria's mother's concerns, Maria got a job through a provider frying french fries at a local fast food restaurant. The provider gave very minimal training and support, and before long, she lost the job. Though relieved not to have to work there anymore, Maria was devastated by the experience of being fired and leaving her co-workers.

Maria's mother reshuffled family priorities and responsibilities to have Maria at home. Maria sat at home for many months until the provider found her another job. Given Maria's boredom and increasing depression at home, and the fact that the family was juggling schedules to try to provide support for Maria, everyone decided together to accept the job even though it was another food service job. Maria and her mother both made it clear that Maria was not really thrilled about that particular job; rather, she was interested in exploring some other options, maybe with one of the community centers, or craft stores, or something more in line with her interests. The provider indicated that these goals might be unrealistic, noting that they have great success with people in food service and janitorial jobs. They said they would consider other options down the road, but this was all that was available now. Maria and her mother heard that as a quid pro quo: You do well with this job; we'll look for something that suits you later.

Maria's new job was scrubbing pots and washing dishes at a girl's boarding school. She worked the lunch and dinner shifts, with a 2-hour break in between, during which she hung out in the cafeteria. She hated that downtime; she hated the work. It was hot and dirty. She felt isolated in the dish room. Co-workers were impatient and bossy. And she never really did well at the job—not a surprise given the situation.

She worked for several months and tried several times to tell her employment specialist that she did not like the job and wanted to look for a different job. Each time, she was told that she had chosen to work there, that she needed to do a good job and keep the job, that she had to prove she could work this job if she expected a better one, or that she obviously did not want to work any job. She would apply herself for some time, hoping to prove her desire for another job, but could not sustain the effort given how much she truly despised everything about the job and the workplace. Her mother was not aware of these issues because the employment specialist did not tell her and Maria was not able to voice her worries to her mother. She was left highly disempowered.

Eventually, she started developing behavioral problems and even became physically ill. She would drop loaded bus pans, spill things on the floor, and snap at people. She was often sick, complaining of headaches, stomachaches, and back pain, and insisted she had carpal tunnel syndrome (something her sister had recently and was able to miss work for several weeks following surgery). Her employment specialist saw the various maladies as behavioral attention-seeking issues, and told co-workers to ignore it and send Maria back to work.

When she started complaining about her back at home and wanting to call in sick, her mother asked what was going on. Maria managed to tell her mom that she hated the job and described the problems, even letting her mom know that the employment specialist had told her to "work this job or else...." When Maria's mother asked her why she never told her any of this, Maria could not explain very well, and could only say, "But you like my job." Maria's mother interpreted this to mean that Maria was acquiescing to her mother's relief and apparent happiness since Maria started working. Maria's mother would say, "Did you have a good day at work?" or something of the sort, and Maria would give the answer she thought her mom wanted: "Yes." Acquiescence—the response of the truly powerless.

Maria's mother helped Maria resign from her job. She rearranged the family life and structure to again accommodate Maria. Maria continued to complain about her back, and upon visiting a doctor, found that she had a slipping disk that required medical treatment. Maria's mother had to take a leave of absence from work to deal with the medical treatment, therapies, and recovery.

At this point, Maria's mother had some words with the provider organization, and as you can imagine, she was not at her best when she did it. This was the moment when she was defined as "the impossible mother." Throughout her conversations with the agency's leadership, she never felt that her concerns were heard or validated. Though the employment specialist was terminated, the organization was, understandably, on the defensive. The relationship crumbled. Maria spent a few years at home.

The family moved to a neighboring county where other families reported that services were better. However, due to funding cuts shortly after their move, individual jobs were temporarily on hold. The only option for Maria at that time was the workshop. She was reluctant to have Maria in a shop, but she had just uprooted the entire family, hoping for a better situation for Maria. Maria's younger siblings were changing schools. They were stuck with no truly acceptable choices. Mom advocated, got assurances that the hold on jobs was only temporary, and made clear that their goal was real employment. She felt the new provider was listening and cooperative, and it wouldn't be too long before Maria got a job.

Now it's been 8 more years, and Maria still doesn't have a job. Maria and her family have sat through countless meetings where agency staff talked about her inability to stay on task, her refusal to follow directions, her intolerably low production rate, and her increasing tantrums requiring timeout. She was labeled "not ready" for work until these issues were remediated. The family, mostly her mother, advocated for a job and finally got them to refer her for a vocational evaluation as a first step toward employment. Maria's mother was glad for anything different and Maria went through evaluation. The evaluation only confirmed that Maria was "not ready."

Maria's mother continued to patiently try to build relationships and advocate by teaching people about Maria's capacity and how to work with her. Her comments went largely unheeded by the organization, and when she found people who would listen and try new things with Maria, they weren't around for long. There were so many people in and out of their lives that it all became a blur. And they had to start over with every new staff person.

They finally got the janitorial crew job, but it was a hollow victory. Somebody threw them a bone; it was not what they wanted. And to top it off, somebody who worked at the organization from the other county, where things had gone so poorly, joined the staff at this organization. She brought with her the history and mythology about the impossible mother. Maria's mother has continued to advocate, but nobody has really tried to do any of the things she suggested. So, they tolerated the work crew. Maria's mother ran out of steam about 3 years ago. She's a grandmother now. Her grown daughter lives nearby with two little ones of her own. Even though Maria's situation isn't perfect, Maria's mother needs to focus elsewhere.

So now there's been a leadership change, and the organization is ready to give Maria a shot at employment. They approach Maria and her family, thinking she's going to be really excited about it. Her response surprises them. While Maria doesn't like the crew she's presently working with, she's no longer sure she wants a job. She's internalized all the things she's heard over the years: that she's not capable of working. Her mother is dismayed. The same people who have been telling her Maria isn't ready are now saying she is. Those that said she needed certain protections, and so forth, are now saying she doesn't. Those that have seen her as incapable are saying she can contribute.

The staff say they are changing direction, learning new skills to be able to help people achieve real jobs and real outcomes to improve their quality of life. One of the newer staff members even tells Maria's mother that Maria has no business being on a work crew. Her mother feels like they want her to believe that they have magically changed their thinking, their ability, their views of Maria, when everything in her experience screams otherwise.

Maria and her entire family are experiencing a multitude of thoughts and feelings, everything from gratification and validation, to excitement about the opportunity, to hope, to fear, to hope yet again, to anxiety about losing the balance they've achieved, to absolute fright about the ability to survive another try and another failure, to utter distrust and lack of confidence in the staff, to profound disbelief in the staff's competence to actually do what they are saying they can do. The list goes on.

Although expecting the family to maybe have some concerns, the provider believes they will jump at the opportunity. The family's reluctance and questions are perceived as confirmation that the mother is impossible, hard to please, and unrealistic. New staff members perceive her as overprotective and unwilling to take a risk. Reality is very different for Maria, her mother, and her family. It has been 34 years of risk and struggle for very little reward. And every risk, every change, every ending requires the family to reshuffle and pick up the pieces. The family has the lifetime commitment. And nobody tries to really understand Maria, her family, or their perspective. Instead, they label it and move on.

Eventually, Maria's mother contacts the new executive director, who is very open to talking with her and Maria. The executive director understands that they are asking Maria and her family for what she calls "an undeserved leap of faith." She gives realistic assurances, saying they will do their best while noting that they might not get it perfect right away, that there will be some trial and error, and that the staff is learning. She explains that they just want to start by getting to know Maria via some discovery activities and that the family will be part of the team from the start. She connects Maria with a staff member who will serve as team facilitator by selecting a staff person she felt would stay with the organization. She assures Maria's mother that she and Maria can interview this person and if they don't think she is a good fit for Maria, they can interview someone else. The executive director also assures them that she will make sure that Maria's team facilitator will get lots of guidance and mentoring as she learns the new strategies.

The new team facilitator and Maria's team members, along with the supervisor and executive director, work with Maria and her mom to build confidence and a solid working relationship. The team recognizes that change for the family is inherently stressful. At the same time, Maria and her family are able to understand that the team members are themselves learning and trying new things. Both the family and team understand that a certain amount of trial and error can be expected. That everyone involved collaborates as a team and takes the time to allow change to occur naturally are two significant factors that build confidence for everyone.

Eventually, Maria does go to work. During the school year, she works at a private elementary school assisting the arts and crafts teacher with her classes. In the summer, she works for the department of parks and recreation, assisting that same teacher with arts and crafts at day camps.

## Comments

While this story may seem somewhat extreme or unusually awful, it is unfortunately not that uncommon. Clearly, everybody's situation is different. However, the themes of conflict, frustration, challenges within the family, disrespect, erosion of confidence, incompetence of the provider agency, the family catching the remains of a bad experience, feeling unheard or misunderstood, balancing personal and overall family needs versus the individual's needs, labeling, surrender, and so on are common among families.

Much of this can be avoided. Strong partnerships between the schools and adult providers can provide an adequate transition for community connection and contribution. Building life experience driven by individual interests (as opposed to that of the family unit) can be accomplished with peer support. The individual can leave school with not only a decent first job, but with some direction for a career path.

Solid families are vital partners. They have history, influence, and the knowledge and resources to greatly benefit the process.

## When There Is No Family Support

There are, unfortunately, situations where there really is no family support. Sometimes the family is deceased or incapacitated. Sometimes the family simply expects the system to take care of the person, or there may be other issues at play. The person may not have a family, or may have a family that is overwhelmed with other family issues, such as financial issues, other children with disabilities, a family member who is sick, parents living in another state, or parents who are deceased. Perhaps a sibling is trying to be involved but is also dealing with his or her own family unit. Parents may be unemployed or underemployed, there may be some dysfunction in the family, or they may be simply struggling to make it every month. When there is little family involvement, it is important to try to connect with the family and begin to build a relationship wherever possible. Family involvement can be nurtured and developed, particularly when they see potential for the individual becoming more successful and independent. Work with the family to see what they can realistically contribute, perhaps even on a time-limited basis.

There are times when these efforts are not successful, or there is truly no way the family can or will be involved. In such circumstances, it is necessary to try to build a support system around the individual. This may take some effort and creativity, starting with getting paid staff invested in mentoring and assisting the individual to engage in community activities where she can contribute and be with people who share her interests. From this point, more relationships can be facilitated.

## Working with Families: Tips for Professionals

### Don't Make Assumptions

Professionals must guard against making assumptions and judgments about families. Presuming to know what motivates any particular behavior you observe is unfair. For example, if a parent is not happy with a particular job or has concerns with their son or daughter going to work, don't assume it is because the father is overprotective or controlling. Instead strive to understand the parents' concerns. Once an assumption is made, it colors all other interactions. It is important to understand each different family from its perspective.

### Leave the Attitude Behind

Acting on assumptions is even worse than making them in the first place. For example, take the case of a parent who is resisting employment efforts. Staff are making the assumption that the parent is overprotective. The provider responds by trying to convince the parent of the safety of work and discusses concepts like dignity of risk. When the parent continues to resist, the provider sees the parent as an obstacle and becomes increasingly frustrated. The parent feels this attitude, and communication between the parties may become hostile.

Perhaps the reason for the parents so-called resistance is actually 1) concerns about benefits and 2) not clicking with the particular employment specialist assigned to work with them. These issues will never be identified and understood if the provider gives in to the assumption that the parent is just an obstacle.

Do listen. Work to correctly understand the issues at play. The more clear the issues, the more effective are the parties' ability to resolve them. In this example, getting a solid benefits analysis and changing the employment specialist would go a long way to fix the resistance.

### Listen and Observe

There is much more to communication than words. It is quite possible that the words spoken don't fully convey the intended message, and the communication will not progress. Issues will not be resolved until the real or full message is communicated.

If you've ever been married or been in a long-term relationship, chances are you've experienced this, even around the most mundane issues. You know—she wants him to take out the trash; he wants her to leave him alone during the game. Before long, it is a ridiculous argument, disproportionate with the issue at hand. Both parties leave the disagreement angry and nothing has been resolved. Neither feels their issue was heard. Communication and, consequently, action failed. Sometimes there is more to the issue than the mundane statement. For example, she really wants him to notice when the trash needs to go out and do it without her asking; he really wants her to stop asking and to understand that he will do it, but his timing for chores is different from hers.

With the focus on families, it is critical to listen carefully to what is said and to observe, because these will help you identify the issues, build trust, and move toward resolution and cooperation.

### Work at Relationships

Give time to communicating and building rapport with families. Experienced practitioners know that building and maintaining successful employment is much easier with family support and can be very difficult when the family is not on board. At the same time, they respect a family's privacy and take care that professional involvement does not become intrusive.

### Be Competent

Too much cannot be said about provider competence, at both the individual and organizational level. The organization as a whole must develop and maintain a relationship with the community and a reputation for respectful, cooperative relationships with the individuals they serve and their families. Likewise, individual staff working with job seekers or employees and their families must demonstrate both understanding and respect through their actions, a desire to work cooperatively, and the ability to do the things they talk about. This builds the trust required to move forward effectively.

### Build Community Presence

The organization and its staff members must be seen as valuable, contributing members of their community. The organization needs an identity beyond "that program for special people." Its presence in the community should signal its value to the community at large. Once the organization has respect and credibility within the community, networking opportunities will multiply. There are many ways this can be accomplished.

- Hire staff from various communities to work within your community or within some subset of the larger service area. Those staff members can focus on building and nurturing relationships within that community.

- As part of your interviewing and hiring process, ask the applicant about his or her community relationships and membership in various service clubs, recreational clubs, or civic groups. When making hiring decisions, consider the applicant's community connections.

- Require staff to be actively involved with at least one community group—not just business groups—and pay them for these few hours a week. Think of it as job development time because the networking time will turn into jobs.

- Participate in community events like ones associated with Habitat for Humanity, take various cause-related walks or runs, participate in local election groups, as well as in clean-up or planting projects. Take people with disabilities along—one person with one mentor—into situations where they can contribute and participate along with other community members. This not only establishes the organization's presence, but it also helps show that people with disabilities are competent and contributing members of the community.

- Contribute to membership groups, clubs, and business organizations by joining committees and work groups. Attending meetings is passive participation. Active participation is required in order to build the value and presence of your organization and its staff in the community at large.

## Active Roles for Families

Families often ask what they can do to prepare their children with disabilities for the workforce and adult life. The answer lies in assisting their children to engage in the same sort of process everyone goes through in finding and developing their careers. Most people go through a fairly organic process in determining what they want to be when they grow up. Some people grow up and change careers more than once in a lifetime. People have different life experiences that mold and expose them to a variety of interests, and they gain information along the way that guides them toward their career choices.

For many people with disabilities, particularly people with developmental disabilities, that experience is truncated, curtailed by the lack of perceived potential and opportunity that comes with having a disability. This can be attributed in part to the various therapies and medical treatments that may be routine in the day-to-day reality for people, where they grow up in the microcosm of hospitals and treatment rooms. For others, it can be attributed to some level of segregation experienced by virtue of segregated classrooms and community attitudes that the person is different and needs special care or treatment, and by practices that keep the individual, from an early age, from participating fully in society and being embraced as part of the fabric of the community.

Further, children with disabilities don't have the same opportunities for independent life experiences that are typical for most kids, largely because there remains some need for supervision or assistance in new environments and activities, and because these kids don't learn to drive. In short, they don't have the ability or the opportunity to get out and get the experience and exposure that is so important to career development. Whereas many families fully engage their family member with a disability in their family and community lives, the important distinction here is that those activities are typically driven by the family and rarely are they driven by one member's desire. These factors contribute to limiting independent life experience.

The goal is to build and nurture as much independence, peer connection, and mentored experience as possible from early on, though even if someone is older, it's never too late to start! Transition plans should include these strategies as well, as they are very powerful tools to opening opportunity.

### Build Responsibility and Engage in Independent Self-Care and Domestic Chores

Most people have something they can do within a household. Sometimes people with disabilities do not take on a reasonable portion of the responsibilities and chores that go with family life, often because families just get in the habit of doing everything for the individual. That's not to pass judgment on families. Sometimes in the rush of family life, it is easier to help the person get dressed, cut his or her meat for, clean up his or her dishes, or do his or her laundry than it is to dedicate the time necessary to teach him or her the new task and allow them to do it independently.

However, participating in the flow of the household has multiple long-term benefits for the individual that may outweigh the short-term gain of everyone keeping to the old routines of assisting with basic self-care and domestic chores. First, it establishes a sense of confidence, competence, and normalcy for the person and the family in the long term. The success that comes from being able to take on small tasks and perhaps increasingly larger ones helps people and family members see that the individual can learn more than was perhaps originally anticipated. Second, having regular responsibility makes the person part of the family. They are able to engage in reciprocal relationships through the contribution of domestic labor, becoming one of the cogs in the family structure. Just as with any child, that contribution and responsibility builds for the future. Third, people are empowered by doing for themselves and contributing within the group. Both give them a sense of control and ability to manage life. Fourth, young people build skills that will overlap with their adult domestic life and may affect adult work life. Taking on responsibility for oneself and domestic chores within the household sets the stage for self-confidence and future exploration.

### Explore Interests

If a young person or adult with disabilities expresses or shows interest in something, attend to that interest. Even when the interest seems far-fetched, or is not an interest that others in the family share, it is important that the person get opportunities to engage in that interest on whatever level possible. It is not necessary for a person to be able to complete an entire task in order to participate; rather, consider small steps or partial ways the person can engage.

For example, if somebody shows an interest in baking, he does not have to be able to do all the tasks from beginning to end, or even be expected to learn all the tasks eventually. The person can participate partially. For example, he could learn to measure out and pour the ingredients into the mix. If measuring is not a major skill, and he is having a hard time learning it, measuring cups could be marked with color-coded levels. Likewise, measuring spoons could be marked. Somebody else could do the mixing and then he could be involved in kneading the dough or spooning out the cookies while somebody else deals with the oven. Tasks are selected based on the individual. If an individual is really interested in something, he or she may surprise everyone by learning more than ever expected.

Likewise, interests outside of the home should be explored. The bottom line is to help people with disabilities look for interests, create opportunities to try different things, and nurture those interests that sustain focus and enjoyment.

### Join Groups Where People Have Like Interests

One of the best ways to explore an interest is to join groups where people share the same interests. Most communities have an abundance of these opportunities. There is a group for just about everything. Clubs and classes can be found through YMCAs, local recreation departments, community newspapers, community centers, churches, and the Internet. Also, do not overlook local bulletin boards in grocery stores, restaurants, and other community gathering places; these are frequently quite interesting to check out.

In addition, many opportunities exist for developing friendships and connections within the community. People engage around commonalities, and folks who share a real interest or even passion for something are often willing to talk about it with others, and maybe even teach them a few things. Many people with developmental disabilities may need a mentor to help them get started with the experience. Whenever possible, the mentor should be someone who also shares that interest or someone who is "valid" in that environment (i.e., somebody who fits in well in that particular group or community). Clearly, this is not always possible from the outset, in which case a trusted friend or family member can help the person get started, taking them to meetings, helping them meet people and get conversations started. The family member could do some subtle modeling of how to talk to the person and treat them in an age-appropriate way, and then back off and let things begin to develop. In many cases, a mentor emerges from the group, and the person can engage more independently.

These experiences give not only the critical opportunity to explore something of interest, but also the opportunity to develop some ability and confidence. Equally valuable is the learning about the area of interest and how it may relate to work possibilities, and the development of a network of friends and colleagues. These are all immeasurable in their value for customizing employment.

### Build Individual Life Experience

As discussed elsewhere in this chapter, individual life experience guides all of us to careers and various choices throughout life. Creating and taking advantage of opportunities to try different things in life gives an individual more to draw from when considering options and possibilities in life. Further, it gives providers more to go on when trying to identify and develop "goodness of fit" in customizing employment. Life experience can be built by following an individual's interests and using some of the other strategies outlined in this section.

### Develop Peer Mentors

For many people, accessing various groups, clubs, and other organizations, as well as community events and social functions, may be easier with, or may even require, a peer mentor. This is something that can start early and continue into adulthood. With many high schools and colleges requiring volunteer service hours for graduation or admission, it is likely that students could become peer mentors to other students with disabilities. Students could receive a brief orientation to help them understand their role of friend and mentor as opposed to caretaker and then could serve as valuable mentors to assist students to participate in sports, clubs, art, cultural events, and other extracurricular school activities, as well as activities outside the school community.

Be alert in looking for individuals who might take a natural interest in the individual with a disability and work to facilitate connection between them. Within any activities, clubs, events, or groups, look for that connection to emerge and nurture it. For example, a teenager could participate in the Pep Club at school but may need a mentor. If no connection is immediately available to help at school, somebody else may need to accompany the person the first few times. The parent is obviously not the person to go along to help somebody fit in to a high school pep club. A sibling, however, even an older or younger one, would do better. And of course, the best fit would be a neighbor or friend—another student who is already a member of the Pep Club.

### Build the Individual's and the Family's Network

Start building a network early. Make yourselves and the family member with a disability known around the community. Doing this requires active participation in activities and events, not just attendance. Given that time is often in short supply within families, it helps to focus on one or two weekly activities where time is committed. Find ways the individual with a disability can contribute.

Church youth groups can be a good place to start. They are generally open to participation. The key is getting a mentor (maybe a sibling or friend) or just the youth group leader to guide initial participation. Find a way the person can contribute to service projects. For example, some youth groups hold bake sales or car washes, some rake yards or take care of yards once or twice a year to benefit the church's elderly or sick members, or as a service to folks who could use the help in the general community. Chances are there is something the person can do to contribute to those events. For example, someone with a physical disability may not be able to vacuum a car interior, but she can spray and wipe interior glass or spray the hose to rinse the car. By establishing membership and contribution, social value is established and social connections occur.

This is the beginning of a network. Family members can do the same. The more people you know, the more resources and connections will lead to opportunity.

### Use Your Network

Once you have a network, use it. People tend to help out when asked. It does not have to be a big deal. Just letting people know that you are looking for certain information, contacts, and resources is a way to use your network Many people will not be able to come up with anything, and that's okay, but somebody might come up with something.

Consider this example, one that is mundane but a common experience—that of moving to a new home. Every resource involved in the move has come via use of networking. The house in the new community was found before it went on the market because family members told people of their intent to move and purchase a home in the particular community. Family doctors and health care professionals, veterinarians, insurance agents, car mechanics, home repairmen—each of these came at the recommendation of people within the network. Although the family knew very few people initially, it was the connections (networks) of those few people that led to the answers and resources needed.

Whereas this is a very simple example, networking for other resources—mentors, opportunities, jobs, and so on—works in a similar fashion. The sphere of influence and opportunity expands exponentially through a network.

### Use a Team Approach

Look to use a team approach wherever possible. This helps the individual to have a variety of contacts and prevents one person from having complete responsibility for managing this process. Of course, one person needs to keep things moving and facilitate communication. But it is the use of multiple resources and supports that will bring the individual the most opportunity.

## CONCLUSION

There is much that families can do to develop an individual's network and contribution to the community early on in his or her life. This active role is probably just as important as any in customizing employment and building the resources, teams, experience, and opportunities that are so valuable to the process of customization. Even if an individual has not had those early experiences, it is never too late to start. Good working relationships and active partnerships between schools or provider organizations and families, along with other critical team members, are key to uncovering individual talents and capacity and opportunity in the community.

# 11 Organizational Commitment to Customized Employment

## The Role of Leadership in Facilitating Careers

*Cary Griffin, David Hammis, and Tammara Geary*

Customized employment (CE) and supported employment (SE) are depicted in literature and practice as frontline service delivery approaches that, if performed studiously, foster individual career opportunities for job seekers with disabilities. This narrow view fails to acknowledge the existence of human services management and delivery systems that play vital enabling roles in the employment process. Leaders of community rehabilitation programs (CRPs) and school-to-work transition programs—including principals, special education directors, and school board members—who do not create, adapt, or change management systems to embrace activities that facilitate the development of community employment can thereby subvert the inclusion process. Frontline and mid-level staff can develop community employment options only to the point that systems and leadership beliefs are willing to allow (Deming, 1986; Kohn, 1993; Wehman, Inge, Revell, & Brooke, 2006). Without top-level administrative buy-in and support, employment outcomes risk being haphazard and mediocre. This chapter presents a framework for organizational change and a challenge to leaders at all agency levels to drive internal priorities that promote employment outcomes.

## COMMUNITY IMAGE

Organizational support for the implementation of CE engages a wide variety of leadership and managerial concepts. Image, for example, plays a crucial role in developing

CE for individuals with significant disabilities (DiLeo & Langton, 1993; Ries & Trout, 1987). When an employment specialist develops a job for an adult with disabilities in a local business but fails to involve the individual in an interview, a barrier is established between that employer and the new worker that signals special circumstances and care regarding supervision and training. Inadvertently, the employer—and her employees—are removed from direct interaction with the new worker, indicating the possible need for an intermediary. Fading from the worksite becomes difficult at this point, employment support costs and stigma go up, individual job satisfaction for the new worker goes down, and the relatively understandable concept of job placement is made complex to the community of employers. Co-workers, in this circumstance, may likely be reluctant to interact with the new worker, especially during the initial training period, and supervision may be directed through the employment specialist to the new worker, further establishing a behavior pattern that reinforces exclusion from worksite interactions with co-workers and supervisors (Callahan & Garner, 1997; Hagner, 2000).

The results of such mechanical and symbolic actions are often not realized until the employment specialist fades. Suddenly, co-workers and supervisors face the realization that they are not equipped with the so-called special skills required to teach, direct, and interact with individuals with disabilities. Job loss is often the result.

Similar scenarios play out in residential and school settings. In many communities across the United States, individuals with disabilities live, work, and learn in congregate settings with others carrying similar labels or at similar functioning levels. Residents of group homes consistently report that they have little or no interaction with neighbors, and the reaction of many neighborhoods to these clusters illustrates that such groupings indicate a need for people with disabilities to be congregated for medical or training reasons, and that people with disabilities would rather be with their own (Allen, 2004; Braddock, Hemp, Parish, & Rizzolo, 2002; Shapiro, 1993). The community is separated from people with disabilities by well-meaning programs using isolating and stigmatizing service models, reinforcing differences and fostering negative stereotypes (Harris Poll, July 5, 2000; Kotler & Roberto, 1989; Torrey, 1988).

The image held in American society of people with disabilities is generally negative. Individuals with psychiatric disabilities are considered dangerous; people with physical disabilities are to be pitied; and people with developmental disabilities are friendly, but incompetent. The result of these beliefs can be loneliness, poverty, and unemployment. And it is the schools and human services industry that reinforce these images through exclusionary training, pity-based fundraising, and poorly supported inclusion efforts.

Two strong contemporary examples of bias appeared recently in the popular media. Both examples illustrate the insidiousness of well-meaning but harmful portrayals. The first involves the documentary *Murderball*. In this award-winning film featuring the U.S. Paralympics wheelchair rugby team, a team member is confronted with a comparison to Special Olympics. The team member reacts strongly, proclaiming his distaste for Special Olympics because he is not after hugs; he is after true championship status and a gold medal. The comparison was not meant to ridicule or devalue the Olympian, but that was the result, all the same. And so it is with much of the prejudice fostered by well-meaning professionals and programs that project images of disability. The intentions are good, but the results are devastating. Note that the team member displays his own distaste for being associated with people with developmental disabilities.

The other example involves the young New York State student with autism, who, on the last day of the season, is elevated from team assistant to high school basketball team player. The young man is called in from the bench with 4 minutes left in the final quarter of the game and sinks several shots in succession. Both the home team and visiting spectators are on their feet as he sinks basket after basket, racking up 20 points. The news clip runs over and over for a week. Surely the young man was good enough to make the team and should have played all season. The stories that followed consistently pointed to the tragedy of autism, noting that there is no known cure (Drehs, 2006).

These examples are telling in that they raise the promise of inclusion and competence, but somehow explain away the feats as incredible and miraculous, while subtly suggesting that unless people with a disability have some remarkable talent, they are of little use (e.g., the movie *Rainman*). Critical to changing this pervasive image of people with disabilities in the eyes of neighbors and employers is changing the operational and market image of special education and community rehabilitation organizations. This is accomplished by

- Practicing good public information management
- Developing a stable, well-trained work force
- Utilizing typical community resources and citizens
- Connecting service consumers to others in the community
- Entering into partnerships with other organizations to accomplish mutual goals for both devalued and valued populations
- Utilizing organizational economic and political power in constructive and business-like ways
- Creating an atmosphere of mutuality with those receiving services and their families
- Operating ethically and professionally
- Eliminating obvious dehumanizing symbols, such as congregate settings; segregated activities, such as segregated recreation and fund-raisers that emphasize pity; and agency names that present images of need and "specialness," such as The Helping Hands Center, the Center for the Retarded, the Crippled Children and Adult Camp, and the Psychosocial Center.

## Broken Windows

The image people have of individuals with disabilities has a direct impact on employment rates (Shapiro, 1993). The images promoted by the disability field have a significant impact on employer perceptions; therefore, organizational values, actions, and priorities must address the remediation of negative stereotypes and portrayals (DiLeo & Langton, 1993). In his book, *The Tipping Point*, Malcolm Gladwell described the law enforcement concept known as the *Broken Windows* theory. This theory was most notably employed in New York City during the 1990s, in response to a soaring crime rate. The concept holds that if someone breaks a window in a neighborhood, and it stays broken, others passing by assume that it is all right to break windows in this area of town. Soon all the windows are broken. The theory suggests that while these may appear as small crimes, their tolerance assumes a lack of law enforcement, resulting in the occurrence of major violations. By cracking down on minor infractions, the message is clear: No violations of law will be condoned (Gladwell, 2000).

Adapting this theory to the realm of disability offers community leaders an understanding of the sustained exclusion of people with disabilities from the community as well as the challenge to change this reality. Children in public schools pass by the special education resource room daily. They may witness a group of students labeled as *special needs* entering the cafeteria together or playing together on the playground. These students without disabilities may grow up assuming that it must be proper to keep people with disabilities separate from their own neighborhoods and businesses. Employers who drive by the sheltered workshop in their community each day may make a similar assumption: This building provides a safe and caring place for people with disabilities, so there is no need to reach out and employ anyone lucky enough to attend such a center. These programs are the broken windows, and they reinforce in the public's mind that segregation is good. Leadership can stop this misconception and open the community to opportunity.

## Social Capital

Instead of erecting walls, leadership should focus on building social capital at both the individual and organizational levels. The term *social capital* is defined by Robert Putnam (2000) as "the collective value of all social networks and the inclinations that arise from these networks to do things for each other." Throughout this chapter, the suggestions offered are predicated on leveraging knowledge, wealth, and cooperation through collaborative relationships among internal personnel and throughout communities. Building social capital is predicated on mutual benefit and growing trustworthiness. This is not a passive activity; it entails sustained mutual effort, risk, and investment. It also means doing business in new ways, guided by these principles.

1. **Pursue partnerships and collaboration anticipating mutual benefit.** For example, transportation is often seen as a barrier to employment for people with disabilities. In reality, transportation is a community issue affecting all commuters. In many communities, as a matter of fact, there is too much transportation, leading to massive traffic snarls. There is in these cases an improper allocation of resources, not a lack thereof, so reframing the problem and working with transit leaders and stakeholder groups to solve a distribution problem may hold promise for people with disabilities. For example, a transportation cooperative could pool vehicles owned by several nonprofit organizations in a community to create a fixed route or on-demand option.

2. **Practice the politics of cooperation.** While the concept of social capital contains the potential for corruption and cronyism, the purpose of cooperation is to counteract the growth of distrust and cynicism. Working cooperatively with government leaders and stakeholders can overcome "good old boy" networks. Public policy and practice can be refined through both civil and civic conversation. Habitat for Humanity presents a fine model of pooling local construction company talents and resources, having them collaborate instead of compete, providing specialized building services beyond the capabilities of the typical housing volunteer (Fuller, 1999).

3. **Support people and places, not structures.** The power of honest and egalitarian stakeholder efforts is in the clarification of policy and practice. Engaging the disability community in true conversation and action concerning the bureaucratic trappings found evident in even the smallest programs illuminates the desired results, and under progressive leadership, leads to streamlined strategies that assist people in getting what they need. Administrators showing good faith get good faith in return, thereby reducing complaints, challenges, and legal threats. A smart social capital developer sees opportunities for building good faith. The rush-hour driver allowing a person to merge in front of him or her increases the likelihood that the person will repay the favor to someone else at the next on-ramp. While it may not immediately benefit the original driver, he or she has set in motion the opportunity for more civil driving in the future, where the culture changes from one of road rage to one of cooperation. Take personal action for change, think one person at a time, and think long-term investment; then apply these principles to daily issues of concern.

In a recent all-too-concrete example in the Rocky Mountain West, economic development agencies were approached by a CRP and asked to build them a new, larger building. Instead of focusing on what each individual wanted, the CRP lumped all people with disabilities together, presented their case that sheltered work was the best option, and without investigation into best practices, the grant was awarded. Little opportunity was given for the development of social capital, and people were removed from their places (community). Ironically, the community in question suffered from a labor shortage, and an incredible opportunity to use the same grant money to accommodate workers with disabilities and build social capital between the new workers, the CRP, and the business community was lost (*Bozeman Daily Chronicle*, 2006).

4. **Create continuous learning inside and out.** Uneducated or unprincipled staff members rely on whatever information they have that gets them through the task at hand. Mistakes are made; interruptions to fix problems multiply; important work suffers; staff feel inadequate and leave; turnover costs mount; more bodies are hired for quick coverage; low wages result from turnover and mistrust of frontline staff; and the cycle repeats. An investment in training is essential for good service delivery and for sending the message to the community and stakeholders that the organization (i.e., leaders) values people with disabilities. Well-trained staff represent the organization in the community and are capable of energizing the growth of social capital (Brooks-Lane, Hutcheson, & Revell, 2005). Poorly performing personnel undermine the best efforts of the organization and people with disabilities.

Customizing employment depends upon each individual associated with the agency in question. The word organization springs from the root *organic*. As such, human services entities are living, breathing, and changing (adapting) organisms. Organizations that support individuals with significant disabilities should prepare for broadened community presence by reviewing their corporate culture first in terms of stated values versus actual practice and outcomes (Griffin, 1999; Kilmann, 1989). Generally, there is a significant gulf between the publicly stated organizational desire for community-based outcomes and the actual practices utilized to accomplish those goals. School and rehabilitation organization managers often find themselves stuck between what they know they should support and publicly profess (real jobs, real homes, friendships for people with disabilities) and the realities of poorly conceived or outdated funding policy and procedures. As well, internal schisms are certainly visible when organizations rethink service delivery and support modalities. Unsatisfying and destructive organizational dissonance occurs that can only be addressed through significant attention to values.

Many organizations address changes in the rehabilitation market by reacting to the most vociferous or influential people. Sometimes these are angry neighbors near a group home, sometimes parents and consumers demanding more control, but typically it is a funding agency. Human services is riddled with scarcity models of management, influenced and designed by professionals with scarcity mindsets (Griffin, 1999). *Scarcity thinkers* tend to react to the most stressing situations on a crisis basis and are particularly prone to view any threat to funding as reason enough to act. Unfortunately, scarcity thinkers rarely see the big picture that *abundance thinkers* see.

Abundance thinkers create organizations that are adaptive, involve customers in product and service design, and recognize that management systems determine the efficacious delivery of quality service, not just the people closest to the customer (Griffin, 1996; Hammer & Champy, 1993). In short, scarcity thinkers are dependent on those people and systems they view as more powerful than themselves and often use these entities as their excuse for not making progress. Abundance thinkers, on the other hand, create the future and recognize the world as having limitless possibilities (Friedman, 2005; Griffin, 1996).

## First Steps

Many human services leaders now understand the vital need for organizational planning. A first step to clarifying organizational direction and necessary outcomes involves values alignment rather than the typical goals alignment so often used in strategic planning (Mintzberg, 1994; Ringland, 2002). In other words, before an agency determines its desired outcomes and goals, it must determine what the organization believes and how it gets others, internally and externally, to believe these things also (Griffin, 1999; Kilmann, 1989). As noted earlier in this chapter, social capital is defined as the collective value of all social networks and the inclinations that arise from these networks to do things for each other. Building social capital assumes that the organization is focused, trustworthy, and honest. The values an organization showcases and exhibits through its outcomes build the reputation that collaborators require. For external constituents, such as employers, neighbors, taxpayers, and funding agencies, rational explanations of the inclusion direction must be developed. Allies and early adopters who will support this refocusing or radical change in direction must be identified (Kotler & Roberto, 1989).

Internally, conspicuous values discussions must occur. These discussions occur throughout all levels and in all agency departments, with the chief executive officer, principal or special education director, or the board of directors playing key roles to ensure that open discussion and debate occurs at all personnel levels. It is critical at this point that leadership is strong, available, visible, conversational, clear of thought, and empowering (Griffin, 1996). One way to prompt such meaningful discussions is to measure organizational outcomes against the values statements common in most modern strategic plans. For instance, if an agency declares that its mission is to promote the employment of people with disabilities in the community, meetings of the board, management, and teams should focus on organizational accomplishments in promoting said employment. This mission can be measured on a regular basis and dissected into specific measures of

- Wages earned

- Career growth and job advancement

- Hours worked

- Fringe benefits received

- Worker satisfaction

Reinforcing the message of the mission is accomplished through diverse methods, including staff meetings, small team meetings facilitated by the agency leader, focus groups, interactive policy forums, and other internal events or media exposure. Although the symbolic image of leadership and management is always critical to any change or realignment process, the most critical aspect at this point is the message.

A clear range of values points must be defined and articulated. The following are key values concepts (see Chapter 1) used by successful organizations as they engage the community in growing social capital and increasing the inclusion of individuals with significant disabilities (Griffin, 1996). Each values point has both direct service and organizational implications, while serving as guiding boundaries relative to the work being performed.

### Zero Exclusion

The direct service implication is that all people, regardless of complexity or type of disability, have the right to live, work, and recreate in integrated settings in their chosen community. Job development must be adapted to each person to highlight their contributions, to ferret out their ideal conditions of employment, and to guide the job developer in creatively thinking beyond typical employment scenarios.

The organizational implication is that systems must, in all aspects, respect the fulfillment of this belief, and management actions should direct the replacement of congregate and segregated facilities and programs with options based on consumer desire and the presence of people without disabilities. Further, the organizational implication contains the directive that staff and stakeholders must be involved, or have a true representative voice, regardless of position, in agency decision making, planning, and operations.

## Partial Participation

The direct service implication is that all people have something or some part of something that they can do and enjoy doing. It is the role of human services leaders to see that this personal genius or skill is utilized to begin the development of real work and civic involvement. The organizational implication is that staff, as well as families, townspeople, job seekers, and other interested and affected people are involved to the degree in which they wish to be involved to assist in building a better, more inclusive community.

## Zero Instructional Inference

The direct service implication is that for many people with disabilities, the best place to learn is in environments where the target skills are utilized. Therefore, the use of developmental continuum, or mastering skills and behaviors in simulated environments before being allowed to participate in community activities, or earning the right to a job or a social activity is eliminated based upon the solid evidence that preparatory training typically has little validity (Brown et al., 1979; Callahan & Garner, 1997). Segregated settings are not necessary and are indeed a detriment to teaching and learning (Brown et al., 1979). The organizational implication is that all segregated sites need to be rethought and probably eliminated. This allows the organization to deputize others in the community as partners in training through the use of businesses and other private and public places for teaching and employment. This tenet suggests that staff will learn better by doing and necessitates staff involvement in designing management systems that encourage decentralized accountability. Furthermore, because staff are in the public eye, skills necessary to facilitate relationships and situations for service consumers must be taught.

## Mutuality

The direct service implication is that we must at all times attribute thinking and feeling to all people regardless of level or type of disability. The Golden Rule should be strictly enforced in all planning and all interactions with people with disabilities and their families. Service alternatives should not be proposed that individuals with disabilities or anyone else find undesirable. The organizational implication is that policies that restrict individual freedom, allow aversive and cost-response behavioral interventions, allow the hiring of ill-equipped staff, or continue to promote segregation in its many forms can no longer be tolerated. Further, mutuality means that staff at all levels are respected, paid, educated, and involved to such a degree that they truly provide world-class customer service and have an active role in organizational direction and operations.

## Interdependence

The direct service implication is that all people rely on social networks that assist them in daily life and in times of personal crises. People with disabilities often have very limited social networks and few friends. The opportunity to be present and participate in a variety of settings with typical citizens is critical to the establishment of such relationships (Condeluci, 1991). The organizational implication is that services and supports should be designed to occur in integrated and nonstigmatizing, noncongregate settings. Further, organizations should become interdependent to create social capital for use in solving predominant problems. There are many opportunities for partnership and collaboration available in even the smallest, most rural, most economically depressed regions. Abundance thinkers create social capital by enlisting and involving others. Scarcity thinkers remain aloof, alone, and unchanged. The movement of individuals to inclusive lives necessitates the interdependence of organizations and the staff members who provide the life blood of those organisms (Griffin, 1994).

## TRANSFORMATIONAL LEADERSHIP

The adoption of CE requires the above realignment of values and the absolute necessity of creating new management priorities and systems that foster the transformation to the community. Organizations are the sum total of all those who work in, are served by, and are impacted or influenced through the actions and image of that entity. Therefore, the living and symbolic components of the agency must be acted upon through leadership, leadership that respects and recognizes the needs of all constituents and works for the greater good of the whole (Block, 1993; Collins, 2001; Kouzes & Posner, 1987; Murphy & Rogan, 1995).

The scope of this chapter is far too limited to address all the process variations and implications requisite in organizational transformation and quality leadership; however, there is a great need for continued discussion regarding the concern that organizations are perhaps not the best vehicle for fostering inclusion. In fact, some argue that by improving organizations through transformational leadership these agencies become more embedded in people's lives and drain off resources that are better directed by individuals with disabilities, their families, and friends.

Today's reality recognizes that thousands of people are to some degree controlled by organizations, and with the improvement of these organizations, doors are opened for people with disabilities to enter more interdependent situations. Closing down agencies historically led to homelessness, continued poverty, and increased victimization (Torrey, 1988). Most human services personnel are good people who gladly welcome the emancipation of people with disabilities, and progressive systems change reveals the opportunity to accomplish this goal without further injury to those served. This process for becoming organizationally interdependent leads to system designs that foster professional roles as conduits or facilitators, connecting consumers with other generic systems and citizens. This transitional change may be too slow for many, and rightly so.

Experience in the field reveals many strong advocates in leadership roles for people with disabilities. Unfortunately, there are many others who have lost touch with those served and their staff and community, and consciously or subconsciously subvert, through policy, funding, or management style and systems design, the inclusion process. Many frontline staff, families, and consumers report that they are slowly subverting misguided management, but without power and control they find the options are difficult to exercise (Griffin, 1996).

Policy makers, funding agencies, boards of directors of CRPs, and citizens must become educated about what is possible in the lives of people with disabilities. This may return rehabilitation organizations to true community entities. The solutions are time-intensive and difficult. But, there are safe methods available to job seekers and frontline staff for subverting bad leadership (Alinsky, 1971; Bell, 1992; Kohn, 1993).

## Identifying the Critical Initiatives of Change

This step in the change plan process generates a set of critical initiatives aimed at improving community employment outcomes. An adaptation of Edwards Deming's Fourteen Points for Quality Improvement (modified to encourage management change) serve here as a starting point for identifying worthy activities (Deming, 1986).

1. *Create constancy of purpose based upon a long-term commitment to continuous improvement.* How: Making this part of operations means that CRPs measure both process and outcomes data in order to pinpoint job development methods that work; they collect time and effort statistics in order to determine costs, and they invest in staff development that delivers high performance and consistency to their various customers.

2. *Adopt a new policy of leadership visibility and commitment to improvement.* How: The CEO carries a caseload so that he or she is never too far removed from service delivery, can monitor progress, and can witness firsthand how policies and practices inhibit or augment positive outcomes.

3. *Cease dependence on external inspection (i.e., quality assurance).* Enable personnel to do tasks right the first time and create systems that allow personnel and customers control over quality. How: Study process variation to determine best practices and invest in staff training that grooms a cadre of high performance employment specialists. Ensure through investment in staff that they do their jobs right the first time, thereby reducing complaints, increasing customer satisfaction, and reducing costs.

4. *Create long-term partnerships with internal and external suppliers to strengthen the value-chain.* How: Engage funders and referral agents, such as vocational rehabilitation counselors, in designing processes that satisfy the needs of their systems, that make referrals consistently easy to accomplish, and that teach employment specialists the quality indicators important to these suppliers.

5. *Decrease waste (cost) by constantly and forever improving processes and systems.* How: Institute written procedures for assessment, job analysis, and placement tasks and train staff to follow these procedures.

6. *Institute relevant on-the-job training.* How: Form training alliances with local colleges and universities, develop grant-funding training programs, develop staff recruitment plans that place an emphasis on talent, not availability, and ask the state for assistance with this mutual goal of retaining staff and increasing employment.

7. *Institute leadership at all organizational levels.* How: Demystify board meetings by inviting staff to attend and schedule different staff or departments to showcase their work regularly, develop a line item in the budget for self-advocacy efforts and feedback loops from families and consumers to upper management (a simple 1-800 number into a dedicated voice mail box accessed only by the board president is one strategy), use a diagonal slice of the organization to develop teams for strategic planning.

8. *Drive out fear.* How: Have staff collect and analyze their own performance data, explain how funding for employment and other programs works, offer public rewards for good work and private correction when necessary.

9. *Break down barriers between departments through cross-functional cooperation.* How: Create a true team-based organization. Most agencies run on teams that are actually committees: groups of people representing their own or their program's interests. True teams are facilitated to focus on a common goal. Teach people how to focus on common goals.

10. *Eliminate slogans and productivity targets. Create systems that support quality work.* How: Numeric goals are valuable, but they need to be flexible to allow for innovation and unique circumstances. One goal, such as placements per month, is not enough. Goals should address the complexity of job development and include customer satisfaction, hours worked per month, and pay and benefits received. Allow teams to achieve their goals collectively, if desired, to encourage sharing job leads and innovative strategies.

11. *Emphasize results and positive outcomes, rather than arbitrary numerical targets.* How: Mix employment data with individual stories of success. Share challenges in team meetings that engage everyone in finding solutions. Demystify the folklore often surrounding the interpretation of rules and regulations by teaching people to ask "why" and "how" more often as a natural part of problem solving and team conversation. Support staff in asking for the help they need by encouraging management to lend a hand.

12. *Remove barriers that rob people of their self-esteem. Replace quality control with continuous quality improvement methods.* How: Showcase individual and team efforts. Make a spectacle of success and promote adventuresome methods. When new processes are developed, replicate the thinking that went into the inventiveness through training.

13. *Institute a vigorous program of education and self-improvement.* How: Hire people who are naturally inquisitive. Make learning a continual part of the job through training and conference attendance, not only for upper management, but also for new hires as well. Hire for the long term and institute methods of self-governance that contribute to a slowing of the personnel turnover rate.

14. *Put everyone to work in the transformation process by communicating what needs to happen and why.* How: Eliminate or substantially reduce time-wasting activities, such as committees and meetings that do not have a direct impact on individual job seeker lives. An organizational audit should be performed annually that identifies time-wasting activities and requests solutions from staff. All activities should be referenced regarding the legal commitments they satisfy and the consumer employment outcomes they encourage.

A change team, composed of a diagonal slice of the organization (e.g., top management, mid-management, frontline staff, consumers) studies these principles as applied to the unique circumstances of an agency and community. In anticipation of moving forward, the team should formally consider the following questions and construct responses based upon the long-term commitment to instituting continuous quality improvement principles. Some of the answers to these questions may not be obvious at this stage in the process. However, asking these questions gives shape to an initial plan.

- How will this organization react to anticipated changes?

- Who will be the supporters of change, and why will they be supportive?

- What are the highest expectations for this organization?

- Where will it be necessary to compromise in process design and change?

- How much time is necessary to make the anticipated changes?

- What is the timetable for change plan implementation?

- How much and what pieces of the organization need to be changed?

- Who needs to know about the plan?

- What are the best methods for informing the various publics?

- Who else needs to be enlisted and who else can help us?

- What milestones and measures will be employed to determine improvement?

Revisit these questions and add new ones as the change process proceeds. The answers help produce a vision of how the organization might react to potential improvement projects and changes. These answers (and the questions, too) will change or need refinement as time passes and corporate culture evolves. Quality improvement is a continuous process of planning, acting, evaluating, and revising (see Figure 11.1).

## Functional Impact

The next step requires identifying major organizational functions or activities and rating them based on their potential impact on performance improvement. The focus of a CRP or school transition program should be successful employment, but over time, these organizations often devolve into preoccupation with their funders, managing personnel, and increasing internal management controls that seek consistency over invention and stability over adventure. Identifying critical organizational functions and their use as levers or catalysts in the change process is done with input from the change team and a variety of stakeholders. One hour discussions in groups of 10–20 people quickly involve most staff and stakeholders in typical agencies. But a well-designed change team with broad corporate representation can also accurately identify key organizational components in need of attention.

Using an Organizational Function Analysis chart (see Figure 11.2), have the group list all major organizational functions in the first column. Recorded items may include community job development, benefits management, financial management/accounting, residential programs, consumer power, board of directors functioning, hiring and recruitment, consumer behavioral support, public relations/marketing, fund-raising, business/community partnerships, accreditation, individualized program planning, consumer training, and transportation, among others. The group discusses and prioritizes through multivoting (a gradual elimination of topics through voting and facilitated discussion) which of these functions need to be change-targets for the agency (Scholtes, 1988). Each individual in the group decides which specific organizational function will cause a great impact, a moderate impact, or little impact on overall quality improvement or change plan success.

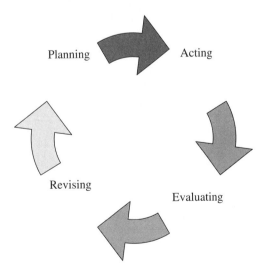

**Figure 11.1.**   Quality improvement process.

| Function | Great Impact | Moderate Impact | Little Impact |
|---|---|---|---|
| | | | |
| | | | |
| | | | |
| | | | |
| | | | |
| | | | |
| | | | |
| | | | |
| | | | |
| | | | |
| | | | |
| | | | |
| | | | |

**Figure 11.2.** Organizational function analysis. Functions should be prioritized as targets of the change program that will have either a *great* impact, a *moderate* impact, or *little* impact on overall quality improvement or change plan success.

At this stage in the change program, some visions of the future start forming for the change team and stakeholders. Strong threats to the change program are likely now as some departments, individuals, and beliefs are identified as subjects for further exploration. Corporate culture clashes are natural and it is in this part of the process that the psychological impacts most often derail change plans. Tempers flare, accusations are made, and overreaction is common on all sides of the meeting table.

Leaders play a profound role at this stage in maintaining objectivity, by acting on facts, not opinions or feelings, and by recognizing that humans are apt to struggle for the maintenance of power and equilibrium. Reactions against change are often predictable, given the widely held belief that changes are instituted only when correction is necessary. These beliefs are rooted in the theory of evolution that an organism's flaws lead to extinction. Fear of mistakes (and punishment) is so emotionally traumatic that many people forget that survival is accomplished by only those who do evolve.

A few observations about human behavior assist change teams, managers, leaders, and co-workers in better understanding some of the predictable reactions to change.

1. Individuals act first. Group action follows someone's lead and endorsement.

2. People choose to change and cannot be forced to do so.

3. People in transition (change) use old, often ineffective behaviors to meet their needs.

4. Change adoption requires that people learn new, more efficient behaviors to meet their needs.

5. Resistance is the movement toward what is known and away from the pain of loss.

6. Change does not happen simply because current methods are not working; there must be compelling evidence to support change.

7. People perform to the level allowed within organizations. Poorly conceived and executed management systems create mediocrity.

8. Personal responsibility has been systematically stripped from people by unrewarding and incomprehensible management systems.

9. Organizations are organic. They exhibit the personalities of those comprising the organization.

10. Healthy organizations reflect an interdependent community working toward a shared purpose.

11. People do not resist change; they resist being changed.

12. Knowing the rules better than those writing the rules is the key to innovation.

13. People want to succeed, to experience joy in their work, and to have authority and responsibility.

14. Perfection is not the point of most lives.

15. Change is easier when past accomplishment is publicly and privately revered by the change agents.

16. People need to know how to change, as well as why to change.

17. Some people will never be convinced that change is necessary, wise, or timely.

18. Some people will leave (Gilbert, 1978; Griffin, 1999; Janov, 1994; Kilmann, 1989; Schaef & Fassel, 1990; Stacey, 1992).

## Identifying Allies and Resisters

At this juncture, the change team knows who supports the initiative and who is resistant, what management structures to investigate, and what policies and procedures must be adapted or abandoned. All of these components involve allowing or asking someone to change. So it makes sense to strategically identify stakeholders, internally and externally, as

a. Promoters (those who will likely act first)

b. Supporters (those who follow the promoters)

c. Neutrals (those who will go along without fanfare or resistance)

d. Analyzers (those who will sharply question each action but may or may not support the change)

e. Resisters (those who will work to actively challenge and even derail the change program)

f. Don't knows (those who cannot yet be classified)

This exercise is not meant to produce an enemies list. Rather, it is an interactive process that identifies people and their reasons for adopting or resisting change. It also helps the change team target efforts to increase interaction, collaboration, education, and training within the change program and to bring serious concerns into focus. Resisters are not necessarily wrong; they often point out serious flaws in thinking, overreaction, and political action. All change teams are strongly cautioned to identify and involve resisters in the process. Human beings have rational reasons for being cautious.

Change is personal. Leaders who forget this create organizational arrest. A key element of successful improvement involves the redesign of employment expectations, duties, and conditions. This is best accomplished through a partnership with those impacted. Meetings with individuals and with teams that outline new work formats are critical for improvement to continue. Areas of key job changes that typically require exploration are

**Core duties:** What tasks must now be done? What does not need to be done? Where is there confusion over assignments?

**Decision making:** How does this change? How much authority does each person have? What processes are to be used? Who has the final say?

**Knowledge and skills:** What new skills do personnel need? Who teaches? How soon?

**Recruitment:** What new staff is needed? What are the knowledge and experience requirements? How are candidates identified, recruited, screened, and assigned? How do they complement and partner with current personnel?

## Evaluating Best Practices

Organizational change is as much about increasing quality outcomes as it is about eliminating waste. The change team should create a best-practices inventory for the organization (see Figure 11.3). This process involves listing those key organizational functions, identifying key quality indicators for these functions, suggesting benchmarks for comparison, and then recommending courses of action that will improve each function over time.

| DEPARTMENT: _____ MAJOR FUNCTION: _____ DATE: _____ | | | | |
|---|---|---|---|---|
| SUBACTIVITIES OF THE MAJOR FUNCTION | QUALITY INDICATORS | WHAT WE'RE DOING BEST | WHAT OTHERS ARE DOING BEST | WHAT WE NEED TO IMPROVE |
| | | | | |
| | | | | |
| | | | | |
| | | | | |
| | | | | |
| | | | | |
| | | | | |
| | | | | |
| | | | | |
| | | | | |
| | | | | |
| | | | | |
| | | | | |
| | | | | |

**Figure 11.3.**   Best-practices inventory.

The change team, individual departments, and other stakeholders first list the major functions and the subactivities that accomplish those functions of the individual departments (e.g., planning, motivation, leadership, communication). Next, participants create a list of quality indicators and rate the work components (i.e., subactivities) by identifying what they are doing best and by recording what others are doing best. Next, columns are compared by identifying items that need improvement. Each department thereby continually evaluates its efforts in comparison to others (internally and externally) and formulates improvement plans to increase quality.

This is a broad-based activity that involves all employees over time. It is an evolutionary process of identifying what works and what needs improvement. Budget reallocations are required to increase staff awareness of best practices through training, visits to other organizations, upgrades in technology and processes, and promotion of collaborative relationships with other potential partners.

Further refining the change programs is possible by asking additional questions. Asking questions gives a variety of stakeholders the opportunity to voice their opinions and share their experiences. Asking questions also helps clarify the issues and better pinpoints improvement efforts: Organizational change should be surgical in nature. Suggested questions include

1.  What information (fact versus opinion) indicates that change is necessary?

2.  Who wants this change to occur? Why?

3.  Are the reasons for the change consistent with our values and purpose?

4.  What stakeholders will benefit from the change? Who might be injured?

5.  Will a higher authority be needed to support the proposed change?

### The Change Program Purpose Statement

At this point, the change team has collected enough information to construct a purpose statement for the change program. The purpose statement is short and focused on what needs to happen and why. A purpose statement for the conversion of a sheltered workshop to 100% CE might read: "Pursuant to the organizational values and mission of Tri-State Services, Inc., we are engaging in a 5-year strategic process that guarantees community employment for all consumers." The change program plan is ready to be drafted.

### The Change Program Plan

Because the preliminary work actively engaged representative stakeholders, the change team can confidently develop the plan and hold meetings to discuss its refinement. A functional change plan details the activities that must occur to achieve the goal of continuous improvement. Plans are not static documents. As one step is undertaken, new circumstances dictate adjustments to reactions, objectives, processes, and goals. The formal plan serves as a reference point—a continually evolving reference point that reflects new knowledge, opportunities, and threats. The following components are required in a workable plan.

1.  An analysis of strengths and weaknesses

2.  Strategies to remediate weakness and to build strength

3.  An analysis of barriers to the changes

4.  An analysis of training and education needs

5. A communications and public relations strategy

6. Concrete goals and objectives with measurable outcomes assigned to key players

7. Milestones and timelines

8. Budgetary impacts and projections

Most organizations are familiar with these components, but some exploration is warranted due to the often negative consequences of proposing massive change. In particular, overcoming the barriers to change proves so difficult that many agencies cease systemic change and fall back on quick-fixes and modest remodeling (Collins, 2001; Deming, 1986; Griffin, 1996). The two most common types of barriers are

**Structural:** Internal and external rules and polices, some of which the organization can change, and some that must be changed by higher authority.

**Cultural:** The combination of tradition, past success, fear of failure, and routine behavior.

Common barriers exemplified by these two categories include

**Senior management lack of commitment:** Any serious change process necessitates leadership endorsement and encouragement to succeed.

**Focus on today:** Management is often crisis oriented. Organizations should find time to change by taking the long view and making a conscious effort to perform tasks that support the change while eliminating work that arrests improvement. Another tactic is to firmly set aside one entire day per week to concentrate on change activities.

**Forgetting the customer:** Internal issues consume organizations. Over time personnel forget whom they work to satisfy. A shift from rule-based management to customer-driven management is necessary.

**Aversion to job-streamlining and elimination:** Non–value-added activities should be identified and eliminated. Poor work processes require improvement through retraining, reengineering, and the use of technology.

**Inconsistent values and work methods:** Management should refine its beliefs and create systems that guarantee success. Education and communication, improved hiring and recruitment, and creative partnerships all play a role in high performance.

**Funding:** Many organizations have dependent relationships with government funders. Blame and political intrigue dominate organizations that fail to leverage the wealth and capacity of the community, collaborative agreements, and creative partnerships. A spirit of scarcity dominates these agencies, preventing experimentation and invention.

## Political Tactics

Politics is defined herein as the interaction of two or more people. Politics is values neutral, but is defined within each organization through its unique set of barriers and challenges. The change plan identifies these barriers specifically. The change team creates goals and objectives, complete with measures and milestones, to overcome, circumvent, or minimize the barriers. The team also utilizes a variety of formal problem-solving approaches over time to address the issues. Such tools include flow charting, Ishikawa diagrams, functional analysis, Pareto charts, storyboarding, and force-field analysis (Griffin, 1999; Scholtes, 1988). In face-to-face meetings with resisters to the change, a few political tactics work well.

**The Pull-Through Technique:** Recurrent conversation is structured to

- Reinforce why the change is required

- Discuss opportunities for small successes and incremental agreement

- Provide accurate information and updates

- Pull resisters into active plan refinement

- Allow for airing of concerns

- Focus on the future by repeating why change is necessary

- Reward those who support the change

- Provide reasonably attainable target goals for resisters to meet

**The Push-Through Technique:** Recurrent communication reinforces the fact that not changing is no longer an option; the decision is terminal. Critical components include

- Explaining the challenges and opportunities as they stand

- Validating the fact that the past was good

- Presenting as clear a picture of the future as possible and answering the "what if" questions

- Specifically indicating what actions are required of the resister and of the organization in order to push through to change process and survive

- Making it uncomfortable to continue resisting

**The Recognition Technique:** This approach moves quickly away from the past by

- Showing that upper management wants the change to occur

- Recognizing and rewarding those who move forward

- Presenting concrete plans for the elimination of old work methods while offering substantial support to help resisters adopt new work routines

Each strategy requires honesty, sincerity, and a firm belief that change is in the customer's best interests. Resistance to change is resistance to being changed. Consider opposition as a sign that typical communication is failing. Reframe these behaviors as messages.

a.   I like my job the way it is.

b.   I don't know how to do that new job.

c.   You are treating that person better than you are treating me.

Change is inherently messy. Planning and communication can make it less so. When the change plan is finally ready for implementation, key components should include

a.   A change purpose statement that is in absolute alignment with overall organizational purpose and values

b.   Clearly articulated goals and objectives with measures and milestones directly related to customer service improvement, work process refinement, organizational design changes, and stakeholder education

c.   An action component for overcoming barriers and challenges

d.  A resource allocation component for supporting the change process

e.  A thorough communications strategy

f.  Acknowledgment that the process is evolutionary and that the plan will need continuous evaluation and refinement

## Final Contradictions

There is no one correct way to plan for change. Every organization is unique. The strategies offered herein are reinforcement for those who know that leadership is a constant process of invention and discovery; that life is pretty messy sometimes and that solutions are seldom permanent; that we are given far more opportunities than time; that change is never isolated or without consequence; that many of those around us prefer to believe what is convenient and not necessarily what is correct; that planning can have the effect of leading us towards what we already know instead of what we need to know; that there is no one right answer or way of getting things done; that our accomplishments are the results of interdependent relationships that must change as circumstances change; and that stability is not the goal of management, improvement is.

CE options do not happen by accident. Creating inventive career opportunities with consistency and quality requires leaders and management systems dedicated to redirecting funds, rethinking policy, changing practices, truly engaging consumers and families, forging partnerships with the public and private sectors, and investing in staff competency and retention far beyond traditional community rehabilitation practice.

The traditional study of management and leadership leads one to believe that the role of top administrators is to set a course and stick to it. Through strategic planning, performance evaluations, formal interdepartmental memos, policies and procedures that consistently support the stated mission, and internal quality measures, leaders attempt to keep the organization stable, predictable, and on course.

Of course, off course is where enlightenment and adventure begin. And this very issue strikes panic into the hearts of those charged with assuring the sustainability of agencies. The challenge for leaders is contradictory: manage for stability while at the same time creating new opportunities and innovations. These mutually exclusive goals guide the best organizations. Leaders capable of supporting the invention of new products and services, creating multilayered networks, and casting off the ballast of rotted management practices while carefully retaining the promising ones achieve lasting results. And, since leadership and management are largely nonlinear undertakings, these are uncharted waters with no apparent one right way and no absolute formulas for success. Great leaders see beyond the horizon, but know they have to adapt along the course as opportunities and obstacles surface.

The following 10 contradictions represent a starting point in rethinking the role of leaders. This is in regards to leaders at all levels of an organization, in families, communities, and in the world at large.

### 1.  Great Leaders Know that the Map Is Just a Suggestion

In other words, leaders are responsible for gathering broad-based support for the strategic vision, but must jettison linear work models that foster straight-line progression. Innovation is generated and nurtured through experimentation that is sometimes wasteful and unfruitful on the surface, but that creates experiences leading to problem solving. An organization that playfully embraces new circumstances (and a new circumstance occurs whenever a customer asks for something new, or when we ask a customer if they would prefer something new) is regularly confronted with side trips that potentially lead to new knowledge, opportunities, and customers but that can also lead to loss, political confrontation, and trouble. Good leaders are prepared for either, and take smart risks.

For instance, the leader that funds a benefits specialist in order to leverage consumer-controlled resources is taking a risk, but is also acknowledging the need for consumer power and new approaches to funding employment services.

## 2. Our Job Is to Spend Money

Contrary to the popular clichés, there are stupid ideas. Great leaders and their colleagues use their intuition and experience to discourage bad ideas, but support marginal ones that just might have a chance at succeeding. A leader who allows for and budgets for experimentation sends a clear signal that personnel are encouraged to find better methods and products. In the long run, profits come to those who innovate, not to those who stay the course. Various skunk works inside innovating corporations such as Canon, Xerox, and 3M have proven remarkably profitable following short-term expenditures to generate and test new ideas. In the same way, an agency that sets aside a revolving loan fund for developing small businesses owned by consumers may find that other funders are more likely to contribute as well since the risk is shared between them. The public trust is not served best by hoarding money in fund balances; it is meant to be spent wisely, to advance and improve the lives of people with disabilities. Sometimes innovation costs money and investing in outcomes reframes and challenges the tradition of buying services.

## 3. The Customer Comes Second

Customer service starts internally. Appreciated and intellectually challenged staff perform better, stay longer, and earn organizations better reputations by treating their co-workers better. Satisfied personnel treat external customers better and happy customers tell their friends. Therefore, staff satisfaction should be among the first concerns of leaders. Job satisfaction comes from reasonable pay, of course, but more so from challenging work, being provided the tools and core competencies to do the work, and from the visible respect of leadership. The authors witness morale improvements often in employment projects that repeatedly train and challenge staff in new techniques. A 360-degree relationship develops over time where appreciation generates high performance, which generates satisfied customers, which generates profits, which generates better pay and new tools for innovation, which generates appreciation. Investment strategies in long-term personnel recruitment and development are a key action step in satisfying customers.

## 4. Lose the Job Descriptions

Whereas we all want to know where our responsibilities begin and end, it is almost impossible to predict what every employee should be doing for all customers in all circumstances these days, especially in a person-centered service environment. Certainly, guidelines spelling out broad categories of work duties, core tasks and competencies, and responsibilities are critical, but allowing discretionary staff effort propels good companies. Rigid job descriptions are based in logic and analysis, which are good tools for managers. But, adaptive and inventive organizations need personnel who also rely on intuition, experimentation, analogy, and the ability to cope with ambiguity. Consider the airline customer who has a canceled flight and cannot get rebooked on another airline because the gate agent repeats, "I am not authorized to help you." The situation is so much more pleasant (and eventually profitable) if gate agents have the power (discretionary effort) to fix customer problems at the point of face-to-face contact. Employment specialists should have the authority and the training to attempt new forms of employment, such as telework or job creation, when the consumer indicates such a need; when families need their child to have a modified work schedule; or when funders are seeking better outcomes for their investment in community rehabilitation. Repeat business from paying customers is critical to even nonprofit success. Showing funders and taxpayers that staff inventively solve problems and create careers leads to happier customers, increased public recognition, and better reimbursement rates.

## 5.  Pay Attention to 20% of Your Customers

While it is true that all customers are critical and important, and want to feel that way, in most circumstances Pareto's 80/20 Principle holds true (Scholtes, 1988). Roughly 80% of an organization's business (profit) is generated from 20% of its customers. Ensure a solid future by paying attention to those specific repeat customers. This keeps the organization focused on critical innovations, problem solving, and opportunities that nurture these select few. When program and budget expansion occurs at the state level, the funders often come to the best, the most conscientious, and the most innovative agencies first. Of course, innovation happens on the fringes, so the other customers are important too, and may very well lead the organization into new service territory. Contradiction at its best.

## 6.  Stand in Contradiction to the Corporate Culture

Corporate culture is made up of all the unwritten and written rules of behavior in an organization (Griffin, 1996). There is comfort and stability in learning, knowing, and practicing the rites and rituals of the corporation. And, as humans and good managers, we seek consistency and predictability because it allows us to move forward without distraction. A stable corporate culture, however, can breed complacency and discourage invention. Questioning, bending, revising, and challenging company procedures, especially by leaders, blurs the lines of conformity and allows for experimentation. Creating new ideas and concepts necessitates that teams create a culture of questioning and positive conflict. From the edges of conflict and anxiety comes innovation. Furthermore, making changes or subtly standing in contradiction to the culture makes the past visible and may reveal fears and traditions that stifle creativity. It has been said that "if you want to understand the corporate culture, make a change" (Deal & Kennedy, 2000). Understanding is the first step in making and managing change.

## 7.  Play Politics

Politics is almost always cast in a negative light. Political relationships conjure up images of corruption, favoritism, power plays, and dishonesty. In reality, the term *politics* implies the interaction of any two human beings. Being politically savvy means thinking about the future and how each action may cause a reaction. Playing politics means managers are considering the impact of their actions on others; that they are using insider information to position the company into a stronger market position; that they are creating alliances and partnerships that offer protection to their organization and enhanced service and value to their customers. Imagine the vocational director and the residential director in the same organization, people who find themselves in policy and practice conflicts, coming together to use their power assisting consumers in asset accumulation. As these two find common ground—people's desire to live ordinary lives—they would emphasize the need for employment and home ownership, not one or the other, and politically join forces to achieve a common goal. Politics keep organizations alive and alerts them to changes in currents and tides. Innovation breeds contempt in others, so being politically astute is critical to survival and growth. Einstein said it best: "Politics is harder than physics" (Primack & Abrams, 2001).

### 8. It's Business/It's Personal

In Western society, people are identified in the community by what they do for a living. Thinking that professional and community/family lives are separate is a strange business school notion. Imagine if the director of an environmental group did not recycle at home. That person is guilty, at the very least, of hypocrisy. Leaders are leaders 24 hours a day, and business relationships are simply human relationships with a profit motive (or perhaps a nonprofit motive). As leaders at all levels, especially in the rehabilitation field, we need to make the passion for economic justice visible and credible by voting for supportive candidates, by shopping in stores that hire people with disabilities, by keeping agency money in accessible banks, and by making certain our friends, our boards of directors, and our neighborhoods reflect the diversity we champion. We must hire and promote people with disabilities to positions of power within our organizations. One is only as good a leader as they are a person.

### 9. Both/And, Not Either/Or

Our society is built on the notion of One God, One President, One Director, and so on. So, sometimes it is difficult for us to imagine more than one route to a solution, or more than one solution to a problem, or even that there is no solution and that we must manage ambiguity for long stretches. In most American schools, the biggest person standing at the front of the class has all the answers, and he or she disapproves of anything but the one right answer. Students are expected to keep quiet, focus on their own work, and keep the desks in a straight line. The real world is not a linear, controllable environment, so managers are constantly challenged by complex circumstances that do not lend themselves well to adopted school rules that inhibit teamwork and experimentation. There are unlimited wealth, knowledge, answers, approaches, and options in the world (Friedman, 2005). Great leaders see this circumstance as invigorating and liberating, while linear thinkers see these options as terrifying and uncontrollable. Consider adopting the Rule of Three: Insist that each staff person or team present three possible solutions to serious problems. This practice generates complex thought, challenges teams to reason together, and opens problems up to unique questioning.

### 10. Move Toward Your Anxiety

Most people attempt to ignore conflict or uncomfortable situations, hoping they will go away or resolve themselves. But, conflict rarely evaporates. Conflict does, however, fester, manifesting itself in other behavioral or organizational aberrations, and eventually grows into a web of time- and resource-wasting complexity. True, not every conflict or hiccup in the organization is worthy of attention, but too often gossip, high degrees of expressed emotion, staff turnover, and overemphasis on internal processes result in people disconnecting from the critical values, mission, and communications that help guide organizations. Leaders, at all levels, have to tune in to these disruptions, address their causes, seek solutions, and build consensus on new ways of working and thinking.

## CONCLUSION

Managing and leading is hard work, which is probably why so many administrators turn to the latest bestsellers for canned answers. The truth is that challenges such as CE demand approaches that allow each action to solve multiple problems. This is accomplished through networks of allies and capable employees, using some of the tried-and-true tools of management. The problem-solving and negotiation strategies of Chapter 7 are useful in managing and understanding organizational anxiety. Much of the time our actions appear contradictory, in the same way a tacking ship catches the wind using an irregular course to move forward. This is the way it should be in a complex, evolving world.

The transformation of traditional transition and rehabilitation services to CE is complex. The process entails much more than good frontline training and implementation. Rather, the development of individualized employment requires an organizational system that allows people with disabilities to choose their own futures and to direct the process that returns economic and civil rights.

Self-advocacy and advocacy pressure, values-based policy and funding strategies, and internal commitment from transition and rehabilitation professionals will play the major roles in creating inclusive communities for those now served in restrictive environments. A strong commitment to the values of inclusion will transform management systems, relinquish control over people's lives, and reposition organizations into support brokerages that truly serve the needs and desires of individuals with disabilities.

## REFERENCES

Alinsky, S. (1971). *Rules for radicals: A pragmatic primer for realistic radicals.* New York: Random House.

Allen, M. (2004). *Just like where you and I live: Integrated housing options for people with mental illness.* Washington, DC: Bazelon Center for Mental Health Law.

Bell, G.M. (1992). *Getting things done when you are not in charge.* San Francisco: Berrett-Koehler Publishers.

Block, P. (1993). *Stewardship: Choosing service over self-interest.* San Francisco: Berrett-Koehler Publishers.

Bozeman manufacturer having trouble finding local workers. (2006, October 3). *Bozeman Daily Chronicle.* Retrieved October 3, 2006, from http://www.bozemandailychronicle.com

Braddock, D., Hemp, R., Parish, S., & Rizzolo, M. (2002). *The state of the states in developmental disabilities: 2002 study summary.* Boulder: University of Colorado, Coleman Institute for Cognitive Disabilities and Department of Psychiatry.

Brooks-Lane, N., Hutcheson, S., & Revell, G. (2005). Supporting consumer-directed employment outcomes. *Journal of Vocational Rehabilitation, 23*(2), 123–134.

Brown, L., Branston, M., Hamre-Nietupski, S., Pumpian, I., Certo, N., & Gruenwald, L. (1979). A strategy for developing chronological age appropriate content for severely handicapped adolescents and young adults. *Journal of Special Education, 13,* 81–90.

Callahan, M., & Garner, B. (1997). *Keys to the workplace: Skills and supports for people with disabilities.* Baltimore: Paul H. Brookes Publishing Co.

Collins, J. (2001). *Good to great: Why some companies make the leap...and others don't.* New York: HarperCollins.

Condeluci, A. (1991). *Interdependence.* St. Augustine, FL: St. Lucie Press.

Deal, T., & Kennedy, A. (2000). *Corporate cultures: The rites and rituals of corporate life.* New York: Perseus Publishing.

Deming, E.W. (1986). *Out of the crisis.* Cambridge, MA: MIT Center for Advanced Engineering Study.

DiLeo, D., & Langton, D. (1993). *Get the marketing edge! A job developer's toolkit for people with disabilities.* St. Augustine, FL: TRN Press.

Drehs, W. (2006). *J-Macs meaningful message for autism.* Retrieved January 10, 2007, from http://sports.espn.go.com/espn/news/story?id=2352763

Friedman, T.L. (2005). *The world is flat: A brief history of the twenty-first century.* New York: Farrar, Straus, & Giroux.

Fuller, M. (1999). *More than houses.* Nashville, TN: W Publishing Group.

Gilbert, T.F. (1978). *Human competence: Engineering worthy performance.* New York: McGraw-Hill.

Gladwell, M. (2000). *The tipping point: How little things can make a big difference.* New York: Little, Brown, & Company.

Griffin, C.C. (1994). Organizational natural supports: The role of leadership in facilitating inclusion. *Journal of Vocational Rehabilitation, 4*(4).

Griffin, C.C. (1996). Organizational evolution: Critical pathways to substantive change. *Journal of Vocational Rehabilitation, 6,* 69–76.

Griffin, C.C. (1999). *Working better, working smarter: Building responsive rehabilitation programs.* St. Augustine, FL: TRN Press.

Hagner, D. (2000). *Coffee breaks and birthday cakes: Evaluating workplace cultures to develop natural supports for employees with disabilities.* St. Augustine, FL: TRN Press.

Hammer, M., & Champy, J. (1993). *Reengineering the corporation: A manifesto for business revolution.* New York: HarperBusiness.

Harris Poll. (2000, July 5). *Many people with disabilities feel isolated, left out of their communities and would like to participate more.* Retrieved January 10, 2007, from http://www.harrisinteractive.com

Janov, J. (1994). *The inventive organization: hope and daring at work.* San Francisco: Jossey-Bass.

Kilmann, R. (1989). *Managing beyond the quick fix.* San Francisco: Jossey-Bass.

Kohn, A. (1993). *Punished by rewards: The trouble with gold stars, incentive plans, As, praise, and other bribes.* New York: Houghton Mifflin.

Kotler, P., & Roberto, E.L. (1989). *Social marketing: Strategies for changing public behavior.* New York: Free Press.

Kouzes, J.M., & Posner, B.Z. (1987). *The leadership challenge.* San Francisco: Jossey-Bass.

Mintzberg, H. (1994). *The rise and fall of strategic planning.* New York: Free Press.

Murphy, S.T., & Rogan, P.M. (1995). *Closing the shop: Conversion from sheltered to integrated work.* Baltimore: Paul H. Brookes Publishing Co.

Primack, J., & Abrams, N. (2001). Gravity, the ultimate capitalist principle. *Tikkum Magazine, 10,* 59–61.

Putnam, R. (2000). *Bowling alone: The collapse and revival of American community.* New York: Simon & Schuster.

Ries, J., & Trout, A. (1987). *Positioning: The battle for your mind.* New York: McGraw Hill.

Ringland, G. (2002). *Scenarios in business.* West Sussex, UK: John Wiley & Sons.

Schaef, A., & Fassel, D. (1990). *The addictive organization.* New York: Harper & Row.

Scholtes, P.R. (1988). *The team handbook: How to use teams to improve quality.* Madison, WI: Joiner Associates Inc.

Shapiro, J. (1993). *No pity: People with disabilities forging a new civil rights movement.* New York: Times Books.

Stacey, R. (1992). *Managing the unknowable: Strategic boundaries between order and chaos in organizations.* San Francisco: Jossey-Bass.

Torrey, J.F. (1988). *Nowhere to go: The tragic odyssey of the homeless mentally ill.* New York: HarperCollins.

Wehman, P., Inge, K., Revell, W.G., & Brooke, V. (2006). *Real work for real pay: Inclusive employment for people with disabilities.* Baltimore: Paul H. Brookes Publishing Co.

# Blank Forms

Griffin-Hammis Customized Employment (CE) Management Plan

Job Analysis Record

Plan to Achieve Self-Support

Quarter 1 Report

Quarter 2 Report

Quarter 3 Report

Quarter 4 Report

# GRIFFIN-HAMMIS CUSTOMIZED EMPLOYMENT (CE) MANAGEMENT PLAN

Name: _____  Date: _____

Mailing Address: _____

Phone: _____  E-mail: _____

URL: _____  Fax: _____

Gender: _____  Ethnicity: _____

Age (optional): _____  Primary/secondary disability: _____

## Ideal conditions of employment (from discovery):

Where I'm at my best:

When and where I need the most support:

People who know me best:

## Current CE Team Members

| Name | Affiliation | Phone/E-mail | Expertise |
|------|-------------|--------------|-----------|
|      |             |              |           |
|      |             |              |           |
|      |             |              |           |
|      |             |              |           |
|      |             |              |           |
|      |             |              |           |

*(continued on next page)*

## CE Team Members, Mentors, or Consultants Needed

| Name | Affiliation | Phone/E-mail | Expertise | Who will contact |
|------|-------------|--------------|-----------|------------------|
|      |             |              |           |                  |
|      |             |              |           |                  |
|      |             |              |           |                  |

## Vocational Profile

Key interests:

Preferred situations/activities:

Situations/activities to avoid:

## Methods for Gathering Additional Vocational Profile Information

| Approach/action | Date(s) of activity | Person responsible | Comments/outcomes |
|-----------------|---------------------|--------------------|-------------------|
| 1.              |                     |                    |                   |
| 2.              |                     |                    |                   |
| 3.              |                     |                    |                   |
| 4.              |                     |                    |                   |

*The Job Developer's Handbook* by Cary Griffin, David Hammis, & Tammara Geary.

207

# JOB ANALYSIS RECORD

Instructions: This form is used to capture the major task steps of each job or project. The recorder should pay particular attention to how the tasks are typically performed, any accommodations, technology, or specialized training strategies that should be employed with the new employee. The task sets are to be recorded as projects so that a discrete training format can be established for each.

Name of worker: _____ Date initiated/date completed: _____

Company: _____

Contact person/supervisor: _____ Phone/E-mail: _____

Person completing Job Analysis Record (JAR): _____

Proposed job title: _____

Major tasks or projects: _____

_____

_____

Proposed work hours/days per week: _____

Anticipated pay rate/benefits: _____

Comments/considerations: _____

_____

_____

## Culture of the company:

Record observations regarding the rites and rituals of the company (e.g., dress code, commonly used language and slang that may be helpful to understand, work hours, break times and lunch behavior, initiation rituals for new hires, social interactions, car pooling)

Notes from observation and conversation:

### *Project one description:*

Task steps:

Quality measures:

Tools required:

*(continued on next page)*

*The Job Developer's Handbook* by Cary Griffin, David Hammis, & Tammara Geary.

Speed and accuracy considerations:

Natural instructors/supervision:

Task duration:

Task acquisition concerns:

---

### Project two description:

Task steps:

Quality measures:

Tools required:

Speed and accuracy considerations:

Natural instructors/supervision:

Task duration:

Task acquisition concerns:

*(continued on next page)*

## *Project three description:*

Task steps:

Quality measures:

Tools required:

Speed and accuracy considerations:

Natural instructors/supervision:

Task duration:

Task acquisition concerns:

## *Project four description:*

Task steps:

*(continued on next page)*

Quality measures:

Tools required:

Speed and accuracy considerations:

Natural instructors/supervision:

Task duration:

Task acquisition concerns:

---

***Notes and recommendations for on-site trainer, resource ownership, universal/assistive technology, further job modification, etc.:***

---

Social Security Administration

Form Approved
OMB No. 0960-0559

# PLAN TO ACHIEVE SELF-SUPPORT

| Date Received |
| --- |

*In order to minimize recontacts or processing delays, please complete all questions and provide thorough explanations where requested. If you need additional space to answer any questions, use the Remarks section or a separate sheet of paper.*

Name _____ SSN _____ – \_\_ – _____

## PART I - YOUR WORK GOAL

A. What is your work goal? (*Show the job you expect to have at the end of the plan. Be as specific as possible. If you cannot be specific, provide as much information as possible on the type of work you plan to do. If you do not yet have a specific goal and will be working with a vocational professional to find a suitable job match, show "VR Evaluation" and be sure to complete Part II, question F on page 4.*)

_____

_____

_____

If your plan involves paying for job coaching, show the number of hours of job coaching you will receive when you begin working. _____ **per** ☐ **week** ☐ **month** (*check one*).

Show the number of hours of job coaching you expect to receive after the plan is completed. _____ **per** ☐ **week** ☐ **month** (*check one*).

B. Describe the duties and tasks you expect to perform in this job. Be as specific as possible.

_____

_____

_____

_____

C. How did you decide on this work goal and what makes this type of work attractive to you?

_____

_____

_____

D. Is a license required to perform this work goal?  ☐ YES  ☐ NO
   (*If yes, include the steps you will follow to get a license in Part III.*)

E. How much do you expect to earn each week/month (gross) after your plan is completed?
   $ _____ **per** ☐ **week** ☐ **month** (check one)

---

In *The Job Developer's Handbook* by Cary Griffin, David Hammis, & Tammara Geary. (Paul H. Brookes Publishing Co., Inc.)

F. If your work goal involves self-employment, explain why working for yourself will make you more self-supporting than working for someone else. _____

_____

_____

_____

_____

**IMPORTANT:** If you plan to start your own business, attach a detailed business plan.
The business plan must include:
- the type of business;
- products or services to be offered by your business;
- the advertising plan;
- a description of the market for the business;
- technical assistance needed;
- tools, supplies, and equipment needed;
- a profit-and-loss projection for the duration of the PASS and at least one year beyond its completion.
Also include a description of how you intend to make this business succeed.
For assistance in preparing a business plan, contact the Small Business Administration, Chamber of Commerce, local banks, or other business owners.

G. Have you ever submitted a Plan to Achieve Self-Support
(PASS) to Social Security?　　　　　☐ YES　　☐ NO　If "no," skip to H.

Was a PASS ever approved for you?　　　☐ YES　　☐ NO　If "no," skip to H.

When was your most recent plan approved (month/year)? _____
What was your work goal in that plan? _____

Did you complete that PASS?　　　　　☐ YES　　☐ NO

If no, why weren't you able to complete it? _____

_____

If yes, why weren't you able to become self-supporting? _____

_____

Why do you believe that this new plan you are requesting will help you go to work? _____

_____

_____

H. Have you assigned your "Ticket to Work"?　　☐ YES　　☐ NO　If "no," skip to Part II.
Show name, address and telephone number of the person or organization it was assigned to.

_____

_____

_____

_____

# PART II - MEDICAL/VOCATIONAL/EDUCATIONAL BACKGROUND

A. List all your disabling illnesses, injuries, or condition(s). _____

_____

_____

B. Describe any limitations you have because of your disability (e.g., limited amount of standing or lifting, stooping, bending, or walking; difficulty concentrating; unable to work with other people, difficulty handling stress, etc.)  Be specific.

_____

_____

_____

In light of the limitations you described, how will you carry out the duties of your work goal?

_____

_____

_____

C. List the jobs you have had **most often** in the past few years. Also list any jobs, including volunteer work, which are similar to your work goal or which provided you with skills that may help you perform the work goal. List the dates you worked in these jobs. Identify periods of self-employment. If you were in the Army, list your Military Occupational Specialty (MOS) Code; for the Air Force, list your Air Force Speciality code (AFSC); and for the Navy, Marine Corps, and Coast Guard, list your rank.

| Job Title | Type of Business | Dates Worked | |
|---|---|---|---|
| | | From | To |
| | | | |
| | | | |
| | | | |
| | | | |
| | | | |
| | | | |
| | | | |
| | | | |
| | | | |
| | | | |
| | | | |
| | | | |

In *The Job Developer's Handbook* by Cary Griffin, David Hammis, & Tammara Geary. (Paul H. Brookes Publishing Co., Inc.)

**D.**  **Select the highest grade of school completed.**

☐ 0   ☐ 1   ☐ 2   ☐ 3   ☐ 4   ☐ 5   ☐ 6   ☐ 7   ☐ 8   ☐ 9   ☐ 10   ☐ 11   ☐ 12

☐ GED or ☐ High School Equivalency     College: ☐ 1   ☐ 2   ☐ 3   ☐ 4 or ☐ more

Were you awarded a college or postgraduate degree?   ☐ YES   ☐ NO

When did you graduate? _____   If "no," skip to E.

What type of degree did you receive? (AA, BA, BS, MBA, etc.)? _____

In what field of study? _____

**E.**  Have you completed any type of special job training, trade or vocational school?   ☐ YES   ☐ NO  If "no," skip to F.

Type of training _____

Date completed _____

Did you receive a certificate or license?   ☐ YES   ☐ NO  If "no," skip to F.

What kind of certificate or license did you receive? _____

**F.**  Have you ever had or expect to have a vocational evaluation or an Individualized Written Rehabilitation Plan (IWRP) or an Individualized Plan for Employment (IPE)?   ☐ YES   ☐ NO  If "no," skip to G.

If "YES," attach a copy of the evaluation. If you cannot attach a copy, when were you evaluated (or when do you expect to be evaluated) and when was the IWRP or IPE done ( or when do you expect it to be done)?

_____

Show the name, address, and phone number of the person or organization who evaluated you (or will evaluate you) or who prepared the IWRP or IPE (or will prepare the IWRP or IPE.)

_____

_____

_____

**G.**  If you have a college degree or specialized training, and your plan includes additional education or training, explain why the education/training you already received is not sufficient to allow you to be self-supporting.

_____

_____

_____

_____

# PART III - YOUR PLAN

I want my Plan to begin _____ (month/year)
(*This should be the date you started or will start working towards your goal.*)

and my Plan to end _____ (month/year)
(*This should be the date you expect to start working in your job goal.*)

List the sequential steps that you have taken or will take to reach your work goal starting with your begin date above and concluding with your expected end date above. Be as specific as possible. If you are or will be attending school, show the number of courses you will take each quarter/semester and attach a copy of the degree program or plan that shows the courses you will study. Include the final steps to find a job once you have obtained the tools, education, services, etc., that you need.

| Step | Beginning Date | Completion Date |
|------|----------------|-----------------|
|      |                |                 |
|      |                |                 |
|      |                |                 |
|      |                |                 |
|      |                |                 |
|      |                |                 |
|      |                |                 |
|      |                |                 |
|      |                |                 |
|      |                |                 |
|      |                |                 |
|      |                |                 |
|      |                |                 |
|      |                |                 |
|      |                |                 |
|      |                |                 |
|      |                |                 |
|      |                |                 |
|      |                |                 |
|      |                |                 |
|      |                |                 |
|      |                |                 |
|      |                |                 |
|      |                |                 |

Form **SSA-545-BK** (11-2005) ef (11-2005)          Page 5

In *The Job Developer's Handbook* by Cary Griffin, David Hammis, & Tammara Geary. (Paul H. Brookes Publishing Co., Inc.)

## PART IV - EXPENSES

A.  Do you propose to purchase or lease a vehicle?
    ☐ YES  ☐ NO

    If yes, list the purchase or lease of the vehicle as one of
    the steps in Part III and complete the following:

    If "no,"
    skip to B
    on Page 7

1.  Explain why less expensive forms of transportation (e.g., public transportation, cabs) will not allow you to reach your work goal. _____

    _____

    _____

    _____

2.  Do you currently have a valid driver's license?
    ☐ YES  ☐ NO

    If "yes,"
    skip to 3

    If no, does Part III include the steps you will follow to get a driver's license?
    ☐ YES  ☐ NO

    If "yes,"
    skip to 3

    If no, who will drive the vehicle? _____
    How will it be used to help you with your work goal?

    _____

    _____

    _____

3.  Do you already own a vehicle?
    ☐ YES  ☐ NO

    If yes, explain why you need another vehicle to reach your work goal.

    If "no,"
    skip to 4

    _____

    _____

    _____

4.  Describe the type of vehicle you propose to purchase or lease:
    Make: _____
    Model: _____
    Year: _____
    Purchase price: _____
    OR Lease price: _____

5.  If the vehicle is new, explain why a used vehicle is not sufficient to meet your work goal.

    _____

    _____

    _____

In *The Job Developer's Handbook* by Cary Griffin, David Hammis,
& Tammara Geary. (Paul H. Brookes Publishing Co., Inc.)

B. If you propose to purchase a computer or other major equipment, describe the computer or equipment you will purchase, including the cost for each item.

_____

_____

_____

C. Do you already own a computer?　　☐ YES　　☐ NO
If yes, explain why you need another computer to reach your work goal.

_____

_____

_____

D. Please explain why you need the capabilites of the particular computer and/or equipment you identified.

_____

_____

_____

E. Other than the items identified in A through D above, list the items or services you are buying or renting or will need to buy or rent in order to reach your work goal. Be as specific as possible. If schooling is an item, list tuition, fees, books, etc. as separate items. List the cost for the entire length of time you will be in school. Where applicable, include brand and model number of the item. **(Do not include expenses you were paying prior to the beginning of your plan; only expenses incurred since the beginning of your plan can be approved.)**

NOTE: Be sure that Part III shows when you will purchase these items or services or training.

1. Item/service/training: _____

   Total Cost: $ _____

   Vendor/provider: _____

   How will you pay for this item _(one-time payment, installment or monthly payments)?_

   _____

   How will this help you reach your work goal? _____

   _____

   _____

2. Item/service/training:_____

    Total Cost: $ _____

    Vendor/provider: _____

    How will you pay for this item *(one-time payment, installment or monthly payments)?*

    _____

    How will this help you reach your work goal? _____

    _____

    _____

3. Item/service/training:_____

    Total Cost: $ _____

    Vendor/provider:_____

    How will you pay for this item *(one-time payment, installment or monthly payments)?*

    _____

    How will this help you reach your work goal? _____

    _____

    _____

4. Item/service/training:_____

    Total Cost: $ _____

    Vendor/provider:_____

    How will you pay for this item *(one-time payment, installment or monthly payments)?*

    _____

    How will this help you reach your work goal? _____

    _____

    _____

5. Item/service/training:_____

    Total Cost: $ _____

    Vendor/provider: _____

    How will you pay for this item *(one-time payment, installment or monthly payments)?*

    _____

    How will this help you reach your work goal? _____

    _____

    _____

6. Item/service/training: _____

   Total Cost: $ _____

   Vendor/provider: _____

   How will you pay for this item *(one-time payment, installment or monthly payments)?*

   _____

   How will this help you reach your work goal? _____

   _____

   _____

F.  Will any of the items, services or training costs be reimbursed to you or paid by any other source, person or organization?　　☐ YES　　☐ NO

   If yes, be sure to complete Part V, question F on page 11.

## CURRENT LIVING EXPENSES

G.  What are your current living expenses each month?　　$ _____ /month

   Include all living expenses:
   - Rent, Mortgage, Property Taxes,
   - Property/Personal Insurance,
   - Utilities, Phone, Cable, Internet,
   - Food, Groceries,
   - Automobile Gas, Repair and Maintenance, Public Transportation,
   - Clothes, Personal Items, Laundry/Dry Cleaning,
   - Medical, Dental, Prescription,
   - Entertainment, Charity Contributions, etc.

H.  If the amount of income you will have available for living expenses after making payments or saving money for your plan is **less than** your current living expenses, explain how you will pay for your living expenses.

   _____

   _____

   _____

   _____

   _____

   _____

   _____

   _____

   _____

   _____

In *The Job Developer's Handbook* by Cary Griffin, David Hammis, & Tammara Geary. (Paul H. Brookes Publishing Co., Inc.)

# PART V - FUNDING FOR WORK GOAL

A. Do you plan to use any items you already own (e.g., equipment or property) to reach your work goal?  ☐ YES  ☐ NO

If "no," skip to B.  If yes, show the items you will use that you already own:

Item _____

How will this help you reach your work goal? _____

_____

Item _____

How will this help you reach your work goal? _____

_____

Item _____

How will this help you reach your work goal? _____

_____

B. Have you saved any money to pay for the expenses listed on pages 6-9 in Part IV? *(Include cash on hand or money in a bank account.)*  ☐ YES  ☐ NO

If "yes," how much have you saved? _____

C. List the income you **receive or expect to receive** below. (*Include Social Security benefits, wages, self-employment, assistance, royalties, pensions, dividends, prizes, insurance, support payments, etc.*)

| Type of Income | Amount | Frequency (Weekly, Monthly, Yearly) |
|---|---|---|
|  |  |  |
|  |  |  |
|  |  |  |
|  |  |  |
|  |  |  |
|  |  |  |

D. How much of this income will you set aside to pay for the vehicle, computer, major equipment and other items, services and training listed in Part IV?

_____

_____

_____

_____

E.  Do you plan to save any or all of this income for a future purchase which is necessary to complete your goal?

☐ YES    ☐ NO If "no," skip to F.

If "yes," you will need to keep this money separate from other money you have. How will you keep the money separate. (*If you will keep the savings in a separate bank account, give the name and address of the bank and the account number.*) _____

_____

_____

_____

_____

F.  Will any other person or organization (e.g., grants, assistance, or Vocational Rehabilitation agency) pay for or reimburse you for any part of the expenses listed in Part IV or provide any other items or services you will need?

☐ YES    ☐ NO  If "no," skip to Part VI.

If "yes," provide details as follows:

| Who Will Pay | Item/Service | Amount | When will the item/ service be purchased? |
|---|---|---|---|
|  |  |  |  |
|  |  |  |  |
|  |  |  |  |
|  |  |  |  |
|  |  |  |  |

**Part VI - OTHER CONTACTS**

Did someone help you prepare this plan?    ☐ YES    ☐ NO

If yes, give the name, address and telephone number of that person or organization:

Name _____

Address _____

City, State and Zip Code _____

Telephone _____

E-mail address _____

Are they charging you a fee for this service?    ☐ YES    ☐ NO

If yes, how much are they charging? _____

In *The Job Developer's Handbook* by Cary Griffin, David Hammis, & Tammara Geary. (Paul H. Brookes Publishing Co., Inc.)

May we contact them if we need additional information about your plan?  ☐ YES  ☐ NO

Do you want us to send them a copy of our decision on your plan?  ☐ YES  ☐ NO
If yes, please submit a Consent for Release of Information, form SSA-3288.

*(If you also wish to authorize this person or organization to act on your behalf in matters pertaining to this plan, please submit an Appointment of Representative, form SSA1696.)*

## PART VII - REMARKS

Use this section or a separate sheet of paper if you need additional space to answer any questions:

_____

_____

_____

_____

_____

_____

_____

_____

_____

_____

_____

_____

_____

_____

_____

_____

_____

In *The Job Developer's Handbook* by Cary Griffin, David Hammis, & Tammara Geary. (Paul H. Brookes Publishing Co., Inc.)

# PART VIII - AGREEMENT

**If my plan is approved, I agree to:**

☐ Comply with all of the terms and conditions of the plan as approved by the Social Security Administration (SSA).

☐ Report any changes in my plan **to SSA** immediately.

☐ Keep records and receipts of all expenditures I make under the plan until asked to provide them to SSA.

☐ Use the income or resources set aside under the plan **only** to buy the items or services shown in the plan as approved by SSA.

☐ Report any changes that may affect the amount of my SSI payment immediately. (For example: income, resources, living arrangement, marital status.)

I realize that if I do not comply with the terms of the plan or if I use the income or resources set aside under my plan for any other purpose, SSA will count the income or resources that were excluded and I may have to repay the additional SSI I received.

I also realize that SSA may not approve any expenditure for which I do not submit receipts or other proof of payment.

**I declare under penalty of perjury that I have examined all the information on this form, and on any accompanying statements or forms, and it is true and correct to the best of my knowledge.**

Signature _____  Date _____

Address _____

City, State and Zip code _____

Telephone:  Home _____

Work _____

Other _____

E-mail address _____

If you have a representative payee, the representative payee must sign below:

Representative Payee Signature _____  Date _____

Form **SSA-545-BK** (11-2005) ef (11-2005)                 Page 13

In *The Job Developer's Handbook* by Cary Griffin, David Hammis, & Tammara Geary. (Paul H. Brookes Publishing Co., Inc.)

# PRIVACY ACT STATEMENT

The Social Security Administration is allowed to collect the information on this form under section 1631(e) of the Social Security Act. We need this information to determine if we can approve your plan for achieving self-support. Giving us this information is voluntary. However, without it, we may not be able to approve your plan. Social Security will not use the information for any other purpose.

We would give out the facts on this form without your consent only in certain situations. For example, we give out this information if a Federal law requires us to or if your congressional Representative or Senator needs the information to answer questions you ask them.

**Paperwork Reduction Act Statement** - This information collection meets the requirements of 44 U.S.C. § 3507, as amended by Section 2 of the Paperwork Reduction Act of 1995. You do not need to answer these questions unless we display a valid Office of Management and Budget control number. We estimate that it will take about 120 minutes to read the instructions, gather the facts, and answer the questions. **SEND THE COMPLETED FORM TO YOUR LOCAL SOCIAL SECURITY OFFICE. The office is listed under U. S. Government agencies in your telephone directory or you may call Social Security at 1-800-772-1213.** You may send comments on our time estimate above to: SSA, 1338 Annex Building, Baltimore, MD 21235-6401. *Send only comments relating to our time estimate to this address, not the completed form.*

In *The Job Developer's Handbook* by Cary Griffin, David Hammis, & Tammara Geary. (Paul H. Brookes Publishing Co., Inc.)

# OUR RESPONSIBILITIES TO YOU

We received your plan for achieving self-support (PASS) on _____ .
Your plan will be processed by Social Security employees who are trained to work with PASS.

The PASS expert handling your case will work directly with you. He or she will look over the plan as soon as possible to see if there is a good chance that you can meet your work goal. The PASS expert will also make sure that the things you want to pay for are needed to achieve your work goal and are reasonably priced. If changes are needed, the PASS expert will discuss them with you.

You may contact the PASS expert toll-free at 1- ( ___ ) ___ – _____

# YOUR REPORTING AND RECORDKEEPING RESPONSIBILITIES

**If we approve your plan, you must tell Social Security about any changes to your plan and any changes that may affect the amount of your SSI payment. You must tell us if:**

☐ Your medical condition improves.

☐ You are unable to follow your plan.

☐ You decide not to pursue your goal or decide to pursue a different goal.

☐ You decide that you do not need to pay for any of the expenses you listed in your plan.

☐ Someone else pays for any of your plan expenses.

☐ You use the income or resources we exclude for a purpose other than the expenses specified in your plan.

☐ There are any other changes to your plan.

☐ There are any changes in your income, help you get from others, or things of value that you own.

☐ There are any changes in where you live, how you live, or your marital status.

You must tell us about any of these things within 10 days following the month in which it happens. If you do not report any of these things, we may stop your plan.

You should also tell us if you decide that you need to pay for other expenses not listed in your plan in order to reach your goal. We may be able to change your plan or the amount of income we exclude so you can pay for the additional expenses.

**YOU MUST KEEP RECEIPTS OR CANCELLED CHECKS TO SHOW WHAT EXPENSES YOU PAID FOR AS PART OF THE PLAN.** You need to keep these receipts or cancelled checks until we contact you to find out if you are still following your plan. When we contact you, we will ask to see the receipts or cancelled checks. If you are not following the plan, you may have to pay back some or all of the SSI you received.

Form **SSA-545-BK** (11-2005) ef (11-2005)                    Page 15

In *The Job Developer's Handbook* by Cary Griffin, David Hammis, & Tammara Geary. (Paul H. Brookes Publishing Co., Inc.)

# QUARTER 1 CUSTOMIZED EMPLOYMENT DEVELOPMENT PROGRESS REPORT

Period: _____ Individual: _____

Average hours worked per week: _____

Average gross revenue per month: _____

Average net revenue per month: _____

Average gross wages per week: _____

Average net wages per week: _____

Employment or business refinements/supports needed or of concern:

Success stories:

Next steps:

Comments:

# QUARTER 2 CUSTOMIZED EMPLOYMENT DEVELOPMENT PROGRESS REPORT

Period: _____ Individual: _____

Average hours worked per week: _____

Average gross revenue per month: _____

Average net revenue per month: _____

Average gross wages per week: _____

Average net wages per week: _____

Employment or business refinements/supports needed or of concern:

Success stories:

Next steps:

Comments:

# QUARTER 3 CUSTOMIZED EMPLOYMENT DEVELOPMENT PROGRESS REPORT

Period: _____  Individual: _____

Average hours worked per week: _____

Average gross revenue per month: _____

Average net revenue per month: _____

Average gross wages per week: _____

Average net wages per week: _____

Employment or business refinements/supports needed or of concern:

Success stories:

Next steps:

Comments:

# QUARTER 4 CUSTOMIZED EMPLOYMENT DEVELOPMENT PROGRESS REPORT

Period: _____ Individual: _____

Average hours worked per week: _____

Average gross revenue per month: _____

Average net revenue per month: _____

Average gross wages per week: _____

Average net wages per week: _____

Employment or business refinements/supports needed or of concern:

Success stories:

Next steps:

Comments:

# Index

Page references to figures, tables, and footnotes are indicted by *f*, *t*, and *n*, respectively.